TAROT
TALISMANS

ABOUT THE AUTHORS

Chic Cicero was born in Buffalo, New York. A former musician and businessman, Chic has been a practicing ceremonial magician for the past thirty years. He was a close personal friend of Israel Regardie. Having established a Golden Dawn temple in 1977, Chic was one of the key people who helped Regardie resurrect a legitimate branch of the Hermetic Order of the Golden Dawn in the early 1980s.

Sandra Tabatha Cicero was born in Soldiers Grove, Wisconsin. She graduated from the University of Wisconsin–Milwaukee, with a bachelor's degree in the fine arts. Both Chic and Tabatha are Senior Adepts of the Hermetic Order of the Golden Dawn. They are the authors of several books published by Llewellyn.

TO WRITE TO THE AUTHORS

If you wish to contact the authors or would like more information about this book, please write to the authors in care of Llewellyn Worldwide and we will forward your request. Both the authors and publisher appreciate hearing from you and learning of your enjoyment of this book and how it has helped you. Llewellyn Worldwide cannot guarantee that every letter written to the authors can be answered, but all will be forwarded. Please write to:

Chic & S. Tabatha Cicero
% Llewellyn Worldwide
2143 Wooddale Drive, Dept. 0-7387-0871-2
Woodbury, MN 55125-2989, U.S.A.
Please enclose a self-addressed stamped envelope for reply,
or $1.00 to cover costs. If outside U.S.A., enclose
international postal reply coupon.

Many of Llewellyn's authors have websites with additional information and resources. For more information, please visit our website at:

http://www.llewellyn.com

TAROT TALISMANS

INVOKE THE ANGELS OF THE TAROT

CHIC CICERO & SANDRA TABATHA CICERO

Llewellyn Publications
Woodbury, Minnesota

First Edition
Fourth Printing, 2017

Cards from the Tarots of Marseille by Claude Burdel © 2000 by Lo Scarabeo and reprinted with permission from Lo Scarabeo
Cards from the Universal Tarot by Roberto de Angelis © 2000 by Lo Scarabeo and reprinted with permission from Lo Scarabeo
Cover image © by Steve Rawlings / digitalvision, inc.
Cover design by Gavin Dayton Duffy
Editing by Lee Lewis
Illustrations from Aleister Crowley Thoth Tarot® reproduced by permission of AGM AGMüller, CH-8212 Neuhausen, Switzerland. © AGM AGMüller/OTO. Further reproduction prohibited.
Illustrations by Llewellyn art department on pages 19, 21–22, 27, 29, 73, 75, 81–82, 86–87, 90, 93, 97, 100–101, 103, 140, 190, 195–202, 212–218, 226, 230, 235, 241, 245–246, 253–256, 258–271
Illustrations by Sandra Tabatha Cicero on pages 76, 78, 117, 127, 132, 135, 183–184, 205–208, 210, 236–237

Llewellyn is a registered trademark of Llewellyn Worldwide, Ltd.

Library of Congress Cataloging-in-Publication Data
Cicero, Chic, 1936–
   Tarot talismans: invoking the angels of the tarot / by Chic Cicero, Sandra Tabatha Cicero.
     p.   cm.
   Includes bibliographical references (p.   ) and index.
   ISBN-13: 978-0-7387-0871-3
   ISBN-10: 0-7387-0871-2
    1. Tarot. 2. Talismans. 3. Angels—Miscellanea. 4. Hermetic Order of the Golden Dawn.
  I. Cicero, Sandra Tabatha, 1959– II. Title.

BF1879.T2.C525 2006
133.3'2424—dc22

2006041025

Llewellyn Worldwide does not participate in, endorse, or have any authority or responsibility concerning private business transactions between our authors and the public.
   All mail addressed to the author is forwarded but the publisher cannot, unless specifically instructed by the author, give out an address or phone number.
   Any Internet references contained in this work are current at publication time, but the publisher cannot guarantee that a specific location will continue to be maintained. Please refer to the publisher's website for links to authors' websites and other sources.
   Cover models used for illustrative purposes only and may not endorse or represent the book's subject.

Llewellyn Publications
A Division of Llewellyn Worldwide, Ltd.
2143 Wooddale Drive, Dept. 0-7387-0871-2
Woodbury, MN 55125-2989, U.S.A.
www.llewellyn.com

Printed in the United States of America

To Oz
with much love and gratitude

CONTENTS

Part Two: *Tarot Angels*

Chapter 4: Gods and Angels of the Tarot Trumps . . . 113

ILLUSTRATIONS

Figures

Tables

INTRODUCTION

We've all seen them—those eerie Hollywood movies where a character consults a gypsy fortuneteller in some dimly lit parlor, asking to have her destiny foretold by a reading of the tarot cards. After shuffling the deck, the gypsy cautiously turns the cards over. One by one the cards predict disaster until at length the card of Death appears! An ominous sign! Turning white with fear, the gypsy stops the reading and quickly hustles the now-frightened and confused client out of the shop, flips the "open" sign over to read "closed", and draws the shades. Ooh . . . very spooky!

While such scenes make cinema more entertaining, they present many blatant falsehoods about the tarot. For instance, any knowledgeable tarot reader knows that the Death card does not literally mean "death," but rather transformation and change. The biggest misconception that Hollywood perpetuates about the tarot, however, is that a card reading portrays a fixed future or predestined "fate" that can't be altered. This is, quite simply, not true.

Next to astrology, tarot is perhaps the most widely accepted of the esoteric arts. In the early 1960s it was difficult for interested students to simply find a tarot deck for sale. Nowadays, tarot enthusiasts can hardly keep track of the number of different decks that are published every year. For those of us who love the tarot, this is indeed a golden age of plenty.

Astrologers have a saying about their art: "The stars impel, they do not compel." The same can be said of the tarot. A tarot reading provides you with tools to help you analyze a specific situation or problem and offers a possible solution. The key word here is "possible." Because you have free will, you are the master of your own destiny. The tarot simply offers you another perspective—a way to look at a given circumstance from another angle—often a spiritual or psychological angle.

The tarot is an illustrated book of spiritual wisdom. It has many uses besides divination—tarot cards are also used for meditation, skrying, pathworking, and ritual magic. A tarot reading is like a road map: it can give you many different routes to take you where you want to go. You always have options. You can take the straight road or the long, winding road. The cards may show that the path you are currently on is full of construction, obstacles, and potholes. A bridge on the road ahead may be washed out. You can choose to stay on the road and take your chances, or get off at the next exit and find another route. Even when the cards indicate a bad time ahead, they also show a way around the situation. The cards always provide a ray of hope and guidance for a better tomorrow. You can always change your future by making different choices or taking a different course of action. But can you do more? How can you help to ensure that your desired goals are manifested and improved upon? How can you help make a beneficial situation continue on into the future? What can you do to generate positive changes in your life in a proactive fashion? The answer: use the cards of the tarot as magical talismans.

A traditional tarot deck contains seventy-eight images that are associated with various divine qualities and astrological energies. The tarot is like a filing cabinet packed with timeless knowledge and magical correspondences. It is a complete system for describing, understanding, and working with the hidden forces of the universe. Some have called the cards of the tarot the "hieroglyphs of the Western Mystery Tradition."

These seventy-eight cards embody a marvelous world of powerful and divine archetypes, universal to all mythologies. This world provides us with esoteric role models, ideals, advice, warnings, and insights that can aid us on every step of our spiritual quest. Every aspect of human life—secular, spiritual, and psychological—is contained within it.

We like to describe the cards of the tarot as seventy-eight "snapshots" of human consciousness at various stages in our evolutionary growth. The different figures portrayed in the cards are archetypal godforms that manifest through the collective spiritual unconsciousness of humanity. The Fool is the innocent pilgrim on a quest for spiritual meaning. The Empress is the Great Mother and nurturing impulse. The Chariot is the victorious warrior. The Star is the eternal capacity for imagination and hope. And so forth. Each card is a visual image of a specific divine power and attribute. Each has its own zodiacal or elemental energy, its own holy name of power, and its own angel or pair of angels.

Far from being omens of unalterable fate, the cards of the tarot are quite the opposite—they are magical tools for initiating change and transformation! Every tarot card can be used as a talisman and ritually charged to accomplish a specific purpose. For every goal that you may wish to manifest, there is a tarot card that will embody it.

Tarot Talismans was written for those who already have an advanced understanding of the tarot basics. We have no intention of neglecting readers who are just beginning to learn this material, however. If you are new to the study of tarot and magic in general, you will be able to refer to the appendix for a resource list of good books where you can find more information on the fundamentals.

Our work is grounded in the tradition of the Hermetic Order of the Golden Dawn, so *Tarot Talismans* will naturally follow in this vein with regard to correspondences and certain ritual practices. Nevertheless, much of the material presented here is purely our own work that has been adapted from Golden Dawn teachings to suit the needs of the topic at hand, and with practitioners from other magical paths in mind.

This book will show you how to use the cards of the tarot as magical talismans for achieving your goals. You will learn the magical correspondences of every card and how to pick the card that is best suited for your purpose. You will learn how magic works and how to do ritual card spreads. You will learn what divine powers and angels rule over your chosen card and the invocations needed to call upon them. You will learn how to create magical images and sigils of the tarot angels to help you connect with these great beings. And finally, you will learn how to consecrate your own tarot talismans using the techniques of ritual magic.

As we described earlier, the tarot is a road map designed to take you wherever you want to go in life. Ultimately, the tarot is a celestial map that you can use to navigate a universe that is divine in essence. You are now in the driver's seat with your hands on the steering wheel. Do you have a destination in mind? Do you know where you want to go? If so, grab a tarot deck and get started.

Have a pleasant journey.

PART ONE

Tarot Cards as Talismans

I

TALISMANS, MAGIC, AND TAROT

One of the main reasons why the tarot succeeds so elegantly as the premier tool of divination and talismanic magic is because it provides us with an excellent pattern, model, or paradigm of the universe. Human beings are constantly discovering and creating such patterns in order to understand and shape our environment. The Qabalistic fourfold division of the universe, the four elements of the ancient Greek philosophers, the Ptolemaic ordering of the seven ancient planets, the (current) ten-planet and twelve-house systems of the astrologers, the seven-day week, the twenty-four hour day, and the 365-day year all represent various ways in which humans divide, classify, and organize the world we live in. We use categorization as a tool to help us gain knowledge.

The same is true for the seventy-eight card divisions of the traditional tarot deck. These help the diviner classify and understand what he or she is looking at in a card reading. It is the reader's own knowledge and familiarity with this cosmic paradigm that makes divination possible. A tarot deck works as a tool for divination and magic because *the universe is completely defined or patterned within the context of the seventy-eight cards of the deck*. When we perform a card reading with the tarot, we select a small number of cards from the deck that pinpoint what part of the universal pattern needs to be addressed. In a divination, the "chance" selection of a card determines which aspect of the universe should be examined in relation to the question or subject of the reading. If a divination is performed with the proper spiritual intent and is accompanied by meditation and an invocation to deity, then those of us who believe that the universe is divine and inhabited by a higher intelligence will be led to a "divined" rather than a "random" answer to our questions.

The cards of the tarot do not simply represent various fields of human activity or convenient cosmic divisions—they represent real powers and forces that comprise the universe. The tarot is not just a collection of symbolic images—it is a *living* magical system. The universe depicted in the seventy-eight cards of the tarot is a vibrant ecosystem, if you will, of interconnected particles, substances, energies, and entities. In this divine universe, spirit and matter form a symbiotic relationship that has resulted in life as we know it. Each card symbolizes a specific energy, whether elemental, planetary, or zodiacal. The cards also represent the holy emanations of the Qabalah and the various divine names, angels, and archangels attached thereto. Because of this, the cards of the tarot provide a perfect medium for the creation of magical talismans.

Creating and working with talismans is an important part of ceremonial magic. Several books have been written about talismans and it is common to run across various terms that seem to be synonymous with the word *talisman*. These include *amulet, sigil, seal*, and *pentacle*. Although similar in meaning, there are subtle differences between them.

The word "sigil" comes from the Latin word *sigillum*, meaning "signature" or "mark." A sigil is an abstract symbol usually created from the name of a divine power, angel, or spirit name used in magic. It is considered the signature or symbolic representation of the force behind the name.[1]

Closely related is the term "seal," which comes from the Latin *signum* meaning "signet," "token," or "sign." This is usually an abstract symbol that, unlike a sigil, is not necessarily created from a name. In medieval and Renaissance magic, sigils were often created from the *qameoth* or planetary seals (refer to chapter 6 for these seals), which are themselves based on grids of numbers. Both sigils and seals are considered to have potent magical properties—they may be drawn on paper and used as simple talismans, or they may be drawn on more complex talismans that contain many sigils.

The word "pentacle" or "pantacle" is derived from the Latin word *pentaculum*, which is said by some to mean "small painting." This refers to a small drawn or painted talisman consecrated to a specific magical force. Pentacles are usually circular and painted or engraved with hexagrams, pentagrams, or other symbols. In Western ceremonial magic a pentacle is often used as a symbol of elemental earth. The pentacle can be said to represent a container for the magical forces inscribed on it—it is used to encircle those forces and bring them into physical or earthy manifestation. In the tarot, the suit of pentacles is sometimes called disks or coins.

"Talisman" is a term that comes from the Arabic *tilsam*, which in turn comes from the Greek words *telein*, "to consecrate" and *tetelesmenon*, "that which has been consecrated." A talisman is an object that has been charged or consecrated with magical energies for the achievement of a given purpose. A talisman is considered a lifeless object before the magician magically brings it to life by charging it with specific energies that are usually astrological or Qabalistic in nature.

The word "amulet" comes from the Latin *amuletum* ("charm"), and is probably derived from the Latin *amolior*, meaning "to repel, baffle, or drive away."[2] Other suggested sources include the Arabic words *amula*, signifying a small receptacle used for healing, and *hamla*, an object carried on a person for protection.[3] The word "charm," which is applied to small amulets worn on necklaces or bracelets, is derived from the Latin *carmen* ("song"), which originally indicated the incantation that was intoned over an amulet or talisman to consecrate it and empower it with magical force.[4]

Unlike a talisman, the primary power of an amulet is to protect its possessor from harm:

> The meaning of these two words is entirely distinct. Talisman being the conception in the Arabic tongue of the Greek, meaning the influence of a planet, or the Zodiac, upon the person born under the same. A Talisman in olden times was, therefore, by its very nature a sigil, or symbolic figure, whether engraved in stone or metal, or drawn upon parchment of paper, and was worn to both procure love and to avert danger from its possessor. The latter purpose alone was the object of the Amulet, its Latin signification being to do away with, or baffle, its root being *Amalior*. Pliny cites the word as the country-folk name for the Cyclamen which ought to be planted in every human home, because where it is grown poisonous drugs have no power, on which account they call it the flower, Amuletum.[5]

In ancient Babylon, amulets of stone carved into the image of the wind demon Pazuzu were worn by pregnant women because they were believed to have the power to frighten away the dreaded vampire Lamastu. The ancient Egyptians wore charms in the form of the ankh, the scarab, the Eye of Horus, and many other symbols. Today, neopagans wear silver pentagrams and Christians wear crosses and crucifixes. For some, this is not just an expression of their faith, but also a sign of their belief in the power of these symbols to bring good fortune and protect one from evil or injury.

One school of thought contends that, unlike a talisman, which is considered inert until consecrated, an amulet is usually made from a magically active substance and is often not consecrated at all. An amulet can be either natural or manmade, but its substance or symbolism is *believed* to have magical potency of its own. The primary distinction between the two is this: talismans can be consecrated to any specific purpose but are often used to *attract* something—such as a physical object, a beneficial force, a helpful quality, or a favorable set of circumstances, while amulets are mainly used for a protective purpose, to *repel* something—such as a detrimental force, a harmful quality, or an unfavorable set of circumstances.

Most ceremonial magicians today believe that a commercially bought tarot deck is an inert, manmade object that needs to be ritually consecrated in order to bring out its magical qualities. Since each of the seventy-eight cards has a different correspondence, the tarot offers seventy-eight different opportunities for creating potent magical objects, whether the cards are used for talismanic or amuletic purposes.

THE MAGICAL PROCESS: HOW TALISMANS WORK

Tarot cards are perfect for use as talismans. The most important aspect of a talisman is that it must be "charged" by a suitable means, most often by performing a consecration ritual that imbues the talisman with magical energy. In our book *The Essential Golden Dawn*, we described magic as:

> . . . the art and science of causing change to occur in conformity with will. This change can occur 1) in the outer, manifest world; 2) in the magician's consciousness; and 3) most often in both, for changing one often changes the other. Magical change occurs in a way that is not currently understood by modern science because it works through the Unmanifest—through subtle manipulations of the invisible, spiritual realms. However, the workings of magic are subject to natural law. The effects of magic are sometimes clearly visible in the physical world and other times they are only apparent on a personal, spiritual level. The workings of magic are not limited by the constraints of time and space.[6]

In short, magic is the ability to make changes in your life and in your immediate environment. But how exactly does magic work? We believe that the workings of magic can be described in four "laws," or theories. These are:

1) The Law of Willpower
2) The Law of the Astral Light[7]
3) The Law of Correspondence
4) The Law of Imagination (or Visualization)

In short, these four laws state that human willpower is a *potent force* that can cause real change in the physical world; that an invisible astral substance or *matrix* permeates everything in the cosmos; that certain objects, symbols, or natural substances are *connected with* or correspond to different magical energies; and finally that the human imagination with its capacity for visualization is what *focuses* the human will, chooses the appropriate correspondence, and manipulates the subtle astral blueprint behind the physical world, resulting in an act of magic.

The potency of the magician's willpower is a crucial factor in magic because every physical action has a magical reaction. Even our so-called mundane actions will trigger a magical response. Every cause has an effect, and the effort you put into your magic will determine its ultimate success. For example, if you do a Jupiter talisman ritual to get money, but never once go out of the house to actually apply for a job—your action (or inaction in this case) on the material plane shows a lack of willpower as well as sheer laziness and will defeat your purpose. If you perform a twenty-minute ritual invoking peace and harmony in your household and then spend six hours fighting with your spouse, you will defeat your magic. Negativity will also counteract your magic because magic requires *positive thinking*—if you *think* your magic is going to fail, it will.

The astral plane is the region where the magical process begins. This is an invisible plane of *initial formation* where everything in the physical universe first comes into being as an incorporeal idea or prototypal design. When something is created in the astral light, it will eventually filter down and become a reality in the physical realm. One example of this would be a housewife who dreams of setting up her own real estate business. She has an image in her mind of her goal—first, she imagines herself happily working in a spare bedroom that she wants to set up as a home office. This has the effect of creating her vision on the astral plane. Then she works toward realization of her dream by attending real estate classes, completing the necessary paperwork, etc.—all of which creates energy that both reinforces her visualized goal and directs her willpower toward that goal. Eventually, her dream becomes reality. This is essentially how magic works.

When performing an act of magic such as the ritual consecration of a talisman, the magician puts these four laws into action. For example, let's say that you wanted to use a tarot card as a talisman designed to cultivate communication skills. Your decision to charge a talisman for this end is itself an act of willpower, but one that you will have to reinforce with your thoughts and actions in the mundane world. For an appropriate correspondence, you might choose the card of the Magician, which is attributed to the planet Mercury. You would imagine yourself in the role of the magician and visualize yourself as already possessing the needed skill—in fact, you could visualize yourself in the future as *having already used the skill to accomplish your goal*. This visualization will be created as a living thought-form in the astral light. Finally, the physical act of *performing* the ritual consecration of your tarot talisman is a potent act of willpower—energized and focused through the powerful lens of the imagination. What you plant as a seed in the astral world may then grow and blossom in the material world.

All magic, from the simplest rites to the most complex ceremonies, works in the same way—by taking advantage of these magical "laws." And yet the process of *real* magic, unlike the Hollywood version, often works by taking the easiest route and sometimes even the most mundane route to achieve the magician's goal.

It is important to keep in mind that magic in and of itself is neither black nor white, good nor bad, beneficial nor harmful. Magic is just a process. It is the *intent* of the magician that makes it positive or negative. We should not have to remind our readers that ethical magicians who seek spiritual wisdom do not engage in harmful acts of magic. Therefore, it is wise to remember that whatever magic you send out into the universe is exactly what the universe will send back to you.

Finally, the practice of magic usually involves just that—*practice*. To some people, magic just comes naturally, but to most of us it is an art that requires training, preparation, and repeated practice to become skilled at it.

THE ROLE OF THE DIVINE IN MAGIC: GODS AND ANGELS

At this point, some readers may get the mistaken impression that magic is simply a cold, mechanical formula—just an unusual method for building a better widget. Some may ask, "But where does the *divine* fit into this four-step theory of magic? How is this a *spiritual* process? What about God, the Goddess, the angels, and spirits? If I create a talisman and invoke a deity to bless and charge it, isn't *that* what makes a talisman *magical*? Or does magic work simply because the magician trains him- or herself to become skilled in visualization and the ability to focus willpower?"

The answer to both of the last two questions is yes. This is because ceremonial magicians believe the universe is completely divine.

The divine world of spirit and the physical world of matter are two halves of a symbiotic whole and therefore everything that exists out in the macrocosm, the "greater universe," also exists in the microcosm or the "lesser universe" within the soul and psyche of humanity. They are both connected and what affects one will affect the other. This divine symbiosis is easily recognized by those who have a religious or mystical inclination. It has been plainly yet eloquently described by the Hermetic axiom "As above, so below." Simply put, there exists a nous or universal consciousness that permeates everything. It gives purpose and meaning to all things in creation. Whether one calls this consciousness God, Goddess, deity, the divine, Ain Soph, the oversoul, the eternal source, or the absolute unity—is basically irrelevant so long as the term used is understood to be one's highest idea of pure, transcendent divinity. For the sake of simplicity, this concept will be referred to here as God or the divine.

The divine enlivens the universe and ultimately grants the human mind those creative, psychic faculties needed to perform divinations and other acts of magic. In ritual, magicians usually invoke the highest aspect of the divine before all else. The magician's ability to tap into this universal consciousness will determine the accuracy of his or her divinations, as well as the success of ritual magic.

Magic has been defined as "the method of science, the aim of religion." Science and spirituality are not diametrically opposed to each other as some would believe; rather, they support one another like the black and white (or male and female) pillars of the Qabalistic Tree of Life. Both are essential and interrelated. Thus, the theory of evolution can be described as the process or mechanism by which God continually creates new forms of life on Earth. The "Big Bang" theory of the creation of the universe, along with its resulting expansion of matter, can be described as the process by which the divine caused the cosmos to come into being.

In the same way, magic, which constantly involves the invocation of deities and angels to "look with favor upon this ceremony," simply utilizes the four laws listed above as the mechanism that sets the magical process in motion. But in order to accomplish magic, the magician strives to achieve true spiritual growth and inner illumination *so that his or her will is in a state of alignment with the higher will of the divine.* If it is, then the magician's willpower is immeasurably strengthened. If the magician's will is in conflict with the higher and divine will, then the magic will either fail or go awry.

In keeping with the laws of magic, the deities and angels invoked in ritual are chosen because of their attributions and correspondences. Prayers and powerful invocations recited to spiritual beings for the accomplishment of a specific magical purpose are affirmations that the magician's will is in alignment with the will of the invoked deity. An image of the deity or angel may be created in the astral light through the faculty of the imagination. This image will act as a focal point for the magician's willpower, resulting in the ritual's success.

Angels are spiritual beings that are considered to be specific aspects of God, each with a particular purpose and jurisdiction. The word "angel" comes from the Greek *angelos*, which is itself a translation of the Hebrew word *melakh*, meaning "messenger." They have been described as "messengers of the soul." More precisely an angel is "an intermediary intelligence between the human and the One in the Great Chain of Being."[8] These divine intermediaries work with the magician in two ways: as direct intercessors between the human and the divine, and as governors in the spiritual hierarchies who command lesser angels, spirits, and elementals to carry out the goal of the ritual.

Angels are our companions in the magical arts, working together with us in the Great Chain of Being. They are of particular importance to talismanic work. In Part Two of this book we will explain how to create images of the tarot angels that can be used to help visualize these beings in the astral light.

HRU: THE ANGEL OF THE TAROT

The tarot manuscripts of the Golden Dawn list Hru as "the Great Angel (who) is set over the operation of the Secret Wisdom."[9] He is often invoked by tarot readers for guidance in divination.

Many have assumed that Hru is a form of the Egyptian war god Horus.[10] This is because most amateur Egyptophiles render the Egyptian name of Horus as "Heru" following the scholarly conventions of E. A. Wallis Budge's day. However, Budge himself and every Egyptologist since his time have known that the name of the hawk-headed god was actually pronounced "Hor" or "Hoor." We feel it is unlikely that the founders of the Golden Dawn, who obviously knew that the Coptic form of the name Horus was "Hoor" (ϩⲱⲱⲣ),[11] would have made this kind of mistake. We therefore cannot personally equate the tarot angel Hru as a form of Horus. Since the original "Book T" tarot documents show the angel's name written as H.R.U., the name might actually be an acronym.

Many of the cards in our deck *The Golden Dawn Magical Tarot* show "a radiant angelic hand" holding the various implements of the four tarot suits. We like to think of these images as showing the hand of the great angel Hru guiding and directing the use of the tarot in divination and magical work.

MAGICAL ETHICS

One would think that in magic, a practice that often involves the invocation of divine forces and holy angels, all practitioners would have an intuitive understanding that any magic that is harmful to another person runs completely contrary to the nature of the Great Work. Sadly, this is not always true. In magic, just as in larger arenas of human society, there are always those who think only of themselves and have little regard for others. Dabblers will sometimes pick up a magical book and try to cast black magic spells on people they don't like, or try to win the affections of someone who totally ignores them. Luckily, their efforts are usually doomed to failure since they have little or no understanding of the divine nature and purity of intent that the magical art requires. And, unfortunately, there are some magicians who know better, yet continue to perform negative magic against others. Israel Regardie advised his students to "shun those who practice black magic as you would shun a foul disease."

You don't have to worry too much about anyone casting evil spells against you. Because black magic runs contrary to the divine will, it tends to "boomerang" back on the person who performs it. Wiccans teach that any harmful magic that you send out will return to you three times. Author Carroll "Poke" Runyon has a wonderful analogy on the subject: a black magician is like a person in a phone booth with a hand grenade. He dials the phone number of a person he wants to "curse" and when that person answers the phone, the magician pulls the pin out of his hand grenade. His intended victim may hear the explosion on the other end of the receiver, but it is the magician in the phone booth who takes the full force of the blast. Just remember that whatever you send out into the universe is what the universe will send back to you.

But even magicians with the best of motivations must avoid performing magic that has unintended harmful consequences. The Wiccan Rede, a statement of principles for the Wiccan religion, says: "*An it harm none*, do what you will." But sometimes you can cause harm without knowing it, especially if you try to interfere with the *free will* of another person. For example, if you perform magic to make another person fall in love with you, you are interfering with his or her free will. If you continuously pray that a family member turns away from his or her own faith and adopts your faith, then you are interfering with his or her free will. If you want to create a talisman for other people, you'd better make sure that they want your help, even in a healing, otherwise you are interfering with their free will.

How can these things be considered harmful, you might ask? Well, would you want someone to cast love spells on you? Or perform magic to cause you to lose your faith? As for healing—what if your illness would ultimately result in a profound spiritual vision, life experience, or the working out of karma? Would you want someone else to interfere?

What about the toughest case of all, when someone is causing you harm or difficulty? Don't you have the right to fight back or protect yourself magically? Of course you do, but it's all a matter of how you go about it. You do not have to fight fire with fire, or counter-attack harm with harm. Instead, your magic should be focused on binding the other person's harmful actions—banishing or deflecting his or her negativity away from you. Combined with simple rites of protection to shield you, the threefold law of return will usually take care of the offender.

Always keep magical ethics in mind when you consider the creation and consecration of a talisman. Every case is different, so even with the most seemingly innocuous of talismans, carefully weigh all the issues involved before proceeding.

CHOOSING A TAROT DECK FOR TALISMANIC MAGIC

People tend to choose tarot decks for a couple of reasons. Some pick a particular deck because they are simply attracted to the artwork, while others choose a deck for the imagery it contains, such as gods and goddesses from Egyptian, Celtic, or Greek pantheons. Ceremonial magicians often choose a deck that adheres to the traditional tarot correspondences taught by the Hermetic Order of the Golden Dawn. These correspondences are widely used today by a great number of tarot enthusiasts and they are also the ones we will be using here. Five different tarot decks have been employed to illustrate this book. They include:

- *The Golden Dawn Magical Tarot* by Sandra Tabatha Cicero. This deck is based on the traditional teachings of the Hermetic Order of the Golden Dawn. The trump cards (i.e., the major arcana cards) are rich in symbolism and imagery while the pip cards of the minor arcana, like those of the so-called "medieval decks," are numbered and stylized.

- *The Thoth Tarot Deck* by Aleister Crowley. The Thoth deck is also based on the tarot teachings of the Golden Dawn, modified by Crowley's own system of Thelema. The cards were painted by Lady Frieda Harris and they are gorgeous.

- *The Universal Tarot* by Roberto De Angelis. This tarot is a new rendition of *The Rider-Waite Tarot*, the most popular tarot deck of all time. It is faithful to Pamela Coleman Smith's original cards of the *Rider-Waite* deck, but with softer lines and a more modern and natural style.

- *The Babylonian Tarot* by Sandra Tabatha Cicero. This deck has the familiar Golden Dawn attributions but with Mesopotamian imagery.
- *The Tarot of Marseille* (Lo Scarabeo version). The most popular of the "medieval" tarot decks, the Marseille Tarot dates from the eighteenth century and was the model for many tarot decks that came after it.

The cards of the tarot have specific meanings associated with them and many traditional decks are based on the tarot attributions promulgated by the Golden Dawn. Even among traditional decks, however, there are enough differences in keyword meanings, design, and imagery to influence the manner in which a specific card may be chosen and used as a talisman. The same card in different decks may be used for different magical goals.

For example, the card of the Lovers is associated with the zodiacal sign of Gemini and may be used to invoke any quality that is associated with the sign of mutable air—including versatility, communication skills, and inventiveness. And yet, the visual imagery of the Lovers in each of the five decks listed here suggests that this card may be used for various talismanic purposes depending on which deck is chosen, as in the following examples:

The Golden Dawn Magical Tarot: to gain victory over seemingly insurmountable odds *or* to free yourself from something that binds you.

The Thoth Tarot Deck: to unite opposites successfully and with complete harmony.

The Universal Tarot: to become intuitively aware of the sacredness of sex *or* to better understand the spiritual concept known as the Garden of Eden and what it means for the individual.

The Babylonian Tarot: to learn how to become a more attentive and loving partner.

The Tarot of Marseille: to ensure a successful marriage.

In another example, this time of a pip or minor arcana card, let's examine the Six of Swords. The unique imagery of this card in each of the five decks mentioned suggests a wide variety of uses:

Golden Dawn: to gain success after a period of conflict and struggle.

Thoth: to attain a state of perfect balance *or* to achieve a scientific or technological breakthrough.

Universal: to finally move on after a long time of mourning.

Babylonian (here the card is called the Six of Arrows): to heal after a long illness *or* to become a healer.

Marseille: since the pip cards of this deck are highly stylized and numerical, the Six of Swords in this deck may be used for any of the purposes listed in this paragraph.

Figure 1: The Golden Dawn Magical Tarot.

Figure 2: The Thoth Tarot Deck.

Figure 3: The Universal Tarot.

Figure 4: The Babylonian Tarot.

Figure 5: The Tarot of Marseille.

As you can see, every tarot card can be used for different purposes and these purposes may vary from deck to deck, depending upon which tarot you wish to use. We will list more of these talismanic uses in the next chapter.

PREPARING TO WORK WITH YOUR CHOSEN DECK

Ultimately, whichever deck you pick is not as important as how you interpret its imagery. Tarot symbolism taps into a deep well of spiritual wisdom that is both universal and personal. The choice of a deck is yours to make.

The first thing that any magician should consider when deciding to do ritual work of any kind with the tarot is consecrating a deck of cards. The word consecration means to "make sacred" or to dedicate to a sacred purpose. In a consecration, we charge or give magical life to the cards, just as we would for any other magical tool used regularly in ritual work.

Ambient music playing softly in the background throughout the ritual will help you make the change in consciousness from the mundane to the spiritual. Prior to performing the tarot consecration ritual, you should do a relaxation ritual or at least spend some time in quiet meditation before jumping immediately into the ritual. Taking a ritual bath will also help to put you in a magical frame of mind.

THE CLEANSING BATH

Take a shower to clean the body. Then fill the bathtub with warm water. Add bath salts or perfumed oil to the water. For an added spiritual effect, white candles and incense may be employed in the room. Some soothing music on the CD or tape player wouldn't hurt either.

Simply soak for a few minutes and release any negativity or tension into the cleansing water. Then pull the plug and drain the water while remaining in the tub. Feel your doubts and worries siphon out with the water, leaving you feeling relaxed and energized. Don't rush when getting up.

BANISHING

You should also clear the temple or your sacred space with a banishing ritual. This will cleanse the area of all unwanted energies and set up a circle of protection. The Lesser Banishing Ritual of the Pentagram or LBRP is one of the most popular rituals for achieving this. The LBRP begins with a very short ritual called the Qabalistic Cross.

THE QABALISTIC CROSS

This brief yet potent ritual forms a balanced cross of light within the magician's aura.

Stand and face east. Imagine a brilliant white light touching the top of your head. Reach up with the index finger or blade of a dagger to connect with the light and bring it down to the forehead. Touch the forehead and intone **"Atah"** (*ah-tah*, *"Thou art"*).

Touch the breast and bring the dagger blade or index finger down until it touches the heart or abdominal area, pointing down to the ground. Imagine the light descending from the forehead to the feet. Intone **"Malkuth"** (*mal-kooth*, *"the kingdom"*).

Touch the right shoulder and visualize a point of light there. Intone **"Ve-Geburah"** (*veh-geh-boor-ah*, *"and the power"*). Touch the left shoulder and visualize a point of light there. See the horizontal shaft of light extending from the opposite shoulder to join this point of light. Intone **"Ve-Gedulah"** (*veh-geh-doo-lah*, *"and the glory"*).

Imagine a completed cross of light running from head to feet and from shoulder to shoulder.

Bring the hands outward, away from the body, and finally bring them together again, clasped on the breast as if praying. Intone **"Le-Olahm, Amen"** (*lah-oh-lahm*, *"Forever, unto the ages, amen"*).

THE LESSER BANISHING RITUAL OF THE PENTAGRAM (LBRP)

Begin by performing the Qabalistic Cross. Then, still facing east, use a dagger or the index finger of the right hand to trace a large Lesser Banishing Pentagram (see figure 6). Thrust the dagger tip or index finger through the center of the pentagram and intone **"YHVH"** (*yod-heh-vav-heh*).[12] Keep the right arm extended throughout; never let it drop to your side. The pentagrams should be visualized in a flaming blue or white light.

Turn to the south and trace the same pentagram there. Charge the figure as before, intoning **"Adonai"** (*ah-doh-nye*, *"Lord."*)

start here

Figure 6: Lesser Banishing Pentagram.

Turn to the west and trace the same pentagram. Charge it with **"Eheieh"** (*eh-hay-yay*, "I am"). Turn to the north and draw the same pentagram, this time intoning the word **"Agla"** (*ah-ga-lah*).[13]

Keep the arm up and extended. Turn to face the east. Extend both arms out in the form of a tau cross (T-shape) and say, **"Before me, Raphael"** (*rah-fah-yel*). Visualize before you the great archangel of air rising out of the clouds in flowing yellow and violet robes, carrying a caduceus wand.

Behind you, visualize another figure and say, **"Behind me, Gabriel"** (*gah-bree-el*). See the archangel of water stepping out of the sea, like the goddess Venus, dressed in robes of blue and orange, with cup in hand.

Say, **"On my right hand, Michael"** (*mee-kah-yel*). See another figure to your right, the archangel of fire, dressed in flaming red and green robes, carrying a sword.

Say, **"On my left hand, Uriel"** (*ur-ee-el*). See another figure to your left. The great archangel of earth rises up from the vegetation of the earth in robes of citrine, olive, russet, and black, holding stems of ripened wheat.

Then say, **"For about me flames the pentagram, and in the column shines the six-rayed star."**

Repeat the Qabalistic Cross as in the beginning.

TAROT CONSECRATION RITUAL

In the center of your temple or sacred space you will need an altar that faces east. On the eastern side of the altar, place a black and a white pillar candle (left and right respectively) and a small white votive candle just to the east of them. Place your unopened deck in the center. If the deck has been previously opened and used, before starting the ritual you should wipe each card with a clean white cloth that has been charged for that purpose.

Around your tarot deck, place the following: on the east side, a dagger or short sword; on the south side, a wand; on the west side, a cup or chalice; and on the north side, a pentacle.

Note: a Golden Dawn magician will usually prefer to use the standard elemental weapons—the air dagger, fire wand, water cup, and earth pentacle. Practitioners of other magical traditions may choose any convenient wand for the south and a Wiccan-style pentacle for the north. If none of these items is available, simply use a stick of incense for the east, a red candle for the south, a glass of water for the west, and a platter of salt for the north. In this ritual these implements are meant to represent the elemental suits of the tarot deck itself, so you will need a second wand such as a lotus wand, spirit wand, tarot wand,[14] or any favorite magical wand for invocations and general use. You will also need either a sword, a black-handled dagger, or an athame just for banishing.

To begin the ceremony, spend a few minutes in relaxed meditation. Then perform a banishing ritual such as the LBRP.

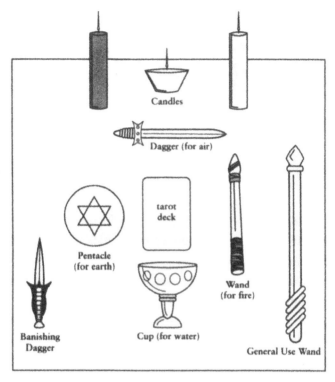

Figure 7: Altar Set-up for Tarot Deck Consecration.

Stand west of your altar, facing east. Trace a circle and a Lesser Banishing Pentagram over the unopened deck of cards. This begins the process of cleansing the cards of any previous mundane influence.

With your general use wand, strike or touch the deck three times and say, **"Eheieh. Yah. YHVH Elohim"** (*eh-hay-yay. yah. yod-heh-vav-heh el-oh-heem*).[15] With each stroke of the wand, intone one of these supernal names. Then say:

"Unto the highest do I *(state your magical name)* **consecrate these cards of art, that they may become true reflected images of thy manifestation and splendor. Not to my name but to thine be the power and the glory."**

Trace a cross over the deck and say:

"In the divine name IAO (*ee-ah-oh*),[16] **I invoke the great angel Hru** (*heh-roo*) **who art set over the operations of this secret wisdom. Lay thine hand invisibly on these cards of art and give them life. Anoint them with the divine science so that through their use I may obtain true knowledge of hidden things, to the glory of the ineffable name. Amen."**

Visualize the hand of a mighty angel held over the deck glowing with a bright white light. The tarot deck should also be visualized in a brilliant halo of light.

Strike the tarot deck again three times with the wand. Then visualize a great white light above you. Fill yourself with its divine power. Then project this energy directly at the deck

Figure 8: Projection Sign (left) and Sign of Silence (right).

using the Projection Sign, also called the Sign of the Enterer: extend your arms up above your head, then bring the hands down close to either side of the head at eye level, fingers extended, hands held flat with palms down. Then step forward with the left foot, at the same time thrust the arms directly forward, and sink the head till the eyes look exactly between the thumbs (see figure 8). Do this projection three times.

Then give the Sign of Silence: bring the left foot back, both heels together—stamp the ground once with the left foot as it is placed beside the right. At the same time, bring the left hand to the mouth and touch the center of the lower lip with the left forefinger—close the other fingers and thumb. Drop the right hand to the side.

If properly performed, you should feel a bit drained at this point, so take a moment to catch your breath.

Now, open the deck and take out the cards. Fan the cards out in a circle on the altar. With your general use wand, trace a cross in the air above the cards and say: **"By names and images are all powers awakened and re-awakened."** Thrust your wand head through the center of the cross.

Gather up the cards and wrap them in white silk or a specially chosen tarot bag. Then say:

"I now release any spirits that may have been imprisoned by this ceremony. Depart in peace. Go with the blessings of Yeheshuah Yehovahshah" (*yeh-hay-shoe-ah yeh-ho-vah-shah*).[17]

Perform the Banishing Ritual again.

Finally say: **"I now declare this temple duly closed."**

The ritual is ended.

---

1 The origin of some sigils, however, especially those found in many medieval grimoires, is not always clear and appears to be derived from skryed visions rather than from the letters of names.

2 Frederick Thomas Elworthy, *The Evil Eye: An Account of This Ancient and Widespread Superstition* (New York: Bell Publishing Company, 1989), 121.

3 Sirdir Ikbal Ali Shah, *Occultism: Its Theory and Practice* (New York: Dorset Press, 1993), 139.

4 Doreen Valiente, *An ABC of Witchcraft Past & Present* (New York: St. Martin's Press, 1973), 6.

5 The Reverend Charles William King, notes from the *Archaeological Journal*, quoted in *The Book of Talismans, Amulets and Zodiacal Gems* (1914) by William Thomas and Kate Pavitt, 10.

6 Chic Cicero and Sandra Tabatha Cicero. *The Essential Golden Dawn: An Introduction to High Magic* (St. Paul, MN: Llewellyn Publications, 2003), 70–71.

7 The Astral Light of Western magic is similar to the Eastern concepts of *prana* or *chi*. It is the spiritual life force of the cosmos.

8 Adam Forrest, "This Holy Invisible Companionship," *The Golden Dawn Journal, Book Two: Qabalah: Theory and Magic* (St. Paul, MN: Llewellyn Publications, 1994), 188.

9 Israel Regardie, *The Golden Dawn* (St. Paul, MN: Llewellyn Publications, 1994), 540.

10 This was Aleister Crowley's assumption as well (see *The Book of Thoth*, page 115).

11 Regardie, *The Golden Dawn*, 352.

12 Four Hebrew letters that stand for the highest, ineffable name of God.

13 Hebrew acronym for the phrase *Atah gebur le-olahm Adonai* or "Thou art great forever, my Lord."

14 These wands are described in our book *Secrets of a Golden Dawn Temple, Book One: Creating Magical Tools* (Thoth Publications, 2004), pages 274–281, 333–336, 341–343.

15 These three godnames are among the highest divine names on the Qabalistic Tree of Life. See chapter 4 for more information on these names.

16 The letters of the name IAO stand for Isis, Apophis, and Osiris, or the cycle of life, death, and rebirth. It is the Gnostic equivalent of *Tetragrammaton*, the holy "Four-Lettered Name," Yod Heh Vav Heh.

17 Known as the *Pentagrammaton* or holy "Five-Lettered Name" equivalent to the five elements of fire, water, air, earth, and spirit.

2
BASIC TAROT CORRESPONDENCES AND TALISMANIC USES

Creating tarot talismans requires a basic knowledge of tarot attributions and the various divine powers that each card represents. Equipped with this knowledge, the reader can create a talisman and charge it with very precise energies, invoking whatever force is needed for its specific influence and effect.

In this chapter we will briefly review the vital forces that are represented by the various cards of the tarot. These include the powers of the elements, the planets, the zodiacal signs, and the Qabalistic Tree of Life. We will also provide a list of talismanic uses for each force.

The correspondences given here are derived from the teachings of the Golden Dawn. Other magical traditions use different attributions that are perfectly valid within their respective teachings. The tarot associations provided in this book, however, constitute the most widely used system known to modern tarot readers and Western magicians.

The two major sections that divide the tarot are known respectively as the major and minor arcana, or the greater and lesser mysteries.

TAROT AND QABALAH

A traditional tarot deck consists of seventy-eight cards that embody the energies of the Qabalah. The main symbol of the Qabalah is the Tree of Life (see figure 9) and all of the cards are assigned to different aspects of it. The more you study the Qabalah, the more you will understand the tarot.

The Qabalah is a Jewish mystical tradition that originated in ancient times and was further developed by medieval rabbis living in Spain and southern France in the twelfth century. During the Renaissance it was adopted by Christian mystics and Hermetic magicians. Today, the Qabalah forms the foundational bedrock of the Western Esoteric Tradition.

The word *Qabalah* means "oral tradition" in Hebrew. Legend has it that the mysteries of the Qabalah were unveiled by God to the angels, who in turn transmitted this knowledge to Adam after his exile from Eden, to teach him how to recover paradise lost. At its heart, the Qabalah is a system for gaining a profound awareness of the divine.

The diagram of the Tree of Life consists of ten spheres called *sephiroth* (the singular form is *sephirah*), which means "emanations" or "numerations." The sephiroth are considered powers or manifestations of divine energy. By describing these divine powers, by giving each sphere a holy name and explaining its various qualities, functions, and attributes, Qabalists have given us a perfect system for making the divine more accessible to our understanding. On one level, the Qabalistic Tree of Life is a symbolic map of the universe. On another level, it is a map of our own inner consciousness. Together, the ten sephiroth and the twenty-two paths that connect them are often referred to as the Thirty-two Paths of Wisdom.

We will return to the subject of the sephiroth of the Tree of Life later. At this stage, it is important to examine another aspect of Qabalah—the study of the Hebrew alphabet. This is because every Hebrew letter, twenty-two in all, is attributed to one of the twenty-two tarot trumps.

THE HEBREW ALPHABET

The Hebrew alphabet is much more than a simple series of letters. It is a complete Qabalistic philosophy and system of its own. Each letter is a glyph or compound symbol with many associated ideas. For example, the first Hebrew letter is aleph, which is equivalent to the letter "A." The meaning of aleph is "ox" and it has a numerical value of one. Aleph is also used to represent the element of air, but in addition, the color yellow and the musical note E-natural are ascribed to it. Thus, from one single letter of the Hebrew alphabet we have obtained many different but connected ideas and sensory images.

Hebrew is a hieroglyphic alphabet of symbols, hidden meanings, colors, numbers, and sounds. This makes it ideal for unlocking the doors of the unconscious, since the subconscious mind speaks to us in symbols and archetypes. By training the conscious mind to understand the meanings of symbols, we are teaching both parts of our mind, conscious and unconscious, how to communicate with each other. This not only leads to the development of a healthier personality but also helps to clear the way for real spiritual growth to occur. The Hebrew letters were intended to be meditated upon as sacred symbols—portals of hidden wisdom through which one can climb the Tree of Life in order to reach its summit.

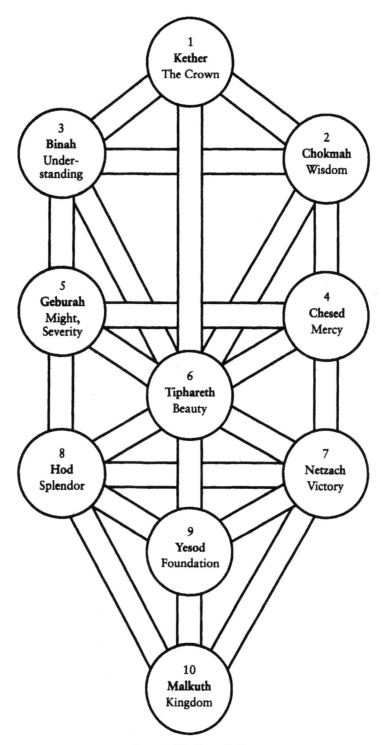

Figure 9: The Tree of Life.

HEBREW LETTERS AND THE TAROT TRUMPS

The twenty-two trump cards of the major arcana (sometimes called the tarot *keys* or *Atus of Tahuti*), collectively tell the story of the human soul on its journey through life. These are the cards that are assigned to the twenty-two Hebrew letters.

One significant feature of the Hebrew alphabet is its three-fold division. The twenty-two Hebrew letters are separated into the *three mother letters,* the *seven double letters,* and the *twelve simple letters.* These divisions are associated with the elements of the ancients, the energies of the planets, and the signs of the zodiac. Each tarot trump has a key number and a path number.[1]

The Attributions of the Tarot Trumps

Key	Path	Trump Name	Hebrew Letter	Astrological Symbol
0	11	The Fool	א aleph	△ Air
1	12	The Magician	ב beth	☿ Mercury
2	13	The High Priestess	ג gimel	☽ Luna
3	14	The Empress	ד daleth	♀ Venus
4	15	The Emperor	ה heh	♈ Aries
5	16	The Hierophant	ו vav	♉ Taurus
6	17	The Lovers	ז zayin	♊ Gemini
7	18	The Chariot	ח cheth	♋ Cancer
8	19	Strength	ט teth	♌ Leo
9	20	The Hermit	י yod	♍ Virgo
10	21	The Wheel of Fortune	כ kaph	♃ Jupiter
11	22	Justice	ל lamed	♎ Libra
12	23	The Hanged Man	מ mem	▽ Water
13	24	Death	נ nun	♏ Scorpio
14	25	Temperance	ס samekh	♐ Sagittarius
15	26	The Devil	ע ayin	♑ Capricorn
16	27	The Tower	פ peh	♂ Mars
17	28	The Star	צ tzaddi	♒ Aquarius
18	29	The Moon	ק qoph	♓ Pisces
19	30	The Sun	ר resh	☉ Sol
20	31	Judgement	ש shin	△ Fire / ⊕ Spirit
21	32	The Universe	ת tau	♄ Saturn / ▽ Earth

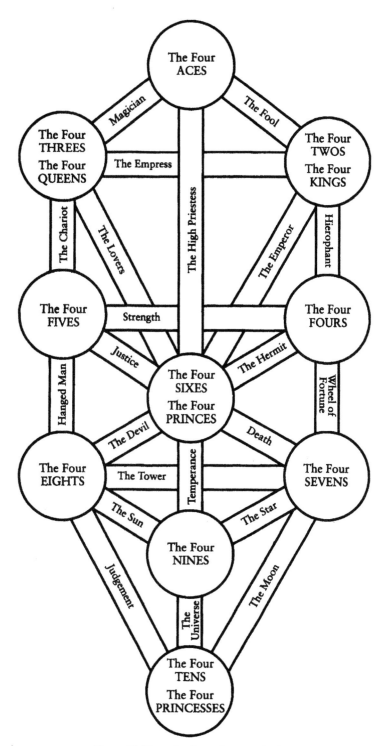

Figure 10: Tarot Cards on the Tree of Life.

THE ELEMENTAL TRUMPS

The three mother letters are aleph **א**, mem **מ**, and shin **ש**, which are attributed to the three elements of the ancients: air, water, and fire. The tarot trumps that correspond to these letters—the Fool, the Hanged Man, and Judgement—are specific conduits of these elemental energies. In the Golden Dawn system of tarot and Hebrew letter correspondences, the letter tau **ת**, ascribed to the card of the Universe, has a double-duty assignment. It is attributed to the element of earth in addition to the planet Saturn.

Interestingly, the three mother letters are also assigned to the three primary colors of yellow, blue, and red, the colors from which all other hues are derived.

ELEMENTAL ENERGIES

Classical Greek philosophers such as Empedocles and Aristotle were among the first to posit the idea that the universe is composed of four elements: fire, water, air, and earth. Not to be confused with the scientific table of elements, these four magical elements are regarded as realms, kingdoms, or divisions of nature. They are the basic modes of existence and action—the building blocks of everything in the universe. Briefly, the characteristics of these energies are:

△ Fire

The principle of animation and action. Fire energy is dynamic, energetic, vitalizing, invigorating, spontaneous, initializing, transformative, illuminating, and regenerating. The element of fire was seen by the alchemists as the "agent of transmutation" because all things are derived from and return to fire. When controlled and contained, fire changes that with which it comes into contact—but when unrestrained, it consumes whatever it touches and breaks down all substances into their basic matter. To pass through fire is symbolic of transcending the human condition. The cardinal point assigned to fire is south, the direction usually associated with the heat of summer.

Fire energy is often described as active and masculine. There is a direct parallel between the concepts of fire and life—fire is an embodiment of energy found at the level of the animal passions as well as the plane of spiritual fortitude. Its action is quick and unpredictable.

Associated Tarot Trump: Judgement.

Talismanic Uses: A talisman consecrated with the energy of fire can be used to initiate immediate action in a given situation. Fire energy can be used to increase one's personal energy, power, and force; to gain dominion, authority, or prestige; to start a new project; to undertake a new spiritual path; to consecrate an object or goal; and to ensure swift movement and rapid action on a matter.

Amuletic Uses: To banish opposition to your plans; to banish hostility and conflict.

▽ Water

The principle of consciousness and creativity. Water energy is all that is receptive, sustaining, subconscious, hidden, mysterious, generative, fertile, fluidic, malleable, limitless, and universal. In an esoteric sense the concept of water implies all liquids. Water energy is usually described as passive and feminine. The so-called "fluid body" of man is translated by modern psychology as a symbol of the unconscious or the archetypal feminine side of the personality. Water is seen as a symbol of the maternal, the Great Mother, the divine vessel or receptacle of consciousness, as well as the great well of wisdom contained within the subconscious mind, encompassing all that is deep, profound, and unfathomable.

The cardinal point assigned to water is west, the direction associated with the approach of night and the mythological "submergence" of the sun into the underworld. Submersion in water alludes to a return to an unformed state. Since water cleanses and dissolves impurities, it is seen as a symbol of spiritual purity, such as in the rite of baptism.

Associated Tarot Trump: The Hanged Man.
Talismanic Uses: The energy of water is ideal for bringing profound spiritual knowledge
  from the depth of the subconscious to the forefront of the conscious mind; to increase
  creativity; to promote fertility and productivity; to gain pleasure and happiness; to
  make friendships or partnerships; and to invoke spiritual purification and wholeness.
Amuletic Uses: To banish frustration, discomfort, misery, or emotional distress.

△ Air

The principle of adaptability and equilibration. Air energy is all that is intellectual, logical, communicative, expressive, and abstract. It is often described as being active, masculine, and changeable. Air is the element of mediation, reconciliation, and bringing together. It is often thought of as a symbol of the spirit—free, unbound, and without limits, permeating all corners of the universe. The cardinal point assigned to air is east, the direction of the dawning sun associated with spiritual light.

Light, flight, scent, and weightlessness are related to this element. In many mythologies it is connected with the idea of creation, the breath of life, and speech. It is a medium for movement and the emergence of life processes.

Air is a volatile element considered to be the offspring of the parental elements of fire and water, thus creating steam. It is the reconciler between the rival elements of fire (male) and water (female)—balancing and equilibrating these two parental opposites. Air also alludes to the rational mind and thought processes that are quick, unpredictable, and abstract. It is a symbol of waking consciousness, as opposed to water, which is a symbol of *un*consciousness.

Associated Tarot Trump: The Fool.
Talismanic Uses: The energy of air is beneficial for increasing one's intellectual capacity
  and powers of perception; to be able to think more clearly; to improve communication

skills and learning; to gain skill in a specific area of study; to invoke good health and convalescence; and to heal disputes.

Amuletic Uses: To banish sickness, trouble, or quarreling.

▽ Earth

The principle of stability and condensation. Earth energy is all that is grounding, stable, slow-moving, manifesting, practical, and mundane. It encompasses all activities of materiality, solidity, fertility, incarnation, mass, and definition. Earth represents the physical, materialized universe in which we live. It is the tangible world around us that we can touch and feel. It grounds and supports us. The cardinal point assigned to earth is north, the direction associated with darkness and stillness.

Earth energy is said to have passive and feminine qualities. It is the daughter of fire and water, just as air is the son. This element encompasses all activities of productivity, fertility, growth, and regeneration. Earth is the fourth and final element and the result of the actions of the other three. It is the ultimate receptacle of all the elemental and spiritual forces that have gone before it. Earth force is the energy of inertia or coming to rest, without which nothing can manifest in the material plane.

Associated Tarot Trump: The Universe.

Talismanic Uses: Earth energy can be utilized for practical matters such as increasing one's money or financial security, gaining employment or career opportunities, or expanding a business. It can also be used to promote productivity in any endeavor; to ground or materialize a product; and to have an idea achieve full physical manifestation.

Amuletic Uses: To banish materialism and greed; to banish inertia; to keep trouble from manifesting.

Although the trumps listed above are important expressions of elemental energies, these forces play a much more significant role in the four suits of the minor arcana, wherein all the wand cards are attributed to fire, all the cup cards are assigned to water, all the swords are ascribed to air, and all the pentacles are allocated to earth. It is in the minor arcana where the powers of the elements come into full expression, especially for use as tarot talismans.

THE PLANETARY TRUMPS

In the Hebrew alphabet, the seven double letters are assigned to the seven planets: beth ב to Mercury, gimel ג to Luna, daleth ד to Venus, kaph כ to Jupiter, peh פ to Mars, resh ר to Sol, and tau ת to Saturn. These double letters are so-called because they each have two sounds associated with them—one hard and one soft, and they also have a double esoteric meaning. The seven double letters are assigned to the seven rainbow colors of light reflected in a prism.

The word *planet* comes from the Greek word *planasthai*, "to wander." The planets were referred to in ancient times as "the stars that wander" because unlike the so-called fixed stars, the planets were always changing their position around the night sky. The ancients recognized only seven planets beyond Earth: Mercury, Mars, Venus, Jupiter, Saturn, and the luminaries of the sun and moon, which were also seen to wander.

Planets represent the primary energies involved in the science of astrology—they are the movers and shakers of the horoscope. The planetary spheres are "symbolic expressions of functional principles which are found at all levels of functional existence."[2] These fundamental energies are modified by the various signs of the zodiac. The planets can be likened to the main actors in a celestial drama, while the signs are the various roles that these actors play.

Each planet has a special relationship with one or more of the zodiacal signs it is said to govern. The energy of a planet is strongest and most harmonious in the sign(s) that it rules. Conversely, a sign that is contrary in nature to a specific planet tends to weaken that planet's energy.

Some modern astrologers have assigned the newer planets of Neptune, Uranus, and Pluto to the tarot trumps commonly assigned to the three Hebrew mother letters. This is fine, although astronomers are not yet done finding new planets, and some are even speculating that Pluto is really an asteroid, not a planet. In any event, the fact that new planets have been discovered has no bearing on the validity of the ancient seven-planet system, which like other paradigms of the universe is complete within itself. The time-honored seven-planet system, which matches the tarot correspondences of the Hebrew double letters, is the one we will describe here.

THE PLANETARY ENERGIES

☉ Sol

The principle of inner self. Sol is the Roman sun god and the origin of the word "solar." The sun is the primary source of light and life in our solar system. Sol represents the primary masculine principle and men in general. It is also the fundamental expression of the individual, displaying qualities of success and leadership. The sun's action is energizing and stimulating. It symbolizes the center or power of the higher self, and the principle of self-actualization.

Associated Tarot Trump: The Sun.

Talismanic Uses: Solar talismans govern health and healing; vitality and energy; personal fulfillment, identity, and personal power; willpower and essential principles; and authority, leadership, positions of rank and title, high office, advancement, fame, and general prosperity. They may also be used to dissolve hostility and cultivate friendship.

Amuletic Uses: To banish selfishness, ego-inflation, and delusions of grandeur; to banish illness.

☽ Luna

The principle of change. Luna is a Roman name identified with Diana, goddess of the moon. The moon embodies the primary female principle, motherhood, and women in general. The moon's action fluctuates—it is the principle of change and alternation. This luminary also encompasses the unconscious, instincts, reactions, feelings, habits, tides, phases, reflexes, and reflections. Luna rules needs, desires, personal interests, messages, navigation, recovering stolen property, magnetism, liquids, fertility, and growth.

Associated Tarot Trump: The High Priestess.

Talismanic Uses: Lunar talismans can be used to understand the secrets of dreams, visions, and the subconscious mind; to improve one's instincts, intuitions, and psychic abilities; for maternity and women's affairs; for safe travel over water; and to become more flexible, adaptable, and receptive.

Amuletic Uses: To banish nightmares, hallucinations, phantasms, or delusions; to banish anxiety, stress, and insomnia; to banish wandering thoughts.

☿ Mercury

The principle of expression. This planet is named after the fleet-footed Roman messenger god. Mercury governs communication, reason, intellect, mental functions, thought processes, rationalization, awareness, perceptions, adroitness, skill, opinions, transmission, words, speaking, writing, mailings, and means of articulation. In addition, Mercury deals with family, children, siblings, social contacts, day-to-day activities, travel, and transportation, and it rules trickery, theft, and deceit. This planet's action is rapid, unpredictable, and explosive.

Associated Tarot Trump: The Magician.

Talismanic Uses: Mercury talismans are good for obtaining skill in all forms of communication such as writing and public speaking; for receiving messages; for increased skill in divination, science, and magic; for improving knowledge, intellectual prowess, and study skills; for success in competitive events such as sports or games; for business dealings, bookkeeping, and merchandizing; for safe travel; for teaching; to recover stolen goods; to be able to tell truth from falsehood; to correct a misunderstanding; and for success in diplomatic affairs.

Amuletic Uses: To banish falsehood and deception; to banish thieves, con artists, liars, and charlatans.

♀ Venus

The principle of attraction. The planet of love, named after the Roman goddess, was in ancient times nicknamed the *Lesser Benefic.* It governs the establishment of what we consider to be important or worthwhile—merits, values, and ideals. Venus rules harmony, pleasure, natural love, sensuality, sociability, attraction, interaction, art, music, poetry, drama, song, culture, beauty, possessions, jewelry, sentiments, marriage, relationships, and unions. Its action is mild and harmonious.

Associated Tarot Trump: The Empress.

Talismanic Uses: Venus talismans may be used for love; to find one's life partner; for improved romance and sexual relations between partners; for forming friendships and harmonious partnerships; for moving in social circles; for cultural pursuits; for joyous and pleasant undertakings; for kindness and pleasure; and to excel in any of the fine arts as well as enjoyment of the arts.

Amuletic Uses: To banish lust, infidelity, or betrayal; to banish fantasy-escapism; to avoid a bad relationship or partnership.

♂ Mars

The principle of energy. The Roman name for the god of war, this planet was referred to by the ancients as the *Lesser Malefic.* It governs desires, sexual energies, focused energies, dynamic action, initiative, animal nature, force, will, the desire for power, strife, strain, adversity, work, achievement, competition, and death. Mars also rules weapons, aggression, war, accidents, violence, surgery, tools, iron, and steel. The action of this planet is sudden, forceful, and disruptive. The energy of Mars can be used violently and destructively or with valor and strength.

Associated Tarot Trump: The Tower.

Talismanic Uses: Martial talismans are good for success in conflict; for protection against enemies; for protection in general; to counter an attack; for military success; for justice and integrity; for successful surgery; to purify an infection; to acquire great amounts of energy; to gain courage, valor, and military honor; and for success and protection in firefighting and law enforcement.

Amuletic Uses: To banish arguments, violence, aggression, or warfare.

♃ Jupiter

The principle of expansion. This planet, named after the primary Roman god, was called the *Greater Benefic* by the ancients. Jupiter is the lawmaker, the judge, and the benefactor of humankind. This planet rules leisure time, wealth, growth, prosperity, opportunity, assimilation, indulgence, optimism, big business, morality, the higher (abstract) mind, higher education, ambitions, philosophy, and luck. Jupiter's action is orderly and efficient and fosters growth and increase.

Associated Tarot Trump: The Wheel of Fortune.

Talismanic Uses: Jupiter talismans can be used for obtaining honors and good will; acquiring money, riches, and financial benefits of all kinds; for profitable business dealings and investments; for peace between enemies; for preserving health; for acquiring anything desired; for rest and relaxation; for good relations with leaders and employers; for success in banking, legal matters, and foreign affairs; and for success in general.

Amuletic Uses: To banish over-indulgence, injustice, subjugation, or despotism; to banish something that was badly constructed; to banish poor business practices or underhanded financial schemes.

♄ Saturn

The principle of contraction. The ringed planet, named after the Roman god of agriculture, was called the *Greater Malefic* in earlier times. This planet is known as the taskmaster of the horoscope. It rules organization, discipline, responsibility, security, structure, goals, career opportunities, limitations, conservatism, crystallized focus, restrictions, delays, theories, orthodoxy, tradition, depth, time, memory, patience, endurance, truth, wisdom, aging, inertia, and solidification. Saturn's action is slow and enduring.

Associated Tarot Trump: The Universe.

Talismanic Uses: Saturn talismans are used to improve one's understanding of a problem; to understand and deal with major life issues such as aging or death; for anything having to do with the dead; to ensure that wills, property, legacies, and inheritances are properly taken care of; to obtain more time for a project; to increase or limit time constraints; and to provide focus, structure, and organization to a project.

Amuletic Uses: To banish limitation, imprisonment, or confinement; to banish sorrow or inertia; to banish false memories.

THE ZODIACAL TRUMPS

The twelve simple letters of the Hebrew alphabet are assigned to the twelve zodiacal signs: heh ה to Aries, vav ו to Taurus, zayin ז to Gemini, cheth ח to Cancer, teth ט to Leo, yod י to Virgo, lamed ל to Libra, nun נ to Scorpio, samekh ס to Sagittarius, ayin ע to Capricorn, tzaddi צ to Aquarius, and qoph ק to Pisces. The simple letters have a single sound and an esoteric meaning that describes one of twelve human properties. They embody the symbolism of the twelve signs as well as twelve of the tarot trumps.

The zodiac (literally "circle of animals" or "circle of living beings") is the heavenly belt or ecliptic composed of the twelve zodiacal signs. If the planets can be likened to the greater celestial energies that move through the universe, the signs can be described as lesser formative powers of the cosmos that modify and shape those planetary energies—focusing them upon Earth and on the inner world of humanity. Each of the zodiacal signs symbolizes the discharge of a specific *quality* of cosmic energy as well as the expression of a particular archetypal field of human activity.

THE ZODIACAL ENERGIES

♈ Aries

The principle of activity. The expression of commencement. Keywords associated with this sign include: quick, impulsive, dynamic, initiating, energetic, enthusiastic, confident, and pioneering.

Element and Quality: Cardinal fire.
Ruled by Planet: Mars.
Associated Tarot Trump: The Emperor.
Talismanic Uses: Aries energy is especially useful in creating talismans for extra energy, vigor, or needed self-confidence; a quick answer to an immediate problem; stimulating new growth; taking control or authority in a situation; and initiating new projects or new ideas.
Amuletic Uses: To banish the tendency to be intolerant, arrogant, or domineering; to banish the tendency to not follow through or complete things.

♉ Taurus

The principle of stability. The expression of self-substantiation. Keywords associated with this sign include: steady, stable, practical, productive, substance-oriented, dependable, thorough, conventional, aesthetic, and sensual.

Element and Quality: Fixed (kerubic) earth.
Ruled by Planet: Venus.
Associated Tarot Trump: The Hierophant.
Talismanic Uses: Taurus energy is particularly suited to creating talismans for needed stability, steadiness, or permanence; to materialize an idea; to manifest an endeavor; to finalize or complete a project; to assure loyalty and dependability; to acquire goods; and to stand firm and hold your ground under pressure.
Amuletic Uses: To banish the tendency to be greedy, possessive, stubborn, or self-indulgent.

♊ Gemini

The principle of versatility. The expression of communication. Keywords associated with this sign include: adaptable, dexterous, dual, inventive, intelligent, inquisitive, literary, quick-witted, and sociable.

Element and Quality: Mutable air.
Ruled by Planet: Mercury.
Associated Tarot Trump: The Lovers.
Talismanic Uses: Gemini energy is beneficial for creating talismans to improve communication and writing skills; to better express yourself to others; to improve concentration,

intellectual powers, the capacity for rational thought, and creative thinking; and to become more flexible and versatile.

Amuletic Uses: To banish the tendency to be reckless, impulsive, indecisive, unreliable, or scatterbrained.

♋ Cancer

The principle of dedication. The expression of emotion. Keywords associated with this sign include: nurturing, devoted, parental, familial, domestic, understanding, supportive, receptive, sympathetic, sensitive, and emotional.

Element and Quality: Cardinal water.
Ruled by Planet: Luna.
Associated Tarot Trump: The Chariot.
Talismanic Uses: Cancer energy is especially useful in creating talismans that will support domestic life in every way; to be a good provider for your family; to be a good parent to your children; for peace and harmonious relations with your extended family; and for a happy marriage. Cancer energy is also good for emotional support, nursing care, empathy, and sensitivity to the needs of others.
Amuletic Uses: To banish the tendency to be hypersensitive, pessimistic, self-pitying, or selfish.

♌ Leo

The principle of magnetism. The expression of willpower. Keywords associated with this sign include: ambitious, enthusiastic, charismatic, dramatic, optimistic, enterprising, confident, generous, and idealistic.

Element and Quality: Fixed (kerubic) fire.
Ruled by Planet: Sol.
Associated Tarot Trump: Strength.
Talismanic Uses: Leo energy is used for creating talismans that will attract fame, honor, and recognition; courage, strength, and self-confidence; positions of authority and leadership; and the aptitude for creativity in the fine arts. Leo energy is also good for charity work, developing organizational skills, and developing social skills.
Amuletic Uses: To banish the tendency to be vain, pompous, overbearing, or status conscious.

♍ Virgo

The principle of analysis. The expression of practicality. Keywords associated with this sign include: discriminating, scientific, systematic, fact-finding, methodical, studious, analytical, pragmatic, and diligent.

Element and Quality: Mutable earth.
Ruled by Planet: Mercury.
Associated Tarot Trump: The Hermit.
Talismanic Uses: Virgo energy is ideal for making talismans to gain mental sharpness; for aid in any project that demands accuracy, precision, and fine detail; for finding practical solutions to difficult problems; and for obtaining work or employment that is challenging and enjoyable. Virgo energy is also good for scientific, engineering, or medical work, teaching, and research.
Amuletic Uses: To banish the tendency to be overly critical, pedantic, obsessive, or self-centered.

♎ Libra

The principle of balance. The expression of harmony. Keywords associated with this sign include: fair-minded, judicial, even-handed, reasonable, diplomatic, tactful, cooperative, agreeable, and sociable.

Element and Quality: Cardinal air.
Ruled by Planet: Venus.
Associated Tarot Trump: Justice.
Talismanic Uses: Libra energy is particularly suited for creating talismans to obtain balance and harmony; to restore equilibrium and stability; for seeing all sides of a problem; for an unbiased look at different viewpoints in a given situation; for being the peacemaker between quarreling parties; for putting an end to arguments and conflicts; for successful negotiations or fair arbitrations; for developing "people skills"; and to obtain social justice and equality.
Amuletic Uses: To banish the tendency to be fickle, indecisive, apathetic, or easily deterred.

♏ Scorpio

The principle of motivation. The expression of awareness. Keywords associated with this sign include: intense, profound, resolute, penetrating, resourceful, purposeful, persistent, focused, determined, mystical, and transformative.

Element and Quality: Fixed (kerubic) water.
Ruled by Planet: Mars.[3]

Associated Tarot Trump: Death.

Talismanic Uses: Scorpio[4] energy is beneficial for creating talismans that focus on obtaining your ultimate goals; to channel all of your talents and natural resources into a specific objective; for penetrating to the depths of a difficult problem; to explore your passions; to channel sexual energy into other activities; to explore the secret forces of nature; to develop personal magnetism; to become a mystic; to "die" to an old way of life and be transformed into a new way of life.

Amuletic Uses: To banish the tendency to be temperamental, jealous, vengeful, violent, intolerant, secretive, or suspicious.

♐ Sagittarius

The principle of education. The expression of inner vision. Keywords associated with this sign include: philosophical, religious, scholarly, intellectual, progressive, prophetic, visionary, broad-minded, just, straightforward, ethical, and optimistic.

Element and Quality: Mutable fire.

Ruled by Planet: Jupiter.

Associated Tarot Trump: Temperance.

Talismanic Uses: Sagittarius energy is especially useful in creating talismans that will increase your understanding of philosophical matters, spiritual mysteries, or religious doctrines; to gain access to higher education or higher learning; to obtain a scholarship; to gain occult knowledge; and to study new subjects. Sagittarius energy is also good for sporting events and games; for traveling; for speaking your mind; and for going on adventures.

Amuletic Uses: To banish the tendency to be argumentative, overly talkative, impatient, reckless, pushy, or hot-headed.

♑ Capricorn

The principle of perseverance. The expression of ambition. Keywords associated with this sign include: disciplined, reliable, responsible, patient, steady, industrious, productive, determined, perfectionist, orderly, methodical, practical, careful, conventional.

Element and Quality: Cardinal earth.

Ruled by Planet: Saturn.

Associated Tarot Trump: The Devil.

Talismanic Uses: Capricorn energy is ideal for making talismans that will improve your career interests, business, financial investments, and economic security; for making sound plans and improving your organizational skills; for developing a better work ethic; for attaining your goals in a careful, step-by-step manner; for learning patience;

for gaining status and prestige; and for cultivating the ability to persevere through hardship.

Amuletic Uses: To banish the tendency to be egotistic, fatalistic, stubborn, inhibited, unforgiving, or status-seeking.

♒ Aquarius

The principle of imagination. The expression of thought. Keywords associated with this sign include: intellectual, logical, inventive, scientific, intuitive, analytical, progressive, independent, diplomatic, and altruistic.

Element and Quality: Fixed (kerubic) air.
Ruled by Planet: Saturn.[5]
Associated Tarot Trump: The Star.
Talismanic Uses: Aquarius energy is beneficial for creating talismans to improve your intellect and capacity for logical thinking; to improve your powers of imagination and creativity; for gaining independence and self-reliance; and for pursuing humanitarian causes and social reform. Aquarius energy is also good for flying, writing, scientific pursuits, electronics, and technology of all kinds.
Amuletic Uses: To banish the tendency to be cold, impersonal, unpredictable, or temperamental.

♓ Pisces

The principle of understanding. The expression of the mystical. Keywords associated with this sign include: introspective, intuitive, psychic, clairvoyant, ethereal, mystical, religious, philosophical, emotional, artistic, compassionate, and gentle.

Element and Quality: Mutable water.
Ruled by Planet: Jupiter.[6]
Associated Tarot Trump: The Moon.
Talismanic Uses: Pisces energy is ideal for making talismans to increase your psychic abilities and capacity for clairvoyance; to invoke visions; to explore the spiritual sciences; to become a mystic; to explore your dreams; to improve your creativity and imagination; to gain skill in all of the fine arts; and for aid in divination. Pisces energy is good for careers in nursing, medicine, social work, and counseling.
Amuletic Uses: To banish the tendency to be timid, inhibited, impractical, melancholy, indolent, or procrastinating.

THE SEPHIROTH AND THE MINOR ARCANA

According to Qabalistic tradition, the essence of the divine began to unfold its energy into the universe as we know it through ten different stages or levels. These were the ten sephiroth or "emanations" of the Tree of Life shown in figure 9. Each successive level became denser than the previous one. This divine energy originated from nothingness, acquiring substance as it descended into the different stages of manifestation. The energy issuing forth followed a cyclical pattern of emanation, limitation, expansion, and overflow until, at length, the energies solidified. The tenth level of emanation was the last, resulting in the physical universe as we know it.

The ten sephiroth have been described as a divine means and pattern for existence, vessels of divine power, and the ten principal aspects of God. The ten sephiroth do not represent divisions of the divine, but rather they indicate God's sequential manifestation as if one candle were lit from another without the emanator being diminished in any way. They are one with God, yet they are also distinct from one another. The ten emanations are the diverse expressions and mind-states of a single divine unity. Each sephirah represents one specific aspect of god-energy, holy essence, or a particular mode of consciousness. The sephiroth express divine attributions that are organized into an archetypal pattern that is the model for everything that has come into being.

It is no small coincidence that there are ten sephiroth and ten pip or numbered cards in every tarot suit. Each pip card is assigned to the sephirah whose number matches it (see figure 10). The energies and attributes of the ten sephiroth can be accessed through the pip cards and used to invoke very specific aspects of divine energy for the purpose of creating talismans. The following list can be consulted as a handy reference to these associations.

CORRESPONDENCES OF THE SEPHIROTH

1. Kether

The principle of existence and *the principle of unity.* The first sephirah is Kether, meaning the "crown" at the top of the Middle Pillar, the central Pillar of Equilibrium on the Tree of Life. Kether is pure, brilliant essence. It is a monad of pure energy—androgynous, pure unity without a trace of duality or separation. All of the other sephiroth—and in fact, all of creation—emanate from the primal source, which is Kether. The first sephirah is simply *the One.* It is essentially indescribable although we tend to think of it as pure spirit. It is often symbolized as a point of radiant light. The first sphere represents the highest goal of all mystical experience. Traditionally, Kether has no astrological attribution because the *primum mobile* ("first whirlings") that initiated the creation of the universe is attributed to this sphere.

Elemental Quality: Air.
Gender Quality: Androgynous, uniting.

Planet Assigned to Sephirah: None.

Associated Tarot Cards: The four Aces. The Aces generally represent the power and root force of spirit.

Talismanic Uses: Ketheric energy is beneficial for creating talismans for unity, continuity, perfection, and pure spirituality in its highest sense; to gain an understanding of the concept of infinity and the creation of the universe; to gain an awareness of the divine; to complete the Great Work; to attain union with the divine.

Amuletic Use: None.

2. Chokmah

The principle of action. Chokmah or "wisdom" is the second sephirah, which is situated at the top of the Pillar of Mercy, also called the male Pillar of Force. If Kether can be described as a point, then Chokmah can be portrayed as a straight line—an extension of the point into space. The energy of Chokmah is active and forceful. Chokmah signifies the divine thought of God in self-contemplation. It represents the divine's will to create as well as the catalyst needed to put that will into action. It creates by expanding its energy outside of itself, thus changing from a unity to a duality—the Creator and that which is created. As the archetypal masculine energy, Chokmah is the father of created things who puts all into motion. The second sphere is often symbolized by the image of the Heavenly Father. Rather than having a planet attributed to this sphere, the entire wheel of the zodiac is assigned to Chokmah.

Elemental Quality: Fire.

Gender Quality: Masculine, outpouring.

Planet Assigned to Sephirah: None.

Associated Tarot Cards: The four Twos. The four Kings. The Twos generally imply the initiation and insemination of a matter. The Kings represent the beginning of material forces, as well as a swift, powerful force that quickly fades.

Talismanic Uses: Chokmaic energy can be used to initiate swift action, movement, activity, expansion, and force; to gain spiritual wisdom; to increase one's capacity for spiritual devotion; to better understand masculine energy; to venerate God the Heavenly Father.

Amuletic Use: To banish the tendency to dominate and control.

3. Binah

The principle of receptivity. The third sephirah of Binah, or "understanding," is the feminine counterpart of Chokmah. It sits at the summit of the Pillar of Severity, also called the female Pillar of Form. Binah creates by taking what is outside of itself *inside*—it receives and confines the active energy pouring forth from Chokmah. This limiting of Chokmah's energetic force is actually a form-building mechanism because energy that is contained can take on shape and purpose. The third sephirah is symbolized by the great mysterious sea and the image of the Heavenly Mother whose womb is the container that gives form to all things in the universe. Binah represents unity in diversity and the unfolding of what was once hidden. Together, Chokmah and Binah are God the Father and Goddess the Mother— the two dual powers of manifestation which give birth to all creation.

Kether, Chokmah, and Binah form a unique trio of spheres on the Tree of Life known as the supernal or heavenly triad. One source tells us "the Holy One with Three Heads (or principle aspects) which form only one" and "all the mysteries are contained in them."[7] Another source describes these three sephiroth as the three aspects of true knowledge: The crown of Kether is *knowledge* itself, containing all that can be known. Dynamic Chokmah is the *knower* who can look back at the source of Kether and realize divine truth. Binah is that which is *known*. She is the full differentiated expression of what Chokmah knows. It is in the third sphere that knowledge becomes recognized and comprehended.[8]

Elemental Quality: Water.

Gender Quality: Feminine, containing.

Planet Assigned to Sephirah: Saturn.

Associated Tarot Cards: The four Threes. The four Queens. The Threes generally imply the realization of a matter and action definitely commenced. The Queens represent a slow but unshakable force that endures.

Talismanic Uses: Binah energy is ideal for creating talismans that build structure and form; to maintain control; to better understand the necessity of limitation and boundaries; to gain understanding of profound spiritual mysteries through experience; to understand the virtue of silence; to cope with sorrow; to better understand feminine energy; to venerate Goddess, the Heavenly Mother.

Amuletic Uses: To banish avarice.

4. Chesed

The principle of extension. Chesed or "mercy" is the fourth sephirah located on the masculine Pillar of Force. It represents the offspring of Father-Chokmah-wisdom and Mother-Binah-understanding, which results in mercy and compassion. Chesed is "God's love which created the world . . . when he leans over the possibility of his creation, his bliss becomes kindness of kindnesses, goodness, mercy, that is, grace."[9] In Chesed the divine energy of pure being first extends itself beyond the two-dimensional level and takes on physical manifestation. This is because four points of reference are needed to define height and depth, the prerequisites for three-dimensional space. As the number four, Chesed is the structural support of all that is manifested. It makes physical reality possible. All expressions of order, law, and organization, as well as the divine's compassion toward humanity, are attributed to the fourth sephirah.

Elemental Quality: Water.

Gender Quality: Masculine, outpouring.

Planet Assigned to Sephirah: Jupiter.

Associated Tarot Cards: The four Fours. The Fours generally indicate the completion and perfection of a matter.

Talismanic Uses: Chesedic energy can be used to initiate construction, creation, expansion, improvement, growth, and increase; to build something; to organize one's thoughts and plans; to bring an invention into being; to establish an idea; to secure a project; to enforce laws; to better understand the concept of obedience; to invoke pure and unconditional love; to improve one's memory. The power of Chesed is also good for securing joy, empathy, mirth, and happiness.

Amuletic Use: To banish bigotry, gluttony, tyranny, and hypocrisy.

5. Geburah

The principle of limitation. Geburah, which means "power" or "severity," is the fifth sephirah, located on the feminine Pillar of Form. It is sometimes referred to as the "strong arm of God." Geburah is the sphere of justice and control. It limits the abundant energy of Chesed by applying strict discipline in the manner of a purifying fire that burns away all that is useless or obsolete, making the energy suitable for the next stage of emanation and clearing the way for further evolution and growth. It is here that energy is rendered free of any weakness or impurity. Geburah is the contraction of the divine will, keeping in check the ever-expanding energies of Chesed so that there is always a crucial balance between the opposites of mercy and severity. The number five also brings in the dimension of time and, by extension, decomposition and loss. All expressions of God's might, movement, or righteous wrath, as well as conflict and destruction, are assigned to the fifth sphere.

Elemental Quality: Fire.

Gender Quality: Feminine, containing.

Planet Assigned to Sephirah: Mars.

Associated Tarot Cards: The four Fives. The Fives generally denote struggle, strife, and opposition to the matter at hand.

Talismanic Uses: Geburic energy can be used for strength, power, force, courage, energy, and vitality; to fight fear and anxiety; to exercise influence or control over something; to make a final judgment in a matter; for purification or cleansing; to understand why power must be used wisely; to observe or enforce discipline; to prevail in a conflict; to exercise one's willpower.

Amuletic Uses: To banish cruelty and destruction; to banish violence and warfare.

6. Tiphareth

The principle of multiplicity and *the principle of reconciliation.* Tiphareth or "beauty" lies at the very center of the Tree of Life on the Pillar of Equilibrium. As the offspring of Chesed-mercy and Geburah-severity, the sixth sephirah represents God's harmony, peace, and love summed up in the concept of divine beauty. Like Kether above it, Tiphareth is a balanced point of stillness, light, and perfection. The sphere of beauty reconciles between the right- and left-hand columns of the Tree. But Tiphareth is also seen as a unifying link between higher and lower states of being, joining that which is above to that which is below. It is an inner mediator between the higher divine self and the lower self or the ego of the individual human being—between the infinite and the personal—between the singleness of the One and the multiplicity of the many. In Tiphareth we receive the sure knowledge that all the gods are one God, all the goddesses are one Goddess, and that God and Goddess are One. Tiphareth also has a major role in transforming the energy of the Tree of Life by the diversity of the paths that connect and unite the sephiroth. On the human level, the sixth sphere corresponds to the imagination.

Tiphareth is often symbolized by the image of the savior god, as well as by solar deities and gods associated with beauty, who are often gods of sacrifice and resurrection. All expressions of mysticism, healing, inner peace, and human love for the divine are assigned to the sixth sephirah.

Elemental Quality: Air.
Gender Quality: Androgynous, uniting.
Planet Assigned to Sephirah: Sol.
Associated Tarot Cards: The four Sixes. The four Princes. The Sixes indicate definite accomplishment and the carrying out of a matter. The Princes represent a force that is both rapid and enduring.
Talismanic Uses: Tipharetic energy is used to promote balance, harmony, reconciliation, and peace; to understand the connectedness of all things; to understand the mysteries of self-sacrifice; to promote health and well-being; to improve one's imagination; to obtain mystical awareness of self; to obtain illumination and enlightenment; to achieve spiritual rebirth.
Amuletic Uses: To banish egotism, vanity, and spiritual pride; to banish guilt.

7. Netzach

The principle of connection. Below Tiphareth, the Tree of Life begins to establish the manifestation of what humans often think of as "the real world," although it has not yet arrived at the realm of physical matter. Reality here means the level of the human personality. Netzach means "victory" but it is also sometimes called "eternity" and "endurance." It is the enduring victory of God's creativity as well as the realm of human emotions, instincts, and desires. Netzach symbolizes the passionate side of human nature. It also corresponds to the collective or group mind of humanity, from which it derives the principle of connection. Netzach is a connecting force that is expressed as the power of love—love for humanity as well as love for the gods in all their diverse splendor.

The seventh sephirah is considered a dynamic force that inspires us and drives us. All expressions of human passion are attributed here, as well as all of the creative arts—music, dance, and poetry.

Elemental Quality: Fire.

Gender Quality: Feminine (containing/attracting), but also outpouring.

Planet Assigned to Sephirah: Venus.

Associated Tarot Cards: The four Sevens. The Sevens generally signify a powerful force which requires one capable of handling it. They also show a possible outcome for good or ill—depending very much on the action taken.

Talismanic Uses: Netzach energy can be used to achieve victory and success; to gain inspiration; to learn how to be generous and unselfish; to improve creativity and artistic abilities; to learn how to express emotions; to increase energy, vitality, enthusiasm and zest for living; to obtain pleasure and satisfaction; to fulfill one's heart's desire.

Amuletic Uses: To banish lust; to banish depravity, addiction, obsession, or abuse; to rid oneself of an unhealthy emotional dependency; to curb anger, jealousy, or hatred; to rid oneself of depression and despair.

8. Hod

The principle of separation. Hod means "splendor," "glory," or "majesty." It represents another portion of the human personality, the "glory" of the divine mind as well as the human mind that is its reflection. It is the intellectual part of the mind that balances the fiery emotions of Netzach. Hod is assigned to the left side of the brain, the reasoning mind, just as Netzach corresponds to the intuitive right side of the brain. It also corresponds to the individual mind, as opposed to the group mind of humanity in Netzach. It is the individual mind from which Hod derives the principle of separation. Hod is the rational mind that separates, organizes, and labels—making distinctions between things so that we can better understand them. All expressions of writing, language, communication, magic, mathematics, and science are assigned to Hod.

Elemental Quality: Water.

Gender Quality: Masculine (outpouring), but also containing/limiting.

Planet Assigned to Sephirah: Mercury.

Associated Tarot Cards: The four Eights. The Eights generally indicate short-term success.

Talismanic Uses: Hod energy can be utilized for sharpening intellect and brainpower; to increase capacity for rational thought and abstract thinking; to engage in scholarly, literary, and educational pursuits; to invoke the truth; to aid in the study and practice of magic and divination.

Amuletic Uses: To banish lies, dishonesty, and falsehood; to rid oneself of an unhealthy detachment from people; to banish divisiveness; to banish the tendency toward escapism through intellectual pursuits.

9. Yesod

The principle of involvement. Yesod, the "foundation," completes the final triad on the Tree of Life. It represents the reproductive power of the divine, both masculine and feminine. Yesod supports and absorbs the energies of all three pillars on the Tree of Life before they reach final manifestation. The ninth sephirah is the sphere of the astral light—the etheric blueprint upon which the physical universe is built. Yesod receives the energies from all of the sephiroth above it, which are then combined into a type of pattern for the physical world to follow.

In Yesod, the divine puts into action the principle of reproduction as it prepares to give birth to the material world. One of the holy names of this sphere is Shaddai El Chai, which means "Almighty Living God." This indicates that the divine infuses itself into every aspect of our universal blueprint, making every living thing a vessel for its holy power. In this manner, the divine becomes a fully involved participant in every aspect of all physical life.

Yesod is the expression of divine intuition, the foundation of reality. At the level of the human personality, the ninth sphere corresponds to the instincts and the unconscious mind. All expressions of human intuition, precognition, and revelation, as well as dreams and visions, are assigned to the ninth sphere.

Elemental Quality: Air.
Gender Quality: Androgynous/hermaphroditic, uniting.
Planet Assigned to Sephirah: Luna.
Associated Tarot Cards: The four Nines. The Nines generally represent very great fundamental force and executive power, for good or ill.
Talismanic Uses: Yesodic energy can be employed to build a foundation, craft a blueprint, or lay the groundwork for a project; to promote reproduction or procreation; to explore the mysteries of sex; to better understand the invisible mechanism of the universe; to gain independence; to sharpen instincts; to increase psychic powers; to improve capacity for visualization; to develop clairvoyance.
Amuletic Uses: To banish idleness, laziness, and aimlessness; to avoid becoming an "astral junkie."

10. Malkuth

The principle of manifestation. Malkuth "the kingdom," is the tenth and last sephirah. It is the final container of all the energies of the entire Tree of Life, wherein all of the powers of the sephiroth come to completion and final manifestation. This is the so-called "real world" or the material universe as we know it. Malkuth is the only sephirah that has achieved stability and rest. On the human level, the tenth sphere is represented by the physical body and the five bodily senses. All expressions of corporeal existence and physical sensation are assigned to this sphere.

Elemental Quality: Earth.

Gender Quality: Feminine, containing.

Planet Assigned to Sephirah: Earth, divided into the four elements.

Associated Tarot Cards: The four Tens. The four Princesses. The Tens show a matter thoroughly and definitely completed, for good or ill. The Princesses represent a potent and permanent force manifesting in the material plane.

Talismanic Uses: Malkuth can be used to ground energy; to learn the value of discrimination; to gain an understanding of the four elements; to maintain the health of the physical body; to sharpen the five ordinary senses; to manifest an idea in the physical plane; to materialize a project; to bring something to final completion.

Amuletic Uses: To banish avarice and material greed; to banish lethargy, apathy, and inertia; to keep trouble from manifesting.

ADDITIONAL TALISMANIC USES FOR THE TAROT

The tarot decks described in this book all follow the same basic attributions, with a couple of exceptions. All of these decks, therefore, can be used in the exact same way when it comes to divination or the creating of tarot talismans. However, each deck has its own distinct artwork and symbolism that can provide for a more nuanced interpretation in divination. In addition to the many talismanic uses already mentioned, the exact artwork of each individual card can also provide a variety of talismanic uses, including ones that are quite specific. The following is a list of how the various cards in the five tarot decks used to illustrate this book can be employed as talismans. Of course, these are not the only such uses that can be applied to each card. We encourage readers to experiment and come up with their own unique ways of employing the cards as talismans.

Please note that the talismanic uses listed here for *The Universal Tarot* also apply to the popular *Rider-Waite Tarot*. Also, some of the more complex cards may lend themselves more to amuletic uses than to talismanic ones.

The Fool

Golden Dawn: To develop new ideas; to regain the innocence of youth; spiritual rebirth.

Thoth Tarot: To develop self-control and willpower; to become impervious to the negativity of others; to learn the virtue of silence.

Universal: To detach oneself from all troubles and worries; to begin a new spiritual journey; to attain spiritual freedom; to become an optimist; to take a chance.

Babylonian: To evolve a new way of thinking; to evolve to a higher level of being; to develop new social skills; to gain a higher social status.

Marseille: To detach from worries; to become light-hearted; to become an entertainer or diplomat.

The Magician

Golden Dawn: To develop skill in magic; to become a visionary; to put thought into motion; to direct strength and willpower into action.

Thoth Tarot: To be able to juggle many responsibilities at the same time; to multi-task.

Universal: To become the magician; to become a shaman or visionary; to take control of one's life; to reach beyond one's limitations.

Babylonian: To become a magician; to obtain occult knowledge.

Marseille: To develop autonomy; to embrace the spirit of initiative; to become an illusionist or an entrepreneur.

The High Priestess

Golden Dawn: To facilitate change; to attain spiritual wisdom; to become a priestess; to understand the mysteries of the moon; to better understand the subconscious mind and its content.

Thoth Tarot: To understand the true meaning of virginity.

Universal: To be able to facilitate change; to become a sturdy anchor in a sea of change; to become a wise woman; to understand the mystery of life; to develop clairvoyance.

Babylonian: To become a priestess or prophetess; to understand the celestial mysteries; to develop the faculty of intuition.

Marseille: To study and understand abstract spiritual matters.

The Empress

Golden Dawn: To explore the sacred feminine; to better understand the concept of the Holy Spirit.

Thoth Tarot: To better understand the alchemical principle of salt.

Universal: To discover how to make one's ideas and plans blossom and grow; to explore and express one's emotions; to understand the mysteries of motherhood; to understand the laws of nature; pregnancy.

Babylonian: To facilitate childbirth; to create new life; to create a prototype; to better understand the laws of nature; to foster agriculture and gardening.

Marseille: To develop sensitivity; to invoke fertility.

The Emperor

Golden Dawn: To become a good leader; to initiate new plans; to use power and influence wisely.

Thoth Tarot: To better understand the alchemical principle of sulfur.

Universal: To govern with wisdom and compassion; to understand the importance of the laws of society; to develop and uphold a just and ethical code of conduct.

Babylonian: To develop strength and self-assurance; to become a better leader, champion, or protector.

Marseille: To develop willpower; to gain authority.

The Hierophant

Golden Dawn: To invoke a teacher; to become a teacher; to put what one has learned to practical use; to better understand the mystery religions of the ancients.

Thoth Tarot: To begin to develop a personal awareness of God; to release one's inner child; to begin a new phase of one's life.

Universal: To uphold tradition; to return to orthodoxy; to maintain the status quo; to lay down the law; to become a priest or minister; to give a blessing; to offer guidance.

Babylonian: To become a priest or minister; to develop writing skills; to write one's own destiny; to become skilled in divination.

Marseille: To have faith; to learn tolerance; to have mercy and compassion for others.

The Lovers

Golden Dawn: To gain victory over seemingly insurmountable odds; to free oneself from restrictions or limitations; to free oneself from the material.

Thoth Tarot: To better understand the parable of Cain and Abel; to better understand that every action has a reaction that is equal and opposite to it; to practice alchemy.

Universal: To become intuitively aware of the sacredness of sex; to better understand the spiritual concept known as the Garden of Eden and what it means for the individual; to learn the joys of love.

Babylonian: To learn how to become a more attentive, sharing, and loving partner; to improve one's relationship.

Marseille: To ensure a successful marriage; to make a new partnership.

The Chariot

Golden Dawn: To invoke spiritual visions; to develop the capacity for astral traveling; to develop willpower; to take control.

Thoth Tarot: To make better use of one's time; to be worthy of the mysteries of the Holy Grail; for protection in travel.

Universal: To become the conquering victor; to exercise control; to develop moral fortitude; to reach maturity on many levels; to look beyond the ego and truly "know thyself;" for protection in travel.

Babylonian: To become the conquering hero in battle; to have the ability to travel; to influence the weather; to invoke rain.

Marseille: To put ambitions into motion; to recognize one's own merits; to learn how to lead.

Strength

Golden Dawn: To gain strength and vitality; to develop a calm, clear state of mind; to allow suppressed emotions to emerge but use them constructively; to tame wild animals.

Thoth Tarot (Lust): To release passion and repressed sexual energy; to practice tantra; to work with the kundalini.

Universal: To release one's deepest emotions but not allow them to take over; to face a difficult period with hope, enthusiasm, and courage.

Babylonian: To invoke courage and strength; to overcome one's animal nature; to become fearless.

Marseille: To develop moral strength; self-mastery.

The Hermit

Golden Dawn: To gain a teacher, counselor, or healer; to be able to receive and share spiritual knowledge and wisdom.

Thoth Tarot: To invoke fertility; to invoke a soul guide.

Universal: To gain a teacher or counselor; to gain a spirit guide; to become a beacon of light for others; to develop one's own inner light; to learn meditation.

Babylonian: To withdraw into a period of quiet reflection and soul-searching; to go on a walkabout; to overcome shyness, social anxiety, or fear of people.

Marseille: To seek solitude; to learn prudence; to become an ascetic.

The Wheel of Fortune

Golden Dawn: To regain order, control, and structure in one's life; to pay off a karmic debt; to reap a karmic reward.

Thoth Tarot (Fortune): To increase personal energy; to invoke the element of luck.

Universal: To invoke good fortune; to learn how to accept and adapt to a new situation or reality; to find meaning and value in an unexpected situation.

Babylonian: To go about one's daily life in peace, free from worry.

Marseille: To be able to endure periods of uncertainty; to understand that a fortuitous circumstance may change; to better understand the natural cycles of time.

Justice

Golden Dawn: To make a decision and stick to it; to invoke fairness and parity; to wield the sword of justice; to maintain one's balance and fairness in a difficult situation.

Thoth Tarot (Adjustment): To better understand that balance is maintained by a series of adjustments between opposing energies.

Universal: To take responsibility for one's actions and choices; for success and fairness in legal proceedings, courts, and trials.

Babylonian: To uphold social justice; to protect the less fortunate; to provide for widows and orphans; to interpret dreams; to practice divination.

Marseille: To succeed in legal proceedings, courts, and trials.

The Hanged Man

Golden Dawn: To be at peace when everyone around you is frenzied; to undergo self-sacrifice for a higher cause or the greater good; to submerge the lower ego so that the spiritual self may flourish.

Thoth Tarot: To withdraw from the world for a period of time for self-reflection; to enter a trance or altered state; to gain a better understanding of the precession of the equinoxes.

Universal: To surrender to the rhythms of life; to surrender all that the ego holds dear and thereby obtain peace; to become open to all possibilities.

Babylonian: To face up to one's responsibilities even when they are unpleasant; to make something good come from a bad situation; to make a sacrifice meaningful and valuable.

Marseille: To endure sacrifice, punishment, or confinement with grace; to practice asceticism; to act on an altruistic impulse.

Death

Golden Dawn: To accept change with grace and tranquility; to recycle the old into the new; to allow oneself to be radically transformed.

Thoth Tarot: To understand the cycles of life, death, and rebirth; to be liberated; to become reborn.

Universal: To overcome the fear of change; to give up old habits; to embrace a new life.

Babylonian: To examine repressed memories; to face one's deepest fears in order to learn and grow from them.

Marseille: To have courage in the face of radical change.

Temperance

Golden Dawn: To become spiritually whole and psychically integrated; to have one foot in the material world and one in the spiritual world; to take the middle path.

Thoth Tarot (Art): To achieve harmony between opposites; to practice alchemy; to gain a better understanding of alchemical symbolism.

Universal: To learn moderation; to become a well-rounded person; to invoke a guardian angel.

Babylonian: To bring balance and symmetry into one's life; to allow one's inner Tree of Life to blossom and bear fruit.

Marseille: To learn moderation; to invoke a guardian angel.

The Devil

Golden Dawn: To develop the power to see beyond illusions; to free oneself from material wants; to laugh at one's fears.

Thoth Tarot: To improve sexual relations; to appreciate the power and attraction of sex; to practice sex magic.

Universal: To free oneself from someone else's control; to recognize one's options; to avoid turning sex into an obsession or addiction; to stop being a slave to one's desires.

Babylonian: To guard against evil, malice, and perversion; to fight depression; to combat black magic; to banish nightmares.

Marseille: To avoid being controlled or manipulated by the magnetism of others; to avoid being charmed or enchanted by a charismatic figure.

The Tower

Golden Dawn: To have a powerful revelation or flash of enlightenment; to rid oneself of old habits and destructive behaviors; to understand vibration.

Thoth Tarot: To completely disrupt; to invoke a drastic change; to shake something up.

Universal: To hear divine wisdom; to release pent-up energy or repressed feelings; to learn a valuable lesson from a period of upheaval.

Babylonian: To push for immediate change; to shake the foundations of the status quo to promote a needed change; to fight for what is right; to banish chaos.

Marseille: To break out of a prison of one's own making; to face the collapse of one's previous convictions; to overcome arrogance and vanity.

The Star

Golden Dawn: To transform old habits and channel wasted energy into new, creative outlets; to gain a high level of spiritual awareness.

Thoth Tarot: To understand that everything in the universe is connected; to allow oneself to become a vessel of divine love and light.

Universal: To develop the capacity for imagination and meditation; to gain healing and wholeness after an emotional storm.

Babylonian: To become an adviser; to give hope to others; to heal the psyche.

Marseille: To receive a favorable omen; to have hope; to gain new ideas.

The Moon

Golden Dawn: To find the courage to strike out on a new path; to evolve beyond current limits; to confront one's personal demons.

Thoth Tarot: To face fears; to overcome illusions.

Universal: To bring a spiritual revelation into the conscious mind without distorting it; to increase powers of imagination; to obtain true visions and banish false ones.

Babylonian: To win the favor of deity; to pray and have one's prayers answered.

Marseille: To invoke dreams and visions; to banish hallucinations; to better understand mysterious attractions.

The Sun

Golden Dawn: To invoke boundless energy and zest for life; to develop a youthful outlook; to discover one's inner Garden of Eden; to develop an inner communication with the divine.

Thoth Tarot: To gain emancipation and true freedom from limitation; to dance.

Universal: To be liberated from one's old life; to be filled with divine light; to return to the innocence of youth; to become one with the natural world; to experience great joy and optimism; to work with horses.

Babylonian: To invoke great power, strength, and vitality; to see one's situation with total clarity; to cultivate horsemanship and work with horses.

Marseille: To strengthen friendship; to resolve problems; to invoke harmony, joy and love.

Judgement

Golden Dawn: To take an initiation; to dedicate one's life to spiritual pursuits; to experience purification and consecration of the soul.

Thoth Tarot (The Aeon): To invoke the divine child within oneself; to invoke the birth of something new.

Universal: To examine the meaning of one's own life; to awaken from spiritual slumber; to remember one's true spiritual identity; to answer the call of spirit; to experience resurrection.

Babylonian: To give aid to strangers; to make amends; to be rewarded for good deeds; to experience astral traveling and astral projection.

Marseille: To undergo a spiritual reawakening and renewal; to initiate an examination of conscience; to have good judgment; to receive a judgment in one's favor.

The Universe

Golden Dawn: To enter the gateway of the mysteries; to better understand the total unity of all existence; to bring something to completion; to focus one's life on the completion of the Great Work.

Thoth Tarot: To better understand that the end is only the beginning; to better understand the cosmic cycle; to experience all life as the dance of spirit; to become the dancer.

Universal (The World): To better understand that the center of the universe is everywhere; to better understand that divinity is all around you and within you.

Babylonian: To return to the source; to better understand the birth of the universe; to invoke perfect unity.

Marseille (The World): To complete an enterprise; to be rewarded or promoted.

Ace of Wands

Golden Dawn: To invoke the powers of fire; to invoke limitless reserves of various types of energy for whatever is needed; to access one's own raw power and natural force.

Thoth Tarot: To invoke limitless reserves of specific energy; to increase vitality.

Universal: To invoke the courage to make a needed change in one's life; to gain strength and a zest for living.

Babylonian: To invoke a strong, protective force; to purify through fire; to consecrate.

Marseille: All of the above.

Two of Wands

Golden Dawn: To establish one's authority in a situation; to govern successfully.

Thoth Tarot: To invoke great power and energy. To control.

Universal: To overcome boredom; to learn the mysteries of the world and the universe.

Babylonian: To develop magical power, spiritual wisdom, and occult knowledge.
Marseille: All of the above.

Three of Wands

Golden Dawn: To invoke what has already been proven to work; to fall back upon one's established strengths; to use what is tried and true.
Thoth Tarot: To increase spiritual virtues. To develop good, noble, and honorable traits.
Universal: To make plans for the future; to become an explorer; to live off the sea; to promote success in sailing, boating, or shipping.
Babylonian: To appreciate what you have already accomplished; to achieve.
Marseille: All of the above.

Four of Wands

Golden Dawn: To finish a project with excellence and perfection; to perfect one's work.
Thoth Tarot: To bring something to completion and final settlement; to create a circle of protection.
Universal: To celebrate; to invoke optimism and joy.
Babylonian: To make sure that one's hard work is rewarded; to help one's family become more active in religious worship; to become more devoted to spiritual practices; to maintain spiritual discipline.
Marseille: All of the above.

Five of Wands

Golden Dawn: To purify; to cause or to banish strife and quarrelling.
Thoth Tarot: To invoke volcanic energy; to cause or to banish strife.
Universal: To be competitive; to be successful in the competition for a job, contract, or sporting event; to succeed in a friendly competition.
Babylonian: To struggle against one's base animal nature; to battle against destructive instincts or habits; to fight against evil and malice.
Marseille: All of the above.

Six of Wands

Golden Dawn: To assure victory and success, especially after strife.
Thoth Tarot: To assure victory and success.
Universal: To assure a triumphal homecoming; to become an optimist.
Babylonian: To assure victory and success; to become a better ritualist; to become a priest; to cultivate a devotional mindset.
Marseille: All of the above.

Seven of Wands

Golden Dawn: To maintain courage under fire; to persevere through difficulty.

Thoth Tarot: To have the courage and raw strength to lay oneself on the line in a crucial situation on behalf of loved ones or beliefs; to be ready to face uncertainties.

Universal: To learn the philosophies and virtues of the warrior; to be ready for combat; to be the strong protector; to enjoy the thrill of competition and a good fight.

Babylonian: To have the courage to face one's deepest subconscious fears; to invoke strength and courage in a dangerous situation.

Marseille: All of the above.

Eight of Wands

Golden Dawn: To receive rapid communication about an important matter; to avoid a breakdown in communication.

Thoth Tarot: To pace one's energy so that it is not quickly squandered; to utilize electricity; to foster any endeavor that involves electricity; to avoid a breakdown in communication.

Universal: To ensure that your proposal is accepted.

Babylonian: To take swift, sure action; to become a messenger or ambassador.

Marseille: All of the above.

Nine of Wands

Golden Dawn: To invoke great power and strength in a stressful matter; to recover from illness; to reach down into one's last energy reserves.

Thoth Tarot: To invoke great strength; to promote recovery from illness.

Universal: To fight back; to be ready for another conflict; to build up one's defenses.

Babylonian: To conquer a larger and stronger opponent; to beat the odds.

Marseille: All of the above.

Ten of Wands

Golden Dawn: To banish oppression and cruelty; to put a swift end to a bad plan; to force a deliberate slowdown.

Thoth Tarot: To banish oppression; to learn to think before acting.

Universal: To avoid taking on too many burdens.

Babylonian: To choose between the lesser of two evils; to seek help from one's "enemy's enemy."

Marseille: All of the above.

King of Wands

Golden Dawn: To gain the initiative; to avoid acting before thinking things through; to avoid "burn-out."

Thoth Tarot: To invoke swift action; to learn to control a fiery temper.

Universal: To learn to take responsibility; to gain a sense of social commitment; to learn tolerance.

Babylonian: To aid in ritual purification; to make rituals more inspiring; to combat negative or harmful magic.

Marseille: All of the above.

Queen of Wands

Golden Dawn: To be comfortable with one's own power and authority; to become more assertive.

Thoth Tarot: To learn not to jump to conclusions; to avoid being quick to take offense.

Universal: To be able to take control in a crisis; to avoid becoming bitter from having to handle too many crisis situations or personal opposition.

Babylonian: To support and complement one's partner in every way, while being completely confident in oneself and one's own abilities.

Marseille: All of the above.

Prince of Wands

Golden Dawn: To invoke great courage and energy; to avoid bragging, egotism, selfishness, and vanity.

Thoth Tarot (Knight of Wands): To become more generous and social; to avoid becoming violent-tempered and cruel.

Universal (Knight of Wands): To combine eagerness with pragmatism; to understand that one does not have to constantly prove oneself to others.

Babylonian: To aid in ritual invocations; to combat negative or harmful magic.

Marseille (Knight of Wands): All of the above.

Princess of Wands

Golden Dawn: To have the ability to start *and finish* projects.

Thoth Tarot: To become more artistic; to avoid becoming superficial.

Universal (Knave of Wands)[10]: To begin a new project; to avoid complexity and the indecision it brings.

Babylonian: To better understand the mysteries of pregnancy and childbirth; to protect pregnant women and their future children.

Marseille (Knave of Wands): All of the above.

Ace of Cups

Golden Dawn: To invoke the powers of water; to receive an influx of divine consciousness.

Thoth Tarot: To invoke the powers of water; to better understand the true nature of consciousness.

Universal: To understand the mysteries of the Holy Grail.

Babylonian: To invoke fertility; to gain pleasure and happiness.

Marseille: All of the above.

Two of Cups

Golden Dawn: To obtain true love or friendship; to better understand the concept of alchemical union.

Thoth Tarot: To invoke true love or friendship; to better understand the concept of alchemical union.

Universal: To invoke marriage; to begin a new romance; to pledge friendship and loyalty.

Babylonian: To implement a loving partnership; to invoke joy and pleasure.

Marseille: All of the above.

Three of Cups

Golden Dawn: To obtain abundance, the fulfillment of pleasure, and fertility; to better understand the mysteries of maternity; to become pregnant.

Thoth Tarot: To invoke abundance; to keep love from becoming stifling and oppressive.

Universal: To learn to enjoy life more; to learn how to share one's experiences with others; to celebrate one's good fortune.

Babylonian: To invoke abundance and plenty; to live off the abundance of nature, to reap a good harvest; to be able to provide food for loved ones or charity for others.

Marseille: All of the above.

Four of Cups

Golden Dawn: To make a positive but short-term situation continue on into the future.

Thoth Tarot: To invoke luxury and extravagance; to implement a long period of rest.

Universal: To avoid wastefulness; to avoid apathy; to make the right choice.

Babylonian: To make the best out of a mixed blessing; to avoid becoming distracted; to fight complacency and indifference.

Marseille: All of the above.

Five of Cups

Golden Dawn: To banish loss in pleasure; to be able to cope with an emotional loss.

Thoth Tarot: To banish disappointment; to cope with loss; to banish the triumph of matter over spirit.

Universal: To accept sorrow and loss; to move on after a period of mourning.

Babylonian: To express one's grief in a healthy release; to better cope with loss.

Marseille: All of the above.

Six of Cups

Golden Dawn: To invoke pleasure and enjoyment; for wish fulfillment.

Thoth Tarot: To obtain pleasure and enjoyment; for sexual fulfillment.

Universal: To invoke memories; to avoid becoming fixated on the past; to remember a past life; to practice past-life regression.

Babylonian: To invoke pleasure, especially sensual pleasure and social enjoyments; for a successful social event, dinner, or party.

Marseille: All of the above.

Seven of Cups

Golden Dawn: To avoid being fooled by illusionary success; to be able to detect the truth when truth is not self-evident; to see through lies.

Thoth Tarot: To not be overcome by ego-inflation and self-deception; to banish drug addiction, lust, or violent tendencies; to banish corruption.

Universal: To appreciate the power of daydreams, but not let them dominate; to choose to focus on what is important in life and not dwell on things that are temporal and fleeting.

Babylonian: To avoid being seduced by temptations; to avoid deception and infidelity in love; to stand above one's animal nature.

Marseille: All of the above.

Eight of Cups

Golden Dawn: To avoid throwing away one's success.

Thoth Tarot: To banish indolence, apathy, and idleness.

Universal: To choose to turn away from things that are no longer needed; to know when it is time to leave.

Babylonian: To maintain focus; to avoid negligence and carelessness; to watch for things going on behind one's back.

Marseille: All of the above.

Nine of Cups

Golden Dawn: To invoke material happiness and success.

Thoth Tarot: To invoke pleasure and sensuality.

Universal: To concentrate on ordinary pleasures; to have a good time; to facilitate parties and celebrations.

Babylonian: To learn to be content with what one already has; to be satisfied and appreciative of the way things are.

Marseille: All of the above.

Ten of Cups

Golden Dawn: To invoke lasting success, joy, and happiness.

Thoth Tarot: To have a better understanding of the Tree of Life.

Universal: To remember, when life is difficult, the beauty and goodness of the universe; to invoke domestic happiness.

Babylonian: To invoke longevity and good health; to obtain complete success.

Marseille: All of the above.

King of Cups

Golden Dawn: To become more romantic and sensitive; to avoid becoming lazy and set in one's ways.

Thoth Tarot: To become brave and daring; to get over past hurts and insecurities.

Universal: To let creativity flow freely; to learn not to repress or bury emotions.

Babylonian: To be comfortable working and directing things behind the scenes and let others be in the limelight; to create something entirely new and different; to become more tolerant of other people's peculiar ways and habits.

Marseille: All of the above.

Queen of Cups

Golden Dawn: To improve social skills; to overcome fear and timidity.

Thoth Tarot: To gain empathy for others; to avoid being used by others.

Universal: To give imagination free reign; to learn not to act on one's emotions in a knee-jerk fashion.

Babylonian: To develop a profound compassion for others; to develop keen instincts; to share the wisdom learned from past experience with others.

Marseille: All of the above.

Prince of Cups

Golden Dawn: To sharpen one's powers of intellect; to avoid the tendency to lie and deceive; to avoid the tendency to ramble or digress.

Thoth Tarot (Knight of Cups): To keep one's naturally intense energy under control; to avoid becoming moody and pessimistic.

Universal (Knight of Cups): To learn how to connect one's feelings with actions; to avoid hypocrisy, self-indulgence, or the tendency for escapism.

Babylonian: To be a good steward or guardian; to take responsibility; to avoid becoming insensitive and cold.

Marseille (Knight of Cups): All of the above.

Princess of Cups

Golden Dawn: To become more expressive, romantic, and artistic; to avoid becoming superficial and melodramatic.

Thoth Tarot: To invoke dreams and visions; to avoid becoming an "astral junkie."

Universal (Knave of Wands): To develop psychic talents.

Babylonian: For accuracy in divination; to aid invocations; to be able to maintain oaths and obligations; to make amends for past transgressions.

Marseille (Knave of Wands): All of the above.

Ace of Swords

Golden Dawn: To invoke the powers of air; to obtain the powers of intellect; to wield the Sword of Justice; to uphold divine authority.

Thoth Tarot: To invoke the powers of air; to implement one's true will.

Universal: To invoke wisdom in order to understand spiritual truth.

Babylonian (Ace of Arrows): To add power to all invocations and rituals.

Marseille: All of the above.

Two of Swords

Golden Dawn: To end a quarrel and restore peace.

Thoth Tarot: To maintain inner peace amidst chaos.

Universal: To become less defensive; to avoid pushing everyone away.

Babylonian (Two of Arrows): To call a truce with one's opponent while remaining on guard against further trouble; to restore peace after strife.

Marseille: All of the above.

Three of Swords

Golden Dawn: To banish sorrow; to avoid letting a third party create disruption.

Thoth Tarot: To banish sorrow; to avoid bending under extreme pressure; to disperse the cloud of depression.

Universal: To accept sorrow and pain and grow beyond it.

Babylonian (Three of Arrows): To banish sorrow; to persevere through great hardship and pain.

Marseille: All of the above.

Four of Swords

Golden Dawn: To rest after a period of strife.

Thoth Tarot: To call a truce with one's opponent.

Universal: To withdraw from the world for a time in order to heal and recover; to shut the world out.

Babylonian (Four of Arrows): To attain a well-deserved rest; to invoke recovery and convalescence; to invoke the healing powers of nature; to learn to appreciate nature; to spend a period of time surrounded by nature.

Marseille: All of the above.

Five of Swords

Golden Dawn: To banish failure and defeat; to scatter; to end cooperation in a matter.

Thoth Tarot: To banish failure and defeat; to scatter; to guard against the triumph of matter over spirit.

Universal: To overcome feelings of humiliation, inadequacy, and impotence.

Babylonian (Five of Arrows): To banish failure and defeat; to scatter; to take back control of one's destiny; to face one's demons with courage and ultimately defeat them.

Marseille: All of the above.

Six of Swords

Golden Dawn: To gain success after a period of conflict and struggle.

Thoth Tarot: To attain a state of perfect balance; to achieve a scientific or technological breakthrough.

Universal: To finally move on after a long period of mourning; to undertake a quiet passage after mourning; to take a healing journey.

Babylonian (Six of Arrows): To heal after a long illness; to invoke recovery and convalescence; to become a healer; to heal others.

Marseille: All of the above.

Seven of Swords

Golden Dawn: To stabilize a precarious situation; to maintain balance and strength in a difficult period; to take strength from small victories; to banish insecurity and anxiety.

Thoth Tarot: To fight the feeling of futility; to remain steadfast under attack or pressure.

Universal: To take responsibility for one's actions even when not proud of them; to avoid acting impulsively when a thoughtful plan is called for.

Babylonian (Seven of Arrows): To invoke stealth, secrecy, and invisibility; to go unnoticed; to remain hidden; to invoke the element of surprise; to facilitate a covert or sting operation; to take a risk.

Marseille: All of the above.

Eight of Swords

Golden Dawn: To banish interference, weakness, and indecision.

Thoth Tarot: To banish interference, weakness, and indecision.

Universal: To banish feelings of confusion, shame, or humiliation; to better understand that sometimes we are trapped in prisons of our own making.

Babylonian (Eight of Arrows): To learn how to live with restriction and limitation; to be able to carry a heavy burden with grace and dignity.

Marseille: All of the above.

Nine of Swords

Golden Dawn: To banish despair and cruelty; to banish mental anguish; to stop physical or mental abuse; to stop hurting oneself; to avoid being one's own worst enemy.

Thoth Tarot: To banish despair and cruelty; to banish mental anguish; to stop physical or mental abuse; to stop hurting oneself; to avoid being one's own worst enemy.

Universal: To banish nightmares; to put an end to agony; to learn the sorrow of the bereaved; to empathize with the sorrows of others.

Babylonian (Nine of Arrows): To actively fight against cruelty and oppression; to stop animal abuse.

Marseille: All of the above.

Ten of Swords

Golden Dawn: To banish ruin; to understand that things are not as bad as they look; to better understand that you are not the only person in the world who has ever suffered.

Thoth Tarot: To banish ruin; to heal a deep emotional wound or heartache.

Universal: To banish hysteria and melodrama.

Babylonian (Ten of Arrows): To avert disaster; to avoid those who mean harm; to soften the hearts of people who act in a heartless fashion.

Marseille: All of the above.

King of Swords

Golden Dawn: To learn how to think on one's feet; to avoid becoming reckless.

Thoth Tarot: To learn how to act quickly and decisively; to avoid taking on more than one can handle.

Universal: To appreciate the wisdom that comes with experience; to be truthful, just, and fair in dealings with others; to avoid becoming remote, domineering, judgmental, or politically correct.

Babylonian (King of Arrows): To be the master of one's own fate; to provide for the welfare of others; to avoid being misunderstood or stereotyped; to facilitate landscaping and agriculture.

Marseille: All of the above.

Queen of Swords

Golden Dawn: To sharpen one's thoughts; to adapt easily to new paradigms and situations; to avoid burning bridges behind oneself; to cut off the past.

Thoth Tarot: To handle authority with ease; to cut off the old in favor of the new; to avoid becoming malicious and cruel.

Universal: To gain wisdom from sorrow; to free yourself from confusion and complications; to let go of the past.

Babylonian (Queen of Arrows): To become a good strategist or coordinator; to move in influential circles; to learn how to hold one's ground; to refuse to put up with nonsense; to avoid becoming ruthless or spiteful.

Marseille: All of the above.

Prince of Swords

Golden Dawn: To sharpen one's mind; to have fresh ideas come rapidly to mind; to avoid being pulled in too many directions.

Thoth Tarot (Knight of Swords): To invoke rapid communication; to avoid the tendency to never finish anything; to avoid extreme nervousness.

Universal: To push beyond limitations; to tackle life's problems head-on; to avoid becoming a fanatic or extremist.

Babylonian (Prince of Arrows): To learn the virtues of the warrior; to avoid hesitation when swift action is called for.

Marseille (Knight of Swords): All of the above.

Princess of Swords

Golden Dawn: To invoke self-assurance; to avoid becoming too aggressive.

Thoth Tarot: To be able to put plans into action; to avoid scaring people off.

Universal (Knave of Swords): To remain vigilant and observant; to avoid becoming aloof or distant; to avoid becoming paranoid or obsessive.

Babylonian (Princess of Arrows): To be a mediator; to stand one's ground when an injustice has been done.

Marseille (Knave of Swords): All of the above.

Ace of Pentacles

Golden Dawn: To invoke the powers of earth; to manifest your plans and ideas; to bring into manifestation.

Thoth Tarot (Ace of Disks): To invoke the powers of earth; to invoke the four archangels of the elements.

Universal: To secure wealth, security, and a joyful life; to better understand how civilization affords us basic protection.

Babylonian (Ace of Disks): To invoke the powers of earth; to manifest plans and ideas.

Marseille: To manifest money; all of the above.

Two of Pentacles

Golden Dawn: To make certain that a change is made with harmony and accord; to ensure a smooth transition; to understand the need for change.

Thoth Tarot (Two of Disks): To invoke a harmonious change; to invoke wisdom; to better understand the nature of time and eternity, continuity, and infinity.

Universal: To find hidden magic in ordinary pleasures and simple amusements.

Babylonian (Two of Disks): To invoke change that brings reward; to better understand the need for change.

Marseille: All of the above.

Three of Pentacles

Golden Dawn: To invoke work and employment; to invoke business.

Thoth Tarot (Three of Disks): To invoke work and business; to invoke the strength of the triad in your endeavor; to better understand the three alchemical principles of mercury, sulfur, and salt; to better understand the symbolism of the pyramid and triangle.

Universal: To become a skilled craftsman or artist; to build or create; to have one's work appreciated by others; to appreciate the work of others.

Babylonian (Three of Disks): To invoke work and business; to become a better craftsman or artist; to build or create; to weave.

Marseille: All of the above.

Four of Pentacles

Golden Dawn: To invoke earthly power; to excel in business; to gain status and honor.

Thoth Tarot (Four of Disks): To invoke earthly power; to invoke the four elements; to maintain vigilance needed for security; to make a secure fortress; to fortify the material realm; to protect one's home.

Universal: To avoid selfishness and stinginess; to realize that greed results in barrenness.

Babylonian (Four of Disks): To invoke earthly power; to make a secure fortress; to fortify the material realm; to protect one's home.

Marseille: All of the above.

Five of Pentacles

Golden Dawn: To banish material trouble; to prevent loss of monetary resources; to better understand that one might be holding onto one's troubles because they have become a convenient crutch.

Thoth Tarot (Five of Disks): To banish poverty; to guard against the triumph of matter over spirit; to avoid elemental instability within the psyche.

Universal: To put aside pride and be able to accept help when in need; to fight hypocrisy; to avoid insincerity; to reject dogma and orthodoxy.

Babylonian (Five of Disks): To banish material trouble; to prevent loss of monetary resources; to avoid committing an act that will be flattering to the ego but harmful in the long run.

Marseille: All of the above.

Six of Pentacles

Golden Dawn: To invoke material success, now and in the future; to succeed in business.

Thoth Tarot (Six of Disks): To invoke material success; to invoke the energies of the macrocosmic hexagram; to better understand the symbolism of the Rosicrucians.

Universal: To be able to give assistance to someone in need; to learn to be charitable; to understand that the more one gives, the more one gets.

Babylonian (Six of Disks): To invoke assistance when you are in need; to give assistance to someone in need; to provide care for animals.

Marseille: All of the above.

Seven of Pentacles

Golden Dawn: To banish failure and material disappointment.

Thoth Tarot (Seven of Disks): To banish failure and material disappointment.

Universal: To improve finances; to look with satisfaction on one's accomplishments; to find meaningful work or an enjoyable career.

Babylonian (Seven of Disks): To banish inertia, laziness, and stagnation.

Marseille: All of the above.

Eight of Pentacles

Golden Dawn: To be able to see what action must be taken when a situation calls for caution and prudence; to be able to discern small details about a matter.

Thoth Tarot (Eight of Disks): To act with prudence; to avoid being "penny-wise and pound-foolish."

Universal: To care more about the quality of one's work than making money; to embrace the skill and discipline needed for high-quality work.

Babylonian (Eight of Disks): To become trained in a new profession; to become highly skilled in one's career; to become an expert astrologer.

Marseille: All of the above.

Nine of Pentacles

Golden Dawn: To invoke material gain, now and in the future; to accumulate whatever provides material comfort; to gain an inheritance.

Thoth Tarot (Nine of Disks): To invoke material gain; to accumulate whatever provides material comfort; to invoke good management; to invoke good luck.

Universal: To gain self-awareness, self-reliance, and self-confidence; to make the right choices in life; to know what really matters in life.

Babylonian (Nine of Disks): To invoke material gain; to cultivate rich soil; to plant seeds; to make fertile; to ensure material gain for successive generations; to promote success in agriculture.

Marseille: All of the above.

Ten of Pentacles

Golden Dawn: To invoke material wealth; to invoke spiritual wealth; to see the magic in ordinary things.

Thoth Tarot (Ten of Disks): To invoke material wealth; to invoke spiritual wealth; to gain a better understanding of the Qabalistic Tree of Life.

Universal: To understand investments; to invest wisely; to learn not to take one's blessings for granted.

Babylonian (Ten of Disks): To complete projects; to bring closure; to forgive one's enemy and make peace.

Marseille: All of the above.

King of Pentacles

Golden Dawn: To become a good provider; to avoid becoming too materialistic.

Thoth Tarot (Knight of Disks): To have a peaceful domestic life; to excel at practical skills; to avoid becoming lazy and obstinate.

Universal: To be close to nature; to enjoy retirement; to avoid thinking that the end justifies the means.

Babylonian (King of Disks): To use the skills one already possesses in new and unusual ways; to not give up if the first attempt is unsuccessful; to ultimately be victorious; to promote success in agriculture.

Marseille: All of the above.

Queen of Pentacles

Golden Dawn: To develop keen instincts; to become fruitful; to avoid being moody.

Thoth Tarot (Queen of Disks): To develop patience; to avoid being too passive.

Universal: To believe in one's own abilities; to be intensely aware of the magic in nature; to avoid becoming isolated and phobic; to banish low self-esteem.

Babylonian (Queen of Disks): To know the value of unselfish loyalty; to remain steadfast under extreme pressure; to have the strength to help someone shoulder a heavy burden.

Marseille: All of the above.

Prince of Pentacles

Golden Dawn: To balance brawn with brains; to avoid the tendency to hold anger inside until one finally explodes in fury.

Thoth Tarot (Knight of Disks): To keep moving steadily forward no matter what obstacles are ahead; to avoid a tendency to move too slowly.

Universal: To avoid becoming too wrapped up in one's work and career; to avoid inertia and depression.

Babylonian (Prince of Disks): To protect the environment; to protect wildlife; to take care of domestic animals or livestock.

Marseille (Knight of Pentacles): All of the above.

Princess of Pentacles

Golden Dawn: To be confident and courageous; to avoid being wasteful.

Thoth Tarot (Princess of Disks): To cultivate one's inner power; to be fruitful; to gain control over bad habits.

Universal (Knave of Pentacles): To become a student; to enjoy higher learning; to gain a scholarship.

Babylonian (Princess of Disks): To enjoy nature; to promote success in agriculture.

Marseille (Knave of Pentacles): All of the above.

Additional Cards

The Babylonian Tarot has five additional cards that can be used as talismans. The talismanic uses of these cards are as follows:

Genesis: To implement a new beginning or a fresh start; to invoke spirit.

Kerub of Wands: To invoke divine protection or divine intervention.

Kerub of Cups: To invoke spiritual love and religious fervor.

Kerub of Arrows: To invoke divine wisdom and spiritual knowledge.

Kerub of Disks: To invoke divine aid; to manifest the spiritual.

---

1 The path number is from the *Sepher Yetzirah,* a Qabalistic text that describes the ten sephiroth and the twenty-two connecting paths as the "Thirty-two Paths of Wisdom." According to the text, the sephiroth are considered the first ten "paths." The twenty-two connecting paths, beginning with aleph/the Fool are numbered from 11 to 32.

2 Dane Rudhyar, quoted by Meyer, *A Handbook for the Humanistic Astrologer* (Garden City, NY: Anchor), 67.

3 Scorpio is traditionally ruled by Mars, although in modern astrology it is said to be ruled by Pluto.

4 Another symbol for Scorpio is the eagle's head ⤳.

5 Aquarius is traditionally ruled by Saturn, although in modern astrology it is said to be ruled by Uranus.

6 Pisces is traditionally ruled by Jupiter, although modern astrology states that it is ruled by Neptune.

7 Leo Schaya, *The Universal Meaning of the Kabbalah* (Baltimore, MD: Penguin Books, Inc., 1973), 42.

8 Charles Poncé, *Kabbalah: An Introduction and Illumination for the World Today* (Wheaton, IL: The Theosophical Publishing House, 1980), 122–123.

9 Schaya, *The Universal Meaning of the Kabbalah,* 47.

10 In the *Rider-Waite Tarot,* the Princess or Knave is called the Page.

3

RITUAL CARD SPREADS
AND CONSECRATION RITES

The previous chapter described the various talismanic uses for the seventy-eight cards of the tarot. This chapter explains how to put that information to work. Here you will learn how to choose and then ritually charge your tarot talisman.

One easy way to work with tarot talismans is to create a *ritual card spread*. The ritual card spread may look like an ordinary card spread, but rather than interpreting the cards as they fall randomly in a divination—here we are *choosing* the cards we want to use as talismans and actively influencing the manner in which we want to manifest our goals. The ritual card spread that we will show here is called the Triangle of Art Spread.

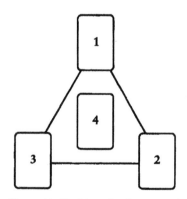

Figure 11: The Triangle of Art Spread.

THE TRIANGLE OF ART SPREAD

This particular four-card ritual spread is based upon the Triangle of Art or Triangle of Evocation, a magical device used for centuries by magicians to call forth spirits to visible manifestation in the center of the triangle. The cards that are used to form the points of the triangle represent those energies or actions that the ritualist wishes to bring into play. The talisman card itself is placed in the center of the triangle to affirm the practitioner's intent to invoke its powers.

This ritual card spread is also based on the figure of the tetrahedron or three-sided pyramid with a fourth side which is the base. The three outer cards used in this spread represent the three points of the tetrahedron while the central card is the apex or summit of the pyramid.

The number four represents manifestation; therefore, the four-card formation of the Triangle of Art Spread is ideal for manifesting your desired goals.

Card 1: *The Significator.* This card represents the subject, which could be the ritualist or someone else that the talisman is being created for.

Card 2: *Initial Action.* This card is what the ritualist wants to visualize as a stimulating magical influence on the process.

Card 3: *Progressive Action.* This card is what the ritualist visualizes as a continuing influence that moves the development of the magic forward on the right track.

Card 4: *Tarot Talisman Card.* The central card is the outcome that the ritualist hopes to bring about. This card is the actual talisman itself.

Of course, it is not necessary to cast a ritual card spread. You could simply choose a tarot talisman and concentrate only on that card. Using a ritual card spread, however, does have its advantages—cards 1 through 3 are used to help facilitate the imagination by providing tools for visualization that will guide the magical process to a successful conclusion. One key element of this ritual card spread is that it works according to the four magical "laws" mentioned in chapter 1.

PREPARING FOR RITUAL

Be certain that you will not be disturbed during the course of your ritual. Once you have selected the cards you will use in your ritual card spread, you will need to prepare everything you need for the ritual. It is a good idea to take a relaxing ritual bath to purify the spirit as well as the body. Ambient music playing softly in the background throughout the ritual will facilitate the necessary change in consciousness from the mundane to the spiritual.

Prepare your altar as shown in figure 12. Place the four cards chosen in a stack with the backsides facing up and card 1 on top. A number of optional magical items corresponding

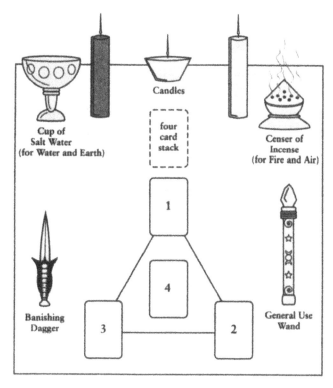

Figure 12: Altar Arrangement for the Triangle of Art Spread.

to your tarot talisman card or your specific goal may be added to your altar arrangement as described in the sample consecration rituals given in this chapter.

Dress in a ceremonial robe and other regalia that puts you in a magical frame of mind. When you are ready, take some time to sit in your temple space for a few moments of quiet meditation. Breathe deeply and slowly in a steady rhythm until you are completely relaxed. There is no rush. When the time seems appropriate, you may begin the ritual.

OPENING CEREMONY FOR
TAROT TALISMAN CONSECRATION

Stand west of the altar facing east. Light the candles and the incense on the altar. With a banishing dagger in hand, move clockwise to the northeast. Raise your dagger high and say: **"Hekas! Hekas! Este bebeloi!"** This is a standard Golden Dawn proclamation in Greek that a ritual is about to begin. If you would rather use the English version, say: **"Far, far away from this place be the profane! Let the sacred rites begin!"** Go back to the west of the altar facing east.

Banishing

Perform a Banishing Ritual such as the LBRP.

Purification

With your right hand, trace an equal-armed cross + over the cup of water. Dip your index finger (or index and middle fingers) into the water and then trace an equal-armed cross + on your forehead. Take up the cup of water and purify the room by sprinkling water three times in each quarter starting in the east and moving clockwise to the south, west, and north. Return to the east, hold the cup high and say: **"I purify with water."**

Consecration

With your right hand, trace an equal-armed cross + over the censer of incense. Take up the incense and use it to trace an equal-armed cross + in front of your forehead. Consecrate the room by waving the incense three times in each quarter, starting in the east and moving clockwise to the south, west, and north. Return to the east, hold the censer high, and say: **"I consecrate with fire."**

The Opening Sign

Place your hands, with palms together, in front of your chest as if praying. Then slowly separate your hands until they are about ten inches apart. Imagine that as you do this, you are opening your psychic faculties and inner awareness. Then say: **"As above, so below. As without, so within. As in Heaven, so on Earth. The divine light connects us all."**

This concludes the opening ceremony. The main working—the ritual card spread and tarot talisman consecration—may now begin. Several samples of ritual card spreads are given in the following pages. After the main working is completed you may perform the following closing ceremony.

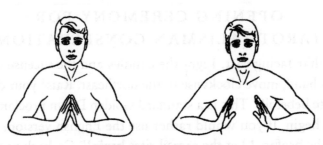

Figure 13: The Opening Sign.

CLOSING CEREMONY FOR
TAROT TALISMAN CONSECRATION

Stand west of the altar facing east. Perform the Qabalistic Cross (see page 19).

Say: "Unto you, sole wise, sole eternal and sole merciful one, be the praise and glory forever, who has permitted me to enter thus far into the sanctuary of your mysteries. Unto you I give thanks. Unto all the divine powers, archangels, and angels who have aided me in this ceremony, I give thanks."

Then say: "As below, so above. As within, so without. As on Earth, so in Heaven. The divine light connects us all."

The Closing Sign

This is the reverse of the Opening Sign. Hold your hands flat with palms facing each other about ten inches apart in front of your chest. Then slowly move your hands toward each other until they are in the "praying" position. Imagine that as you do this you are closing down your psychic faculties and returning to normal consciousness.

Say: "I now release any spirits that may have been detained by this ceremony. Go in peace to your abodes. I now declare this temple duly closed. So mote it be."

SIGNS OF THE FOUR MAGICAL LAWS

The rituals in this chapter call for magical gestures to be made at certain points in the ritual. We have developed these physical gestures to accompany four verbal affirmations that are based upon the four magical laws described earlier. These laws and the affirmations we have assigned to them are as follows:

1) *The Law of Willpower*—affirmation: "I WILL." (Assigned to fire.)
2) *The Law of Correspondence*—affirmation: "I CHOOSE." (Assigned to water.)
3) *The Law of the Astral Light*—affirmation: "I CREATE." (Assigned to air.)
4) *The Law of Imagination*—affirmation: "I SEE." (Assigned to earth.)

Here are the four signs that go along with these affirmations:

The Sign of Willing: Touch the center of your forehead with the first two fingers of your right hand. This symbolizes your mental intent as a potent force.

The Sign of Choosing: Stretch the right arm straight out in front of you, pointing straight ahead with the index finger. This is symbolic of you choosing specific forces and attributions for your magical working.

Figure 14: (Left to right) The Sign of Willing, The Sign of Choosing, The Sign of Creating.

Figure 15: (Left to right) The Sign of Seeing.

The Sign of Creating: Cup both of your hands at chest level, right hand about seven inches above the left, as if you were forming a ball between them.

The Sign of Seeing: Form a triangle, apex upward, on the forehead (over the third eye) with both hands, palms outward. Then thrust the arms straight out and slightly up, keeping the palms downward and held flat, as if you were projecting a mental image out into the universe.

The following is an example of how to use the Triangle of Art ritual card spread. We will employ the *Golden Dawn Magical Tarot* to illustrate this case in point.

SAMPLE SPREAD: TO GAIN SKILL IN MAGIC

Choosing Your Cards

1) Card 1, the significator: This is a card that represents the person who is the subject of the talisman ritual. Most often this will be the practitioner performing the ritual or someone else that the talisman is being prepared for. In the Golden Dawn system, the court cards are most often used as significators, so you could choose a court card that you identify with based upon gender, age, personality traits, zodiacal sign, etc. Certain tarot trumps can also serve as significators so long as you feel a natural affinity with the figure portrayed in the card. For our first example, we will choose the King of Pentacles who, in this case, might represent the ritualist as a mature man who is an earth sign.

2) Card 2, initial action: In order to become the magician, you must open your psyche to the higher powers of the divine and listen to the divine teacher within. Therefore, we

Figure 16: Sample Triangle of Art Spread with the Golden Dawn Magical Tarot.

will choose the card of the Hierophant to represent the initial action of opening the mind to the divine teacher and being able to take in and receive that divine influence from above.

3) Card 3, progression: For the card of continuing development of the matter, we will choose the Hermit. This card is attributed to the sign of Virgo, which is ruled by Mercury. Virgos have a tendency to be meticulous and thorough. Here, the regenerative power of Virgo will be called upon to add continuing, renewing force to the ritual.

4) Card 4, the tarot talisman card: This card is the goal of the ritual—to become the Magician—and the primary focus of the rite. However, all the cards are used for the purpose of visualization leading up to the final desired outcome. You should also notice that the final three cards, the Hierophant, the Hermit, and the Magician, are known in the tarot as the *three magi*—the three great magicians.

A TAROT TALISMAN CONSECRATION RITUAL

So how does one go about performing the ritual for the tarot talisman consecration? In our book *The Essential Golden Dawn* we describe a number of basic steps involved in the working of a Golden Dawn ritual. You can follow these steps exactly as given in that book to design your own ritual, or you could simply perform the following six steps:

1) An opening ceremony that includes a banishing.
2) An invocation to the highest divine powers.
3) Lay down the cards in order, 1 through 4, while using visualization techniques.
4) An invocation of the divine powers represented in your tarot talisman card,[1] including a clear statement of your intended goal.
5) Visualization of your stated goal as exemplified in the final card chosen.
6) A closing ceremony.

The Opening Ceremony

A simple opening ceremony that includes the Lesser Banishing Ritual of the Pentagram has already been covered on page 75.

Invocation to the Highest

An invocation to the highest aspect of deity is performed at this point. Here the ritualist can say a prayer or invocation of his or her own choosing so long as the deity invoked represents the ritualist's highest ideal of the divine source of the universe. For some, the Golden Dawn's simple "Adoration to the Lord of the Universe" will suffice:

"Holy art Thou, Lord of the Universe! Holy art Thou whom Nature Hath not Formed! Holy art Thou, the Vast and the Mighty One! Lord of the Light and of the Darkness!"[2]

Practitioners of some magical traditions may wish to change the title "Lord" to "Creator," "Ruler," or "Source."

Another invocation that could be used here is this:

"O Father! O Mother of Mothers! O Archetype Eternal of Maternity and Love! O Son! The Flower of All Sons! Form of all Forms! Soul, Spirit, Harmony and Numeral of All things! Amen!"[3]

One final example is:

"O Spirit of Spirits! O Eternal Soul of Souls! O imperishable Breath of Life! O Creative Sigh! O mouth which breathest forth and withdrawest the life of all beings, in the flux and reflux of Thine Eternal Word, which is the Divine Ocean of Movement and of Truth!"[4]

Feel free to change these invocations to suit your own spiritual inclination, or use another prayer entirely.

Ritual Spread and Visualization

The cards are then placed face up in the order indicated by the spread on the center of your altar while their imagery is visualized and their energies are invoked in the imagination.

Lay down card 1, the significator and your own self-image card, and visualize yourself with all of the natural strengths that you already possess.

Lay down card 2, the initial action card of the Hierophant, and visualize the teacher within you. Begin to open up your psyche to the sacred knowledge of the divine. See the figure of the Hierophant as your own higher self opening a clear channel for the divine light to descend into your conscious mind. Imagine that your connection to your higher self is greatly improved. Your ability to listen to its divine wisdom is also enhanced.

Lay down card 3, the progression card of the Hermit. Visualize your own higher self holding out the lantern of divine light to guide you. This light is a perpetual source of strength and wisdom that leads you toward your goal.

Invocation of the Talisman's Governing Forces

Lay down card 4, the tarot talisman card. With your lotus wand or general purpose wand, trace a circle over the talisman card.

At this point, you must invoke the energies that correspond to your tarot talisman card. In this example, the tarot talisman card is the Magician, attributed to the planet Mercury. The planets are traditionally assigned to the figure of a hexagram with the sun at its center (see figure 17).

Figure 17: The Planets Attributed to the Hexagram.

Figure 18: The Invoking Hexagram of Mercury.

Trace the Invoking Hexagram of Mercury over the card by starting at the point of Mercury on the upright triangle, going clockwise, then start at the opposite point on the inverted triangle and trace clockwise (see figure 18).

You have the option of tracing the hexagram in silence or you can intone traditional words of power associated with it as follows: As you draw the two triangles that make up the hexagram, intone the word **"Ararita"** (*ah-ra-ree-tah*). This is a name of power that expresses the unity of the divine.[5] Next, intone the Hebrew godname associated with the Mercury hexagram—**"Elohim Tzabaoth"** (*el-oh-heem tza-bah-oth*) which means "God of Hosts" or "God of Multitudes." As you do so, draw the symbol of Mercury in the center.

You could also intone the names of **"Raphael"** and **"Tiriel,"** the archangel and intelligence associated with Mercury. These angelic beings put the magical forces they control into action. (Much more information on Hebrew godnames, archangels, and angels and how to visualize them is given in Part Two.)

At this point you should clearly state your purpose for consecrating the talisman. Use your magical name when you do this. It should be something to the effect of:

"I, *(Frater Veritas)*,[6] open this temple to perform a working in the magic of light. I seek to become the Magician and gain skill in the sacred art of magic. Look with favor upon this ceremony. Grant me what I seek, so that through this rite I may obtain greater understanding of arcane wisdom and thereby advance in the Great Work."

If the tarot talisman card chosen has certain gods or goddesses associated with it, you could recite a special prayer or invocation to that deity at this point in the ritual. In our example, the card of the Magician is attributed to gods of magic and wisdom in several different pantheons: Thoth of the Egyptians, Enki of the Sumerians, Ea of the Babylonians, Hermes of the Greeks, Mercury of the Romans, and many more. A list of the tarot deities can be found in the next chapter. You may choose to invoke any deity of wisdom from whatever pantheon you favor. The invocation can be as simple or elaborate as you wish. The following example is dedicated to the ibis-headed god Thoth:

"Hail Thoth, O great one of wisdom and lord of time! Master of the science of magic! Write well of me in your book of knowledge! Grant me what I seek! Charge this talisman

with your sacred power! May it bring me knowledge and skill in the art of magic! With your divine aid it shall be done! So mote it be!"

Visualize Your Goal

Finally, you should envision your stated goal as exemplified in the talisman card you have chosen. In your mind's eye, see yourself standing in your magical regalia with all the knowledge, skills, and implements of a master magician at your fingertips. Picture yourself performing a successful ceremony that causes an effective change for good. Think of the positive effects that an increase in your spiritual/magical knowledge will have in your life. Remember to always visualize the goal of the talisman card *as if it has already come to pass.* Don't imagine yourself becoming the Magician, envision that you already ARE the magician.

State the following affirmations, giving the Signs of the Four Magical Laws shown on page 78:

"I WILL myself to be the Magician, adept in the high art of magic!
I CHOOSE to invoke those powers that conform to the planet Mercury!
I CREATE a facsimile in the astral light—an undeniable image of what will be!
I SEE myself as I WILL it to be! I have become the Magician."

Closing

Perform the closing ceremony given on page 77.

After performing the tarot talisman ritual, leave the ritual card spread set up on your altar. Or place the talisman card where you will see it often. If that isn't convenient, you can just clean up and put everything away. The ritual will go on working regardless.

Of course, if you prefer, you don't need to lay out a ritual card spread; you could simply consecrate the tarot talisman card itself. The other cards are simply present to facilitate the visualization of achieving your goal.

OPTIONAL RITUAL ITEMS

You may embellish your ritual with a variety of items that correspond to the tarot talisman card. This will enhance the ceremony by providing focus and emphasis on your desired goal. Since the color attributed to Mercury (in the previous example using the Magician card) is yellow, you might wish to add yellow candles to your altar arrangement. For an appropriate incense, try to pick a mercurial one such as mastic, white sandalwood, mace, or storax. Gemstones associated with Mercury include opal, especially fire opal, agate, and serpentine. Ordinary items associated with the planet, such as writing pens and books (particularly magical books), may be placed on or near your altar for added effect. Since the objective in this case is to become a skilled magician, you may choose any number of wands, magical rings, or other magical tools to accent your rite.

None of these additional items are necessary for the ritual to work. If you want to supplement the consecration rite, however, try to choose magical substances that are attributed to your tarot talisman card, or everyday items that are connected with your stated goal. A complete list of colors, gemstones, and incenses is given in the appendix.

The following section provides a number of ritual spread samples designed to create talismans for very specific purposes and the consecration rites that will empower them.

MONEY AND FINANCES: GAINING A PROMOTION

This ritual spread is expressly intended for a general increase in finances—specifically for getting a bonus or promotion at work. We'll use *The Universal Tarot* to illustrate this example.

Card 1: For the significator, choose your own self-image card. Purely for the sake of this example, we will choose the Knave of Cups. This might represent the ritualist as a young, creative woman who is a water sign.

Card 2: For the card of initial action, we will choose the Empress. This card is attributed to the planet Venus, which is often called a "gateway" to new beginnings and is associated with social status. The Empress is the pregnant Great Mother who brings all life into physical existence, thus this is also a card of manifestation.

Card 3: For the card of progression, we will choose the Three of Pentacles. Here we see a sculptor working in a church while a monk and an architect look over his work. It is a card of skill and it signifies appreciation for work well done.

Card 4: For the tarot talisman card, we will choose the Ace of Pentacles. This card indicates the stated goal—monetary gain.

The Ritual

Prepare your ritual space and include any items that might correspond to your tarot talisman card or items that will help you focus on your objective. For gemstones, choose moss agate, rock salt, onyx, or galena—gemstones associated with the element of earth (the suit of pentacles). For incense, use storax. You may include a copy of your paycheck and some coins or currency to indicate your goal of acquiring an increase of money.

Two additional candles may be added to the altar: a white candle for Kether (number one, the Ace) and a black or green candle for earth.[7] If you so desire, you can carve the following symbols into their respective candles: the numeral 1 and an earth triangle ▽. You may also "dress" your candles by anointing them with essential oil: hold the candle horizontally and put a couple drops of oil on the center of it. With your right hand, spread the oil from the center of the candle to the wick. With your left hand, spread the oil from the

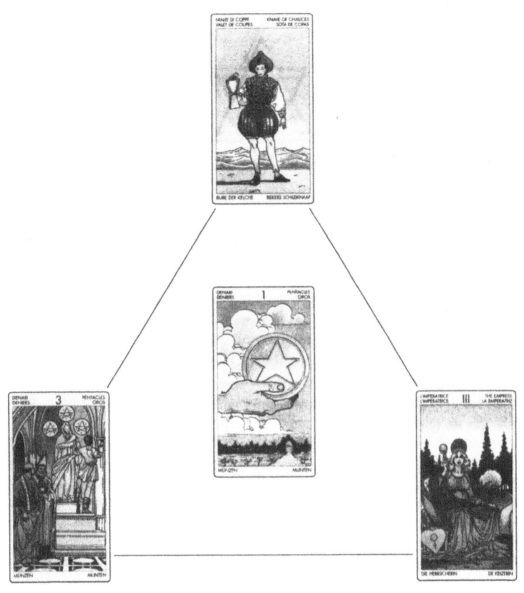

Figure 19: Sample Spread with the Universal Tarot.

center to the candle's base. Turn the candle as you do this, so that its surface is completely dressed with a thin layer of oil. Divine names of the powers represented by the candles may be quietly intoned as you dress them.

Begin with an opening ceremony.

Invoke the highest aspect of deity (as in the examples given on pages 80–81).

Lay out the cards in order and proceed with the work of visualization.

As the significator is placed on the altar, visualize yourself at work, filled with enthusiasm, and eager to display your creative talents to your employers and co-workers.

Figure 20: The Invoking Hexagram of the Supernals (Kether).

Lay down the initial action card and visualize the Empress as the divine force of Venus that helps you move more easily in social circles and improves your "people skills." See yourself as full of confidence, interacting with smiling co-workers and happy supervisors. Picture yourself drawing upon the power of Venus to help you manifest your ideas and projects.

As you lay down the progression card, the Three of Pentacles, visualize your work being admired and appreciated by your co-workers, your supervisor, or your boss. Picture yourself as a problem solver—see yourself working and succeeding in a project that is important to your company. Visualize your boss congratulating you on a job well done.

In the center of the spread, lay down the tarot talisman card—the Ace of Pentacles. Trace a circle over the talisman card.

Next comes the invocation of the energies that correspond to your tarot talisman card. In this case, the tarot talisman card is a pip card, attributed to the sephirah of Kether as well as to the element of earth. Like the planets, the Qabalistic sephiroth are traditionally invoked by drawing the figure of a hexagram. The elements are invoked by tracing the figure of a pentagram. You can therefore invoke the powers of this card by tracing a hexagram and one or more pentagrams.

First, trace the Invoking Hexagram of the Supernals (specifically for Kether) over the card by starting at the point of Saturn on the upright triangle, going clockwise, then start at the opposite point on the inverted triangle and trace clockwise (see figure 20).[8]

You have the option of tracing the hexagram in silence or you can intone the traditional words of power associated with it as follows: As you draw the two triangles that make up the hexagram, intone the word "**Ararita**" (*ah-ra-ree-tah*). Next, intone the divine Hebrew godname associated with Kether—"**Eheieh**" (*eh-hey-yay*) or "I am." As you do so, draw the symbol of Saturn in the center.

Next, trace the pentagrams associated with earth over the talisman card. Practitioners of some magical traditions may prefer to trace only the Invoking Earth Pentagram. Ceremonial magicians, however, will usually opt to trace two pentagrams in this instance—the Invoking Pentagram of Spirit Passive and the Invoking Pentagram of Earth (see figure 21).

Figure 21: Pentagrams for Invoking Earth.

As an affirmation that the highest is always invoked first, the Spirit pentagram is traced first. It acts as a governing force that rules and contains the raw energies of the element. (As a rule, the Passive Spirit Pentagram accompanies the feminine elements of water and earth, while the Active Spirit Pentagram is grouped with the masculine elements of fire and air.)

You have the option of tracing the pentagrams in silence or you can intone traditional words of power assigned to them.

As you trace the Spirit Pentagram, intone the word "**Nanta**" (*en-ah-en-tah*), a divine Enochian name associated with earth. Trace the spirit wheel in the center and intone the divine Hebrew acronym "**Agla**" (*ah-gah-ah*).

As you trace the Earth Pentagram, intone the words "**Emor Dial Hectega**" (*ee-mor dee-al heck-tay-gah*), three Enochian godnames associated with earth. Trace the symbol of Taurus (kerubic earth) in the center and intone the Hebrew godname "**Adonai**," (*ah-doh-nye*, "Lord"), a name often associated with the element of earth.

At this point, you should clearly state your purpose for consecrating the talisman and always be specific when vocalizing your stated goal. It could be similar to this:

"**I, *(magical name)*, open this temple to perform a working in the magic of light. I seek an increase in money through a promotion at my place of employment. *(Be very specific.)* Look with favor upon this ceremony. Grant me what I seek, so that through this rite I may obtain financial security so that I might free myself from the obstacles of the mundane world and thereby advance in the Great Work.**"

If desired you may address an invocation to an Earth god from the pantheon of your choice. For our example, we will use an invocation to Gaia, the Greek goddess of Earth:

"**Hail Gaia, mother of the gods and lady of the green earth! Great goddess who brought the human race forth from the gaping void! Primeval prophetess and essence of the earth! Mother of grain! Fertile Gaia! Bearer of the cornucopia—the horn of plenty! Grant me what I seek! Charge this talisman with your sacred power! May it bring me monetary increase and financial security! With your divine aid it shall be done! So mote it be!**"

You should visualize your stated goal as exemplified in the talisman card you have chosen. In your mind's eye, picture yourself at work, sitting in a larger office, looking forward to new projects and responsibilities. Imagine yourself enjoying the honors that have been bestowed on you. Think of what you plan on doing with the added income. Visualize all of this as if it were a done deal—like it has already happened.

State the following affirmations, giving the Signs of the Four Magical Laws:

"I WILL for myself a career promotion and the monetary increase it will bring me!

I CHOOSE to invoke those powers that conform to elemental earth!

I CREATE a facsimile in the astral light—an undeniable image of what will be!

I SEE myself as I WILL it to be! My work has been rewarded! I have secured financial gain!"

Perform the closing ceremony.

CLAIRVOYANCE

This ritual spread is designed to help develop clairvoyance, higher intuition, and psychic skills. *The Thoth Tarot* will be used to illustrate this example.

Card 1: For the significator, choose your own self-image card. Here we will choose the Princess of Disks. This might represent the ritualist as a practical young woman who is an earth sign.

Card 2: For the card of initial action, we will choose the Moon. This card is attributed to the sign of Pisces, associated with intuition, dreams, psychicism, and mysticism. It is also a card that deals with overcoming illusions.

Card 3: For the card of progression, we will choose the Star. This Aquarian card is associated with developing one's capacity for imagination and meditation. It is a card of inspiration and higher awareness.

Card 4: For the tarot talisman, we will choose the High Priestess, a card that is attributed to the subconscious mind. This card denotes the objective of the ritual—to develop your psychic abilities.

The Ritual

Prepare your temple space and include any items that might help you focus on your objective. The High Priestess is attributed to the luminary of the moon, therefore you might want to adorn your altar with supplemental items that will reflect this: for gemstones, choose moonstone, pearl, fluorspar, or quartz. For incense, pick camphor or jasmine. A blue candle, symbolic of Luna, can be added to your altar—you can carve the symbol of the moon into the candle before dressing it with an appropriate essential oil. Include any magical tools used to increase one's psychic perception, such as magic mirrors, crystal orbs, and skrying symbols.

Begin with the opening ceremony.

Invoke the highest aspect of deity.

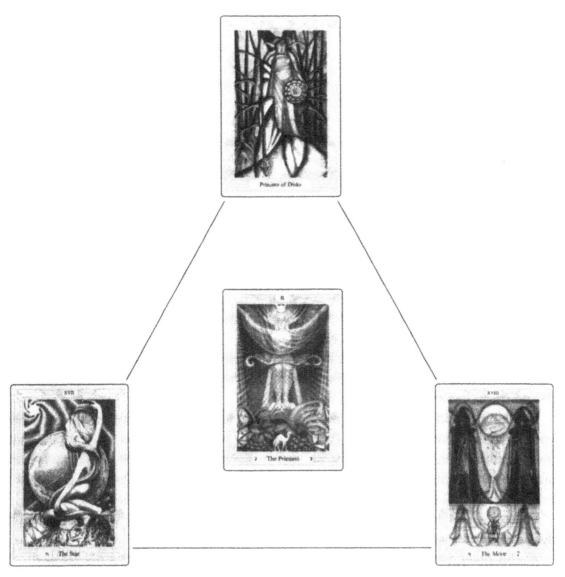

Figure 22: Sample Triangle of Art Spread with the Thoth Tarot.

Lay out the cards in order and proceed with the work of visualization.

As the significator is placed on the altar, visualize yourself standing in your magical regalia, ready to use all of your natural strengths and abilities to sharpen your instincts and hone your awareness.

Lay down the initial action card of the Moon. Visualize a red-violet veil opening before you as you gaze out onto the astral world that exists behind the physical world. Picture yourself fearlessly confronting this misty realm, able to travel on the astral plane, or able to observe the astral world from afar. See yourself as confident and ready to discern truth from illusion, testing any astral vision that seems unreliable or false.

Figure 23: Invoking Hexagram of Luna.

Lay down the progression card of the Star. Visualize yourself standing in a river under a violet starlit sky. Cast your eyes upward and see a large seven-pointed star above you. In your mind's eye, see waves of divine white light streaming down upon you from this star. As it does so, imagine yourself absorbing the energy. Feel yourself being filled with increased powers of imagination and extrasensory perception.

In the center of the spread, lay down the tarot talisman card—the High Priestess. Trace a circle clockwise over the talisman card.

Trace the Invoking Hexagram of Luna over the card by starting at the point of Luna on the inverted triangle, going clockwise, then start at the opposite point on the upright triangle and trace clockwise (see figure 23).

You have the option of tracing the hexagram in silence, or you can intone traditional words of power associated with it: As you draw the two triangles that make up the hexagram, intone the name of unity **"Ararita"** (*ah-ra-ree-tah*). Next, intone the divine Hebrew name associated with the Luna Hexagram—**"Shaddai El Chai"** (*sha-dye el ch'igh[9]*), which means "Almighty Living God." As you do so, draw the symbol of Luna in the center.

You could also intone the names of **"Gabriel"** and **"Shelachel,"** the archangel and intelligence associated with the moon.

At this point, you should clearly state your purpose for consecrating the talisman. Always be specific when vocalizing your stated goal. It could be something like the following:

"I, (*magical name*), open this temple to perform a working in the magic of light. I seek to gain clairvoyant skills and psychic abilities. Look with favor upon this ceremony. Grant me what I seek, so that through this rite I may gain the ability to travel upon the astral plane and see into the etheric realms. Thus may I increase my esoteric knowledge and thereby advance in the Great Work."

The card of the High Priestess is attributed to various lunar goddesses such as Diana and Selene, but also to goddesses of magic and wisdom in several different pantheons. You may add a personal invocation to the deity of your choice here. The following invocation is dedicated to the Egyptian goddess Isis:

"Hail Isis, mother of all! Goddess who art mighty in magic! O celestial queen of heaven! Great lady of wisdom and foresight! Celestial priestess of gods and humans! Grant me what

I seek! Charge this talisman with your sacred power! May it bring me the power of clairvoyance, increased psychic awareness, and the ability to skry into the astral realm! With your divine aid it shall be done! So mote it be!"

You should visualize your stated goal as exemplified in the talisman card you have chosen. In your mind's eye, see yourself as the High Priestess with all the powers and abilities of an accomplished clairvoyant. You are ready to see what lies beyond time, beyond space, and beyond the depths of the subconscious mind. Imagine the feeling of achievement you will experience when your insights prove to be correct.

State the following affirmations, giving the Signs of the Four Magical Laws:

"I WILL myself to be the seer, skilled in all the arts of second sight!

I CHOOSE to invoke those powers that conform to Luna, the moon!

I CREATE a facsimile in the astral light—an undeniable image of what will be!

I SEE myself as I WILL it to be! I have become the High Priestess."

Perform the closing ceremony.

LEGAL MATTERS: A FAVORABLE JUDGMENT

This ritual spread is designed to gain a favorable judgment in a legal proceeding. *The Marseille Tarot* will be used to demonstrate this example.

Card 1: For the significator, choose your own self-image card. For our example, we will choose the King of Cups. This might represent the magician as a mature, sensitive man who is a water sign.

Card 2: For the card of initial action, we will choose Justice. This card is attributed to the sign of Libra, associated with balance, integrity, fairness, and social justice. It is also a card of legal proceedings, courts, and trials.

Card 3: For the card of progression, we will choose the Eight of Wands. This card is associated with swift communication, rapid movement, and the acceptance of proposals.

Card 4: For the tarot talisman card, we will choose Judgement. This card specifies the intended goal of the spread—to gain a legal judgment in your favor.

The Ritual

Prepare your temple space and include any items that might help you focus on your objective. Since the card of Judgment is attributed to the elements of fire and spirit, select supplemental items that will reflect this. For gemstones, choose ruby or fire opal. An appropriate incense would be olibanum (frankincense). Additional candles chosen may be red (fire) or white (spirit) and engraved with the appropriate symbols ($\triangle$ or ✴) before they are dressed with essential oil. Any legal paperwork involved may be placed on the altar under the card spread.

Figure 24: Sample Spread with the Marseille Tarot.

Begin with the opening ceremony.

Invoke the highest aspect of deity.

Lay out the cards in order and proceed with the work of visualization.

As the significator is placed on the altar, visualize yourself confidently sitting in a court of law, fully prepared to successfully argue your case.

As you lay down the initial action card, Justice, visualize the Greek goddess Themis standing behind you. She holds the sword and scales of justice and provides you with wise counsel

start here

Invoking Spirit Active   Invoking Fire

Figure 25: Pentagrams for Invoking Fire.

and support. Visualize other people who are involved in your case—the judge, the attorneys, and the supporting witnesses—being favorable and sympathetic to your cause. Imagine all of them concluding that your case has merit and that you should prevail in the matter.

As you lay down the progression card, the Eight of Wands, visualize your case moving ahead rapidly and effectively, without obstacles or delays. Any terms or proposals that you make are swiftly accepted.

In the center of the spread, lay down the tarot talisman card—Judgement. Trace a circle clockwise over the talisman card.

Trace the pentagrams associated with fire over the card. Practitioners of some magical traditions may prefer to trace only the Invoking Fire Pentagram. Ceremonial magicians, however, may wish to trace two pentagrams associated with fire—the Invoking Pentagram of Spirit Active followed by the Invoking Pentagram of Fire.

You can trace the pentagrams in silence or you may intone traditional words of power associated with them.

As you trace the Spirit Pentagram, intone the word **"Bitom"** (*bay-ee-toh-em*), a divine Enochian name associated with fire. Trace the spirit wheel in the center and intone the Hebrew godname **"Eheieh"** (*eh-hey-yay*).

As you trace the Fire Pentagram, vibrate the words **"Oip Teaa Pedoce"** (*oh-ee-pay tay-ah-ah pay-doh-kay*), three Enochian godnames associated with fire. Trace the symbol of Leo (kerubic fire) in the center and intone the name **"Elohim,"** which is Hebrew for "god(s)," a name often associated with the element of fire.

At this point, you should clearly state your purpose for consecrating the talisman. Be specific when vocalizing your stated goal. It could be similar to this:

"I, *(magical name)*, open this temple to perform a working in the magic of light. I seek to win a favorable judgment in a legal matter. *(Be very specific.)* Look with favor upon this ceremony. Grant me what I seek, so that through this rite I may obtain justice and peace of mind and thereby free myself from the obstacles of the mundane world. Thus may I advance in the Great Work."

If desired, you may address an invocation to a fire deity from the pantheon of your choice. For this case in point, we will use an invocation to Hestia, the Greek goddess of fire. Because her card has a prominent placement in this ritual card spread, we will also invoke Themis, the Greek goddess of Justice:

"Hail Hestia, goddess of the hearth-fire and the public square! Benevolent lady who gives warmth and support! I invoke thee! Grant me what I seek! Charge this talisman with your sacred power, your holy Fire! O Themis, great goddess of justice and righteousness! I invoke thee! May this talisman bring me a favorable judgment in the court of law! With your divine aid it shall be done! So mote it be!"

You should visualize your stated goal as exemplified in the talisman card you have chosen. In your mind's eye, see justice ruling in your favor. The judgment you seek is granted. See yourself being congratulated by those who have stood by your side throughout the proceedings. Visualize the positive effect that this judgment will have on your life.

State the following affirmations, giving the Signs of the Four Magical Laws:

"I WILL for myself victory in court and in all that relates to this legal matter!

I CHOOSE to invoke those powers that conform to elemental fire!

I CREATE a facsimile in the astral light—an undeniable image of what will be!

I SEE myself as I WILL it to be! Justice has declared a judgment ruled in my favor!"

Perform the closing ceremony.

HEALTH AND HEALING

This ritual spread is specifically intended to send healing energy to a sick friend. For this example we'll use *The Babylonian Tarot*.

Card 1: For the Significator, we will choose the Queen of Wands, who in this case might represent the sick friend as a mature woman who is a self-confident fire sign.

Card 2: For the card of initial action, we will choose the Ace of Wands, which will provide a protective, natural force that will begin the process of healing.

Card 3: For the card of progression, we will choose the Six of Arrows (known as the Six of Swords in other decks). Here we see Gula, the goddess of healing, standing over an injured man. She is removing arrows from his side and applying a healing herb to his wounds. The keyword of the card is "Relief."

Card 4: For the tarot talisman card, we will choose the Four of Arrows, which has the keyword of "Rest." This card shows a lioness resting peacefully in a lush garden. It is a card of convalescence and recovery from illness.

Figure 26: Sample Spread with the Babylonian Tarot.

The Ritual

Prepare your temple space and include any items that might help you focus on your objective. For gemstones, choose amethyst or sapphire for Chesed and topaz or opal for the element of air. For incense use galbanum. Two additional candles may be chosen: a blue candle for Chesed and a yellow candle for air. They may be engraved with their respective symbols (the numeral 4 and the air triangle △) before they are dressed with an appropriate essential oil. Fresh flowers may be placed on the altar as an affirmation of vitality.

Begin with the opening ceremony.

Invoke the highest aspect of deity.

Lay out the cards in order and proceed with the work of visualization.

As the significator is placed on the altar, visualize your friend and think about your desire to see her healthy and happy again.

As you lay down the initial action card, visualize the Ace of Wands as a divine, purifying force that is used to root out the source of the disease and destroy infection.

As you lay down the progression card, the Six of Arrows, imagine a great protective goddess standing over your friend and continuously applying her therapeutic powers to heal your friend and provide constant relief.

Finally, lay down the tarot talisman card—the card of "Rest." Trace a circle over it. This is the point at which you would invoke the energies that correspond to your tarot talisman card. In this case, the talisman is a pip card, numerically attributed to the fourth sephirah of Chesed. It also has the zodiacal decanate attribution of Jupiter in Libra. You can therefore invoke the powers of this card by tracing a hexagram for the sephirah and one or more pentagrams for the sign of Libra.

Trace the Invoking Hexagram of Jupiter (attributed to Chesed) over the card. Start at the point of Jupiter on the inverted triangle, going clockwise, then start at the opposite point on the upright triangle and trace clockwise (see figure 27).

You have the option of tracing the hexagram in silence, or you can intone traditional words of power associated with it.

As you draw the two triangles that make up the hexagram, intone the word **"Ararita"** (*ah-ra-ree-tah*). Next, intone the Hebrew godname associated with Chesed and the Jupiter Hexagram—**"El"** or **"Aleph Lamed, AL"**[10] meaning "God." As you do so, draw the symbol of Jupiter in the center.

Our tarot talisman card of "Rest" is attributed to the third decanate of Libra (20°–30°), which is Jupiter in Libra. Pentagrams are always used to invoke zodiacal signs, therefore you would trace the pentagrams associated with Libra over the talisman card.

Practitioners of some magical traditions may prefer to trace only the Invoking Air Pentagram. Ceremonial magicians may opt to trace two pentagrams in this instance—the Invoking Pentagram of Spirit Active and the Invoking Pentagram of Libra. (These are the same two pentagrams that you would normally trace when invoking the element of air. The only difference is that in this instance you would trace the sigil of Libra in the center of the Air Pentagram, rather than the usual Aquarius symbol.[11])

You have the option of tracing the pentagrams in silence, or you can intone traditional words of power associated with them.

As you trace the Spirit Pentagram, intone the word **"Exarp"** (*ex-ar-pay*), a divine Enochian name associated with air. Trace the spirit wheel in the center and intone the Hebrew godname **"Eheieh"** (*eh-hey-yay*).

Figure 27: The Invoking Hexagram of Jupiter.

Invoking Spirit Active   Invoking Air (Libra)

Figure 28: Pentagrams for Invoking Libra.

As you trace the Air Pentagram, intone the words **"Oro Ibah Aozpi"** (*or-oh ee-bah-hay ah-oh-zoad-pee*), which are three Enochian godnames associated with air. Trace the symbol of Libra in the center and intone the divine Hebrew name **"YHVH"** (*yod heh vav heh*), which is ascribed to the four elements but often associated with the element of air.

After tracing these figures, clearly vocalize your intended purpose of sending healing energy to your friend. It could be similar to this:

"I, *(magical name)*, open this temple to perform a working in the magic of light. I seek to send health and vitality to my friend *(Jane Doe)*. Look with favor upon this ceremony. Grant me what I seek, so that through this rite my friend may be completely healed from all illness. Thus will I support and empower my friends and companions and affirm the place of all of humanity in the Great Chain of Being."

You may address an invocation to a Babylonian deity associated with the sephirah of Chesed, such as the god Marduk. An invocation of Gula, the goddess of healing, may be added, especially since her card has a prominent placement in the ritual card spread:

"Hail Marduk, king of the great gods and lord of the storm! Mighty god of mercy and justice whose commands are all-powerful! I invoke thee! Grant me what I seek! Charge this talisman with your sacred and undeniable power! O Gula, great goddess of medicine and healing! I invoke thee! May this talisman bring health and vigor to my friend *(Jane Doe)* for whom it is intended! With your divine aid it shall be done! So mote it be!"

You should visualize your stated goal as exemplified in the talisman card chosen. In your mind's eye, see your friend completely revitalized and glowing with good health. Visualize her sitting in a sunny garden, relaxing peacefully in the fresh air.

State the following affirmations, giving the Signs of the Four Magical Laws:

"I WILL that good health and vitality return to my friend *(Jane Doe)*.

I CHOOSE to invoke those powers that conform to Chesed and Libra!

I CREATE a facsimile in the astral light—an undeniable image of what will be!

I SEE my friend as I WILL her to be! *(Jane Doe)* is completely healed and resting comfortably!"

Perform the closing ceremony.

TO MEND A BROKEN FRIENDSHIP

For this example we'll use the *Golden Dawn Magical Tarot.*

Card 1: For the significator, choose your own self-image card. For this instance, we will pick the King of Wands. This might represent the magician as a mature, active man who is a fire sign.

Card 2: For the card of initial action, we will choose a significator that represents the friend who has become estranged from you. In this case, we will choose the Queen of Pentacles, as if the friend was a mature, practical woman who is an earth sign.

Card 3: For the card of progression, we will choose the Two of Swords. The keyword of the card is "Peace Restored." This card represents the ending of a quarrel in order to re-establish harmonious relations.

Card 4: For the tarot talisman card, we will choose the Two of Cups, which has the keyword of "Love." This card is attributed to the element of water and the sephirah of Chokmah. It symbolizes friendship and natural love.

The Ritual

Prepare your ritual space and include any items that might add emphasis to your objective. For gemstones, choose star ruby or turquoise for the second sephirah of Chokmah, or pick aquamarine or beryl for the element of water. For incense use musk (Chokmah), or onycha or myrrh (water). Two additional candles may be added to the altar: a gray candle for Chokmah and a blue candle for water. If you so desire, you can carve the following symbols into their respective candles: the numeral 2 and a water triangle ▽. The candles can be dressed with an appropriate essential oil. Any item once given to you by your friend may be added to your altar.

Begin with the opening ceremony.

Invoke the highest aspect of deity.

Lay out the cards in order and proceed with the work of visualization.

Figure 29: Sample Spread with the Golden Dawn Magical Tarot.

As the significator is placed on the altar, visualize yourself reaching out with goodwill toward your friend. If you were at fault in the matter, see yourself having the courage to admit it and ask for forgiveness. You also forgive your friend without harboring any lingering resentment.

Lay down the initial action card, the Queen of Pentacles, and visualize your friend reaching out to you, wishing to patch up your differences. If your friend was at fault, see her with the courage to admit it and ask for forgiveness. She also forgives you without harboring any lingering resentment.

Figure 30: The Invoking Hexagram of the Supernals (Chokmah).

As you lay down the progression card, the Two of Swords, visualize the two of you coming together to bury the hatchet and start over. Imagine you and your friend making peace with each other.

Finally, lay down the tarot talisman card—the card of "Love." Trace a circle over it. Now, invoke the energies that correspond to the talisman card. The talisman is a pip card, numerically attributed to the second sephirah of Chokmah. It also has the zodiacal decanate attribution of Venus in Cancer. You can invoke the powers of this card by tracing a hexagram for the sephirah and one or more pentagrams for the zodiacal sign.

Trace the Invoking Hexagram of the Supernals (for Chokmah) over the card by starting at the point of Saturn on the upright triangle, going clockwise. Then start at the opposite point on the inverted triangle and trace clockwise (see figure 30).[12]

You have the option of tracing the hexagram in silence, or you can intone traditional words of power associated with it.

As you draw the two triangles that make up the hexagram, intone the word **"Ararita"** (*ah-ra-ree-tah*). Next intone the divine Hebrew godname associated with Chokmah—**"Yah."** As you do so, draw the symbol of Saturn in the center.

The tarot talisman card of "Love" is attributed to the first decanate of Cancer (1°–10°) which is Venus in Cancer. Trace the pentagrams associated with Cancer over the card. Practitioners of some magical traditions may prefer to trace only the Invoking Water Pentagram.

Ceremonial magicians may wish to trace two pentagrams—the Invoking Pentagram of Spirit Passive and the Invoking Pentagram of Cancer. (These are the same two pentagrams that you would normally trace when invoking the element of water. The only difference is that, in this instance, you would trace the sigil of Cancer in the center of the Water Pentagram, rather than the usual Scorpio symbol.)

You have the option of tracing the pentagrams in silence, or you can intone traditional words of power associated with them.

As you trace the Spirit Pentagram, intone the word **"Hcoma"** (*hay-coh-mah*), a divine Enochian name associated with water. Trace the spirit wheel in the center and intone the Hebrew acronym **"Agla"** (*ah-gah-ah*).

Invoking Spirit Passive   Invoking Water (Cancer)

Figure 31: Pentagrams for Invoking Cancer.

As you trace the Water Pentagram, intone the words "Emp Arsl Gaiol" (*em-pay ar-sel gah-ee-ol*), which are three Enochian godnames associated with water. Trace the symbol of Cancer in the center and intone the name "AL" or "Aleph Lamed AL,"[13] which is associated with water.

After tracing these figures, clearly vocalize your intended purpose of sending reconciling energy to your friend. It could be similar to this:

"I, *(magical name)*, open this temple to perform a working in the magic of light. I seek to mend a broken friendship between myself and *(friend's name)*. Look with favor upon this ceremony. Grant me what I seek, so that, through this rite, peace and friendship may be restored between us. Thus will I support and empower my friends and companions and affirm the place of all of humanity in the Great Chain of Being."

Personalized invocations may be added here. You may address an invocation to a deity associated with the sephirah of Chokmah such as Athena, the Greek goddess of wisdom:

"Hail Athena, great goddess of wisdom! Virgin goddess who sprang fully armed from the head of Zeus! Wise prophetess who foresees all! Protectress and wise counselor, I invoke thee! Grant me what I seek! Charge this talisman with your sacred and undeniable power! May it repair a broken friendship and restore peace between *(friend's name)* and I! With your divine aid it shall be done! So mote it be!"

You should visualize your stated goal as exemplified in the talisman chosen. In your mind's eye, see you and your friend together again. Visualize the two of you smiling and laughing as you make new plans for spending time together.

State the following affirmations, giving the Signs of the Four Magical Laws:

"I WILL that my friendship with *(friend's name)* be fully restored and all hurts forgiven.

I CHOOSE to invoke those powers that conform to Chokmah and Cancer!

I CREATE a facsimile in the astral light—an undeniable image of what will be!

I SEE our friendship as I WILL it to be! There is peace and amity between us!"

Perform the closing ceremony.

Banishing a Talisman

After the tarot talisman card has done its work, you should not let its energies linger or slowly dissipate through neglect. The energies you have invoked should be banished so that the talisman card can be returned to the deck. If you used an invoking pentagram to charge the talisman, you must release it by tracing its *corresponding banishing pentagram* over the card. If you charged the talisman with an invoking hexagram, you must discharge it by tracing its *corresponding banishing hexagram* over the card. All of these figures can be found in the appendix of this book.

Once you have banished the card, simply wipe it off with a clean cloth and put it back in the deck. If your cards are plastic-coated, wipe them off using a cloth dampened by water mixed with a small amount of salt.

AN AMULETIC RITUAL SPREAD

In chapter 1 we described the different views that magicians have concerning what constitutes an amulet as opposed to a talisman. Some believe that if you carry the magical object around with you—it's an amulet. However, talismans are often carried around by magicians, too.

It is our belief that the main characteristic used to distinguish talismans from amulets boils down to this: talismans are meant to attract something to you whereas amulets are made to repel something away from you. Amulets are used for banishing. Therefore we can create tarot amulets by utilizing another ritual card spread that we call the Lesser Banishing Pentagram Spread.

THE LESSER BANISHING PENTAGRAM SPREAD

As its name suggests, this ritual card spread uses the form of the pentagram most commonly used by magicians in the LBRP to banish unwanted energies (see figure 6 on page 19). In this spread, the first card is the tarot amulet card. It represents that energy, situation, or circumstance that the ritualist wishes to banish. The next five cards are used to represent the strongest aspect of each of the five elements. Cards 2 through 6 represent the elemental points of the pentagram. These cards are placed down in the exact order that you would use to trace the figure of a Lesser Banishing Pentagram:

Card 1: The tarot amulet card—the thing you want banished
Card 2: Earth point
Card 3: Spirit point
Card 4: Fire point

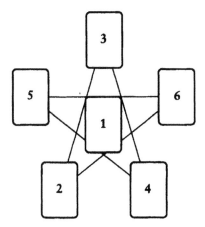

Figure 32: The Lesser Banishing Pentagram Spread.

Card 5: Air point

Card 6: Water point

Any of the earth cards could be used for the earth point, just as any of the fire cards could be used for the fire point, etc. For the sake of simplicity, however, we suggest that you use the Aces, the strongest and purest elemental cards in the deck, for the five pentagram points. These are the divine forces we will symbolically use to banish the central card:

Card 1: Tarot amulet card to be banished

Card 2: Earth: Ace of Pentacles (starting point of the Lesser Banishing Pentagram)

Card 3: Spirit: Judgement (attributed to spirit through the Hebrew letter shin)

Card 4: Fire: Ace of Wands

Card 5: Air: Ace of Swords

Card 6: Water: Ace of Cups

SAMPLE SPREAD: TO BANISH
AN ADDICTION OR BAD HABIT

The Thoth Tarot will be used to illustrate this example. Cards 1 through 5 are the same as those listed on the previous page. For card 1, the tarot amulet card, we will choose the Seven of Cups, which has the keyword of "Debauch." This card sometimes alludes to addictions, obsessions, bad habits, and general overindulgence (see figure 33). We must stress, however, that for particularly harmful addictions such as drug or alcohol dependence, professional help is needed.

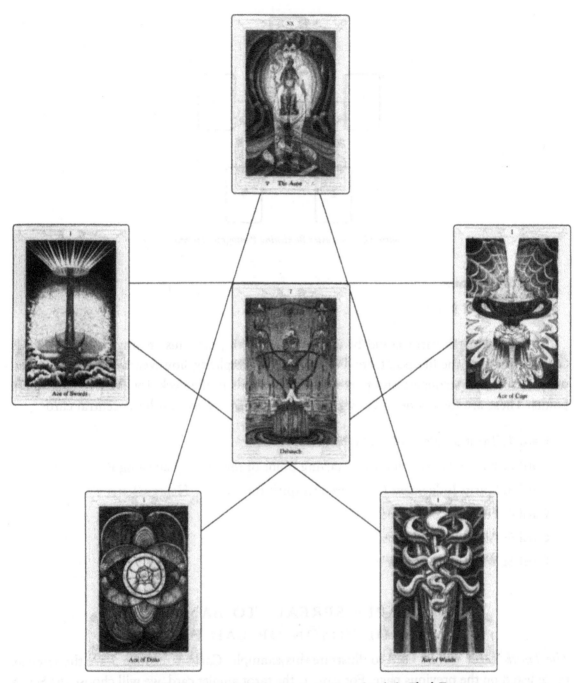

Figure 33: Sample Lesser Banishing Pentagram Spread with the Thoth Tarot.

The Ritual

Prepare your temple space and include any items that might help you focus on your objective—to rid yourself of an addiction. Since it takes a great deal of strength and willpower to resist the temptation that an addiction may have over a person, you may wish to use correspondences relating to the purifying force of elemental fire. For gemstones, choose fire opal or ruby. For incense, use olibanum. Any additional candles may be red, engraved with the fire triangle △, and dressed with an appropriate essential oil.

Begin with the opening ceremony.

Invoke the highest aspect of deity.

Lay out the cards in order and proceed with the work of visualization. As you lay down the first card, picture your addiction, the thing that you want gone from your life. Imagine the various things about your bad habit that you dislike—how this dependency makes you feel, and how it makes those close to you feel. Think of how strongly you want this addiction to stop and how much better you will feel once you have given it up.

With a general purpose wand, trace a circle over the amulet card.

Then lay down cards 2 through 6 in order, following the pentagram formation. As you do this, visualize a white banishing pentagram being traced from one card to the next. Visualize the Aces and the card of Judgement (called "The Aeon" in the *Thoth Tarot*) as living, divine forces of the elements. See these forces containing the addiction. You may also envision five mighty archangels dressed in robes of the elemental colors of black, white, red, yellow, and blue. See these figures holding up the Ace of Pentacles, the holy letter shin, the Ace of Wands, and the other surrounding cards, acting to surround and repel the addiction. Then say the following:

"Hail divine forces of the five elements! Ash—fire, Mayim—water, Ruach—air, Aretz—earth, and the mystical Eth—the spirit that governs all! Look with favor upon this ceremony and grant what I seek. Banished be the powers of the Dukes of Edom, lords of unbalanced force. Banished be the addiction of *(name your addiction, be very specific)*, the compulsive chains that have bound me thus far! They are now broken in pieces like the chaff of the summer threshing fields. Thus may I vanquish what formerly controlled me and thereby advance in the Great Work."

Using your lotus wand or general purpose wand, firmly and purposefully trace the figure of the Lesser Banishing Pentagram over the amulet card. Visualize the pentagram in glowing white light. Then turn the amulet card face down, physically banishing it from your sight.

State the following affirmations, giving the Signs of the Four Magical Laws:

"I WILL that my addiction is now broken and ended.

I CHOOSE to vanquish imbalance with the holy powers of the pentagram.

I CREATE a facsimile in the astral light—an undeniable image of what will be!

I SEE myself as I WILL it to be! Through strength and resilience I have overcome! Compulsion has no more power over me."

Perform the closing ceremony.

Banish the amulet card one final time with the figure of the Lesser Banishing Pentagram. After wiping the cards with a clean cloth, you may put them away back in the deck.

You may wish to follow up an amuletic ritual spread with a separate tarot talisman ritual spread and consecration. This will help to attract energies that will reinforce your willpower. When you banish something harmful, it is a good idea to replace it by invoking something that will be beneficial to you. A card such as Strength or Temperance may be employed as a talisman and carried around with you for additional fortitude to resist the temptation of bad habits.

TO BANISH AN ADVERSARY'S NEGATIVE INFLUENCE

In a perfect world, everyone would realize that we are all brothers and sisters—children of the divine—and would act accordingly with brotherly love, respect, and charity toward all. Unfortunately, we don't live in a perfect world and we often encounter people who, out of jealousy, ignorance, or just bad disposition, act toward us in destructive ways intended to have a harmful influence.

The following ritual does not seek to do your adversary harm, but rather neutralize his or her negativity by containing it, banishing it from your sphere of influence, and sending it back to its source.

Of course, in extreme situations where you may feel physically threatened by another person, it is important to contact the proper authorities.

Instead of using the Aces and the card of Judgement, this time we will use five cards that are unique to *The Babylonian Tarot*. Here we will call upon the kerubim—mighty, divine spirits of protection—to banish the amulet card:

Card 1: Tarot amulet card to be banished

Card 2: Earth: The Kerub of Disks

Card 3: Spirit: Genesis (the spirit of creation)

Card 4: Fire: The Kerub of Wands

Card 5: Air: The Kerub of Arrows

Card 6: Water: The Kerub of Cups

For card 1, the tarot amulet card, you may choose a significator card that would represent your adversary. For the purpose of this spread, we will choose the Nine of Arrows, which has the keyword of "Cruelty." This card sometimes refers to mental abuse and cruelty. Here it will represent your adversary's cruel behavior and will be used to bind and banish these malicious tendencies. In this case, you are only trying to banish the person's negativity and harmful actions, not the person.

The Ritual

Prepare your temple space and include any items that might help you focus on your objective. It wouldn't hurt to have a photo or some personal possession once owned or touched by your adversary. You will also need a small box and two pieces of mirrored glass; the mirrored glass should be big enough to cover the photo, and the box should be big enough to hold the two mirrors. Use whatever additional correspondences seem appropriate to you. If you wish to make your adversary learn a lesson from the experience—to stop, think, and reflect upon his or her actions—then use colors and items that correspond to air. If you want your adversary to begin to feel more empathetic toward you and other people, use objects that are attributed to water. If you want to send your adversary's own negativity back at him or her, use items that correspond to fire.

Begin with the opening ceremony.

Invoke the highest aspect of deity.

Lay out the cards in order and proceed with the work of visualization. As you lay down the first card, visualize your adversary and the malicious, cruel, or harmful behavior that you want to stop. Think of how much you will appreciate not being the focus of this person's destructive thoughts and deeds.

With your lotus wand or general purpose wand, trace a circle over the amulet card.

Next, lay down cards 2 through 6 in order, following the pentagram formation. As you do this, visualize a white banishing pentagram being traced from one card to the next. Visualize the kerubim and the card of Genesis as potent living forces of the elements—great winged guardians who surround your adversary and effortlessly block his or her negativity, deflecting it back to its source. Then say the following:

"Hail divine forces of the five elements! Mighty kerubim who are the strong and divine rulers of the elements! In your midst is the spirit of God who moved upon the face of the waters when the world was formless and void! Look with favor upon this ceremony and grant me what I seek! Contained and confounded be *(your adversary's)* actions of malevolence and cruelty toward me! Banished be his/her power to do harm! May any negativity he/she sends out be deflected back to its source! Thus may I repel the energies of malice and thereby advance in the Great Work."

Using your lotus wand or general purpose wand, firmly and purposefully trace the figure of the Lesser Banishing Pentagram over the amulet card. Visualize the pentagram in glowing white light. Then turn the amulet card face down, physically banishing the card from your sight.

Place the photo between the two pieces of mirrored glass to signify that whatever energy your adversary sends out will be reflected back to him or her. Then place the glass and any of your adversary's personal items inside the box and close it.

State the following affirmations, giving the Signs of the Four Magical Laws:

"I WILL that *(your adversary's)* hostility toward me is blocked.

I CHOOSE to banish *(your adversary's)* harmful intent with the holy powers of the pentagram and the mighty kerubic guardians.

I CREATE a facsimile in the astral light—an undeniable image of what will be!

I SEE my adversary as I WILL it to be! Any negativity he/she sends out is reflected back to him/her."

Perform the closing ceremony.

Banish the amulet card one final time with the Lesser Banishing Pentagram. After wiping the cards with a clean cloth, you may put them away. After a period of time has passed without incident and all problems with your adversary have been resolved, you may release the photo and personal items from the box and put them away.

Using the examples provided here, in addition to the correspondences listed in the appendix, it will be easy for you to devise your own ritual card spreads and consecration ceremonies for tarot talismans and amulets.

Figure 34: Sample Lesser Banishing Pentagram Spread with the Babylonian Tarot.

1 In Golden Dawn practice, certain grade signs are usually given after tracing pentagrams and other figures associated with the divine powers. These grade signs are not necessary for the consecration rites in this book; however, readers who wish to use them with these rituals can find them in several texts, including our book *Ritual Use of Magical Tools*, pages xxxv-xxxvii.

2 Regardie, *The Golden Dawn*, 120. The first three sentences that begin with "Holy art Thou" are usually accompanied with the Projection Sign (see figure 8 on page 22) while the final sentence is followed by the Sign of Silence.

3 Ibid. An excerpt from the "Prayer of the Salamanders," 196.

4 Ibid. An excerpt from the "Prayer of the Sylphs," 165.

5 Ararita is a Hebrew notariqon (acronym) formed from the first letters of the sentence *Achad rosh achdotho rosh ichudo temurahzo achad*, which means, "One is his beginning, one is his individuality, his permutation is one."

6 Your own magical name would be inserted here.

7 The candles chosen may be either black or green since both colors are attributed to the element of earth in various traditions.

8 This same hexagram is used for all three supernals (Kether, Chokmah, and Binah). The only difference is in the specific Hebrew godname intoned for each sephirah.

9 Rhymes with "high."

10 Regardie suggested intoning the Hebrew letters of this short name as a prefix to stretch it out as **"Aleph Lamed, AL."**

11 The standard Invoking Pentagrams of fire, water, air, and earth are normally drawn with the symbols of the fixed (kerubic) signs of Leo, Scorpio, Aquarius, and Taurus in the center.

12 See endnote 8.

13 See endnote 10.

PART TWO

TAROT ANGELS

4

GODS AND ANGELS OF THE TAROT TRUMPS

Each tarot card is associated with a specific energy, whether it is elemental, planetary, astrological, or Qabalistic. Because of this, every card in the deck falls under the authority of certain divine powers, archangels, and angels. The magician can invoke one or more of these entities in a ritual designed to consecrate a tarot card, empowering it as a magical talisman. In the previous chapter we introduced the idea of invoking gods and angels to consecrate tarot talismans. In this chapter we will offer an in-depth look at the various divine forces that are associated with the cards of the tarot.

GOD, GODDESS, ALL THAT IS

Since the dawn of history, humanity has maintained the belief in a divine force that created the world. Although this basic tenet has been expressed in diverse ways, the universal truth at its core unites us all. Some see this divine, eternal force as singular, an indivisible monad—God. Others see it as a diverse tapestry composed of a profusion of deities. What is interesting, however, is that monotheists and polytheists alike share the same basic beliefs, even if they describe those beliefs in different terms.

Most polytheists and pantheists believe in a primal creator being that existed before all other deities (the Babylonian Apsu, the Egyptian Nu, the Greek Chaos, etc.). From these ancient beings, other gods and goddesses were generated. These creator gods, however, were not often seen in ancient times as the most potent nor even the most important of the deities. Eventually, a dominant god and a dominant goddess were born. Other divinities ruled over particular areas of deific influence (the god of war, the goddess of love, the god of medicine, etc.).

Monotheists believe in a single creator god who is all powerful. This divinity created lesser deities known as archangels and angels. These beings have certain duties; they govern a specific area of divine influence—not unlike the lesser gods and goddesses of other pantheons (the angel of childbirth, the angel of death, the angel of annunciation, etc.).

Polytheists and pantheists seem to agree that all the gods are but one god and all the goddesses are but one goddess. In other words, the various goddesses and gods that comprise the pantheons are nothing more than multi-faceted expressions of the archetypal creator beings—the Great Mother Goddess and the Great Father God. But even this idea of a universal duad is a bit of an illusion since ultimately, non-monotheists believe that "All is One." Thus it might safely be said that polytheists and pantheists hold a basic belief in a universal unity that is forever unfolding into various personalized gods and goddesses who are readily accessible to human worshipers. The archetypal images of mother and father are together considered a sacred unity—a union or marriage between two divine halves that by themselves are incomplete. The pantheistic tenet of a "God of gods" is not an affirmation of the Judeo-Christian doctrine, but rather a recognition of the indescribable force that created everything in the manifest universe.

Western ceremonial magicians often profess what might be described as *ultimate monotheism*—the idea that the divine manifests in various diverse forms including gods, archangels, angels, intelligences, and spirits. But ultimately, all of these beings may be traced back to the one divine source of All.

In spite of their differences, monotheists, polytheists, and pantheists are probably more alike in their spiritual beliefs than is generally believed.

THE GODS

Some believe that the gods and goddesses are real and very powerful beings who dwell in another plane of existence and have been around since the beginning of the known universe. Others hold the opinion that the gods are thoughtforms—anthropomorphic images created in the mind of humanity that have been empowered and brought to life by centuries of continuous prayer and veneration. This latter view holds that the divine realities behind the images of the gods and goddesses are enormous reservoirs of energy that are fed by the strong, passionate devotion and focused thoughts of human worshipers. These ancient reservoirs are still in existence, and although centuries of neglect have depleted them, they can yet be re-energized through the ceremonies and invocations of modern-day priests and priestesses. These deific energies may be asleep, but they never cease to be.

The gods are archetypal images that have a life of their own. These divine ideals have had enormous influence over every aspect of human life. Each deity symbolizes one facet of the eternal creative force of the universe. Through the personalization of every single part of the divine, humanity is better equipped to connect with and comprehend the whole, which is so abstract in its sum total that human understanding of it is impossible. Humans will always require some reference point in order to grasp abstract concepts. By giving human form to these divine images, the abstract becomes something that can be related to human experience and deeply felt within the soul.

Gods of the Tarot Trumps

#	*Trump Name*	*Ast.*	*Egyptian*	*Sumero-Babylonian*	*Greek*	*Roman*
0	The Fool	🜁	Bes, Harparkrat Shu *(as 🜁)*	Enkidu *(as fool)* Enlil, Ellil *(as 🜁)*	Pan *(as fool)* Zeus, Aeolos *(as 🜁)*	Pan, Silvanus Aeolus *(as 🜁)*
1	The Magician	☿	Ptah, Thoth	Enki, Ea Nabu *(as ☿)*	Hermes	Mercury
2	High Priestess	☽	Isis *(as priestess)* Khonsu *(as ☽)*	Inanna, Ishtar *(as priestess)* Nannar, Sin *(as ☽)*	Demeter *(as priestess)* Selene, Artemis, Hecate	Ceres *(priestess)* Luna, Diana (☽)
3	The Empress	♀	Mut, Isis *(as mother)* Hathor *(as ♀)*	Ninhursaga, Aruru *(mother)* Inanna, Ishtar *(as ♀)*	Hera *(as queen mother)* Aphrodite *(as ♀)*	Juno *(as queen)* Venus *(as ♀)*
4	The Emperor	♈	Amon *(as king)* Horus *(as ♈)* Khnemu *(as ♈)*	Marduk *(as king)* Nergal *(as ♈)*	Zeus *(as king)* Ares, Athena *(as ♈)*	Jupiter *(as king)* Mars, Minerva
5	The Hierophant	♉	Osiris Serapis *(as ♉)*	Nabu *(as priest)* Gugalanna *(as ♉)*	Dionysos Zagreus	Liber Pater
6	The Lovers	♊	Isis & Osiris *(lovers)* The Merti *(as ♊)*	Ishtar & Tammuz *(lovers)*	Eros & Psyche *(lovers)* Aphrodite & Ares Castor & Pollux *(as ♊)*	Venus & Mars Janus *(as ♊)*
7	The Chariot	♋	Khepera *(as ♋)*	Iskur, Adad, Shamesh	Apollo *(as charioteer)*	Apollo
8	Strength	♌	Sekhet, Bast Neferten *(all as ♌)*	Gilgamesh *(as hero)* La-tarak *(as ♌)*	Heracles *(as hero)* Hestia *(as ♌)*	Hercules *(hero)* Vesta *(as ♌)*
9	The Hermit	♍	Atum *(as hermit)*	An, Anu *(as hermit)* Sala *(as ♍)*	Cronos *(as hermit)* Persephone *(as ♍)* Astraea *(as ♍)* Attis	Saturn *(hermit)* Proserpina (♍) Vesta (♍)
10	Wheel of Fortune	♃	Amoun *(as ♃)*	Marduk *(as ♃)*	Zeus *(as ♃)*, Tyche	Jupiter, Fortuna
11	Justice	♎	Maat	Nanshe	Themis, Athena	Minerva
12	The Hanged Man	▽	Osiris *(hanged man)* Nu, Tefnut, Mut (▽)	Tammuz *(hanged man)* Nammu *(as ▽)*	Adonis, Dionysus Poseidon *(as ▽)*	Liber Pater Neptune *(as ▽)*
13	Death	♏	Nephthys, Anubis	Ereshkigal, Nergal	Thanatos, Hades, Ares	Pluto, Mars
14	Temperance	♐	Neith *(as archer)*	Ishtar *(as archer)* Pabilsag *(as ♐)*	Artemis *(as archer)* Hermaphroditus Chiron (♐), Iris	Diana *(archer)*
15	The Devil	♑	Set, Apep *(as devil)* Min *(as ♑)*	Lamastu *(as devil)* Ninurta *(as ♑)*	Priapus *(as ♑)* Pan *(as ♑)*	Faunus *(as ♑)* Bacchus *(as ♑)*
16	The Tower	♂	Horus, Montu (♂)	Nergal, Erra *(as ♂)*	Ares *(as ♂)*	Mars *(as ♂)*
17	The Star	♒	Sothis *(as star)* Hor Wer *(as ♒)*	Inanna, Ishtar *(as star)* Siduri *(as ♒)*	Hebe, Ganymede (♒) Astraea, Aphrodite *(star)*	Juventas *(as ♒)* Juno, Venus
18	The Moon	♓	Khonsu *(as moon)* Anubis	Nannar, Sin *(as moon)* Adapa, Enki, Ea *(as ♓)*	Selene, Artemis, Hecate Poseidon *(as ♓)*	Luna, Diana (☽) Neptune *(as ♓)*
19	The Sun	☉	Ra *(as ☉)*	Utu, Shamesh *(as ☉)*	Helios, Apollo *(as ☉)*	Sol, Apollo (☉)
20a 20b	Judgement	△ ☸	Neith *(as △)* Neter, Heka (☸) Osiris, Aten *(as ☸)*	Nusku *(as △)*, Shamesh dingir, ilu, "god" (☸)	Hephaestus *(as △)* theios, "divine" (☸)	Vulcan *(as △)* deus "god" (☸)
21a 21b	The Universe	♄ 🜃	Ptah *(as ♄)* Geb *(as 🜃)*	Anki *(as ♄)* Ninhursaga, Aruru *(as 🜃)*	Chronos *(as ♄)* Gaea, Demeter (🜃)	Saturn *(as ♄)* Tellus, Ceres (🜃)

Magicians are able to access the various power reservoirs represented by the gods and utilize them in ritual work. Through willpower, the imaginative faculties of the psyche, and by the active use of symbols such as tarot cards as points of concentration, magicians are able to tap into these vessels of god-energy and invoke them to affect magic.

On the previous page is a list of deities from four major pantheons of the Western Esoteric Tradition corresponding to the twenty-two trump cards of the tarot. This list is by no means complete or authoritative and you may find that your own preferred pantheon is not represented here. It is well beyond the scope of this book to list every pantheon that readers might wish to use, or describe every god or goddess in detail. There are plenty of books available that already cover this material, and we suggest that the reader consult them.

In examining this list, you will find that two or more deities may be given for *different aspects* of a specific card. For example, card 2, the High Priestess, lists two Egyptian deities—the goddess Isis who *is* the High Priestess and the moon god Khonsu, since the astrological correspondence of the card is Luna. In another example, card 21, the Universe, has two different attributions assigned to it: the planet Saturn and the element of earth. Therefore, in the Greek pantheon, Chronos is assigned for the planet Saturn, while Gaea and Demeter are attributed for elemental earth. The exact nature of the tarot talisman chosen will determine which deity best suits your purpose.

DIVINE FORCES OF THE MAJOR ARCANA

The invocation of gods and goddesses corresponding to different cards is an important part of the magic used to create tarot talismans. Assigning deities from ancient pantheons to the tarot cards, however, is an inexact science at best. Since the cards themselves are a product of fifteenth-century Europe, it is far easier to assign to them divine forces from the Qabalistic tradition—the Hebrew godnames, archangels, and angels. A natural affinity exists between the tarot and the Tree of Life. Invoking these forces adds more power to the consecration of tarot talismans.

Angels and archangels have freely crossed cultural and religious boundaries over the centuries. In rabbinic literature, the mighty archangel Gabriel is the prince of justice; in Islam he is said to be the angel who dictated the Koran to the prophet Mohammed; and in Christian scripture Gabriel is the angel of the Annunciation who brings news of the future birth of Jesus.

Yet it is important to remember that angels are neither unique nor exclusive to the monotheistic religions of Judaism, Christianity, and Islam. In the Hellenistic world of late antiquity, pagans also invoked angels. One account tells of a *Michalion,* or Christian shrine to the archangel Michael in the city of Colossae in Asia Minor, said to be the source of a healing spring, where pagans joined Christians to petition the mighty archangel for his miraculous curative power, just as they did their own deities.[1] In fact, many of the holy beings referred to by monotheists

Figure 35: The Archangel Raphael.

as angels and archangels were seen and identified by Hellenistic pagans as gods, as evidenced in the following section of a prayer to the sun god Helios from the *Græco-Egyptian Magical Papyri*:

> . . . I conjure you by the god IAO, by the god Abaoth, by the god Adonai, by the god Michael, by the god Souriel, by the god Gabriel, by the god Raphael. . . [2]

The founders of the Golden Dawn also referred to archangels as gods, as in this description of the four Qabalistic Worlds:

> Briah is creative and originative, and to it certain Great Gods called Archangels are allotted.[3]

Ancient manuscripts such as the *Græco-Egyptian Magical Papyri* reveal that polytheists were quite willing to acknowledge and incorporate the angels of Judeo-Christian tradition, such as in the following invocation to Apollo, the Greek god of the sun:

O lord Apollo, come with Paian[4]
Give answer to my question, lord. O master
Leave Mount Parnassos and the Delphic Pytho
Whene'er my priestly lips voice secret words,
First angel of [the god] great Zeus. IAO
And you, Michael, who rule heaven's realm,
I call, and you archangel Gabriel.[5]

Nevertheless, the Judeo-Christian tradition, especially the non-canonical literature of the Pseudepigrapha and Apocrypha[6] remains a primary source for much of our knowledge of angels and archangels. It is only natural that magicians of Renaissance Europe, such as Henry Cornelius Agrippa, drew heavily upon their own cultural and religious heritage when formulating new lists of angelic beings.

The following explanation of terms, some of which have been only briefly touched upon in previous chapters, will help clarify much of the material that follows.

Godnames: A godname is a potent divine name or "word of power" used to invoke the highest aspects of deity, especially those "holy" names assigned to the ten sephiroth of the Tree of Life. Many of these names are presented in the Hebrew scriptures as the various sacred names of God.

The godnames of the elemental trumps are exactly the same as the godnames given to the elements. The godnames of the twelve zodiacal trumps are also those of the elements, although they are dependent upon the elemental triplicity of the sign in question. The godnames of the seven planetary trumps correspond to those of the Qabalistic sephiroth with which they are affiliated.

Archangels: An archangel is a very powerful, high-ranking angel who governs large groups of lesser angels.

The archangels assigned to the elemental trumps are the well-known archangels of the four elements, visualized in such rites as the Lesser Banishing Ritual of the Pentagram.

The zodiacal and planetary archangels are derived from grimoiric sources such as Pietro d'Abano's (1250–1316) *Heptameron* and Henry Cornelius Agrippa's *Three Books of Occult Philosophy* (1531).[7] The latter text was used as a primary source book for much of the Golden Dawn's teachings.

Angels: The definition of an angel has already been given in chapter 1. The angels that correspond to the elemental trumps are to be found in another important grimoiric source book, *The Key of Solomon the King,* where they are listed as the angels of the elements.[8] The planetary angels are found in Agrippa.[9] The zodiacal angels are listed in a Golden Dawn manuscript entitled "The Schem-Hamphorasch, or the Divided Name."[10] They are also listed in Eliphas Levi's works *The Magical Ritual of the Sanctum Regnum*[11] and *Ritual de la Haute Magie*.[12]

Intelligences: The name for this group of spiritual beings is from the Latin *intelligentia* and it refers to "intelligent/sapient beings" usually of an angelic or archangelic nature. The term was used by pagan Neoplatonists and later by medieval Christian mages. Today the term is most often used to describe planetary angels derived from the *qameoth*, or planetary squares. The planetary intelligences are derived from sources such as Agrippa.[13]

The following is a list of the holy powers and angels that are associated with the twenty-two tarot trumps. Readers may already be familiar with many of these names, but may wonder why certain angels were chosen for specific cards. There are many different lists of angelic hierarchies derived from a variety of sources.[14] Solitary magicians and magical groups of various traditions work quite successfully with assorted lists of angels and a multitude of different ways to describe and perceive these wondrous beings. That being said, the angelic system presented here has proven itself over time to be a productive and powerful source of inspiration for magical work.

A note must be added here about angelic titles. You will notice that the following list shows some archangels who have been given additional titles. This is because different angels, like different people, can have the same name; however, some believe that these angels are one and the same, simply operating on a different plane and taking on different duties. In any event, *Raphael Ruachel* ("Raphael of Air") will have duties, colors, and symbols which are different from *Raphael Kokabiel* ("Raphael of Mercury"). These titles have been added to avoid confusing the angelic hierarchies when they refer to different correspondences.

0. The Fool

Attribution: Air
Associated Godname: (יהוה) YHVH
Archangel: (רפאל) Raphael
Angel: (חשן) Chassan

YHVH: These four Hebrew letters (yod heh vav heh), often called the *Tetragrammaton* or "Four-Lettered Name," stand for the highest divine name of God, whose real name is considered unknown and unpronounceable. Based on etymology, some scholars have suggested possible meanings such as "he is," "he causes to be," and "the mighty one."[20] It also signifies the idea "to be." In the Western Magical Tradition, the name of YHVH is especially related to the element of air because of its association with the godname of the airy sphere Tiphareth (YHVH Eloah ve-Daath).

Godnames, Archangels, and Angels of the Tarot Trumps

Key	Trump Name	Astrological	Godname	Archangel	Angel / Intelligence
0	The Fool	△ Air	YHVH	Raphael *(Ruachel)*	Chassan
1	The Magician	☿ Mercury	Elohim Tzabaoth	Raphael *(Kokabiel)*	Tiriel
2	The High Priestess	☽ Luna	Shaddai El Chai	Gabriel *(Levannael)*	Shelachel[15]
3	The Empress	♀ Venus	YHVH Tzabaoth	Anael[16]	Hagiel
4	The Emperor	♈ Aries	Elohim	Malkhidael	Sharahiel
5	The Hierophant	♉ Taurus	Adonai	Asmodel	Eraziel
6	The Lovers	♊ Gemini	YHVH	Ambriel	Serayel
7	The Chariot	♋ Cancer	El	Muriel	Pakhiel
8	Strength	♌ Leo	Elohim	Verkhiel	Sheratiel
9	The Hermit	♍ Virgo	Adonai	Hamaliel	Shelathiel
10	Wheel of Fortune	♃ Jupiter	El	Sachiel	Iophiel
11	Justice	♎ Libra	YHVH	Zuriel	Chadaqiel
12	The Hanged Man	▽ Water	El	Gabriel *(Maimel)*	Taliahad
13	Death	♏ Scorpio	El	Barkhiel	Sayitziel
14	Temperance	♐ Sagittarius	Elohim	Adnakhiel[17]	Saritaiel
15	The Devil	♑ Capricorn	Adonai	Hanael	Semaqiel
16	The Tower	♂ Mars	Elohim Gibor	Zamael	Graphiel
17	The Star	♒ Aquarius	YHVH	Kambriel	Tzakmaqiel
18	The Moon	♓ Pisces	El	Amnitziel	Vakhabiel
19	The Sun	☉ Sol	YHVH Eloah ve-Daath	Michael *(Shemeshel)*	Nakhiel
20a 20b	Judgement	△ Fire ✷ Spirit	Elohim Eheieh, Agla[18]	Michael *(Ashel)* Metatron, Sandalphon	Ariel[19] Nuriel
21a 21b	The Universe	♄ Saturn ▽ Earth	YHVH Elohim Adonai	Kassiel Uriel	Agiel Phorlakh

Raphael: This archangel was originally known by the name Labbiel before his name was changed to Raphael, which means "healer of God." The Hebrew word *rapha* means "doctor," "healer," or "surgeon." Raphael is the great winged archangel of elemental air and the guardian of the Gates of the East Wind. He is also known by the additional title of *Raphael Ruachel* or "Raphael of Air" in order to distinguish him from *Raphael Kobabiel* ("Raphael of Mercury") and *Raphael Tipharethel* ("Raphael of Tiphareth").

Raphael is said to be one of the four angels "set over all the diseases and all the wounds of the children of men"[21] and in the *Zohar* he is "charged to heal the earth . . . the earth which furnishes a place for man, whom he also heals of his illnesses." Stationed in the east, Raphael is generally visualized as a tall, fair figure standing upon the clouds in robes of yellow trimmed with violet, and holding the caduceus of Hermes, a symbol often used to represent the medical arts (see figure 35).

Chassan: The angel of elemental air. The root word of this name is *chas*, which indicates volatile movement, central fire, and that which seeks to extend itself. Chassan is said to dwell in a tower in a place of rolling hills where it is eternally morning. The sylphs or air spirits bear this angel's messages among all the angels of elemental air. May be generally similar in appearance to Raphael.

1. The Magician

Attribution: Mercury
Associated Godname: (אלהים צבאות) Elohim Tzabaoth
Archangel: (רפאל) Raphael
Intelligence: (טיריאל) Tiriel

Elohim Tzabaoth: The divine name associated with the sephirah of Hod as well as the planet Mercury. It means "God of hosts (armies)" or "God of multitudes." This indicates the unity of the masculine and feminine qualities of the divine in its many aspects.

Raphael: The great archangel of Mercury and the ruler of Wednesday. He is known by the title of *Raphael Kokabiel* or "Raphael of Mercury" and he is an archangel of science and knowledge. Raphael Kokabiel has appeared in many guises, including a Renaissance philosopher with a lyre, a traveler, a merchant, a winged angel, or a horned serpent. He can be envisioned in robes of yellow trimmed with blue and ornamented with the symbol of Mercury or the letter beth inside a hexagram. He may hold various implements, such as a caduceus wand, an abacus, a staff, a stylus, or a scroll. He may be visualized with great wings of pastel yellow and violet feathers.[22]

Tiriel: The intelligence of Mercury. The root word of this name is *ti,* which indicates reflection. He is especially helpful in the consecration of Mercurial talismans and the evocation of Mercurial spirits. He may be generally similar in appearance to Raphael.

2. The High Priestess

Attribution: Luna
Associated Godname: (שדי אל חי) Shaddai El Chai
Archangel: (גבריאל) Gabriel
Intelligence: (שלחאל) Shelachel

Shaddai El Chai: The name *El Shaddai* literally means "God of the uncultivated fields."[23] Shaddai El Chai is the deity name of both Yesod and the moon. It is usually translated as "almighty living God." This also indicates the Supreme Lord of Life and of Lives. In this case the "life power" is to be seen not only as a spiritual essence, but specifically as the driving force behind reproduction and regeneration. Shaddai El Chai is the God-aspect which is concerned with life as a continuation of itself.

Gabriel: The archangel of Luna and the ruler of Monday. Her name means "the strong one of God." She is also known by the title of *Gabriel Levannael* or "Gabriel of Luna." The Sumerian root of the word *gabri* means "governor,"[24] "to be strong," and "to be mighty." The angel of the Annunciation, Gabriel is most often thought of as feminine and is said to instruct the human soul while it gestates in the womb for nine months.

Gabriel has appeared in many guises including a high priestess enthroned, a muse, a Pythian prophetess, a queen in a lunar barque, a white owl, and a white mare. She may be visualized crowned with the lunar crescent and holding a bow. She may also be envisioned in robes of blue (or silver) trimmed with ornage and ornamented with a hexagram containing the sigil of Luna or the letter gimel, holding a lotus wand, a crystal ball, an orb, or a lamp. She may be visualized with great wings of pastel blue and orange feathers.[25]

Shelachel[26]: The intelligence of Luna. The root of this name is *shel,* which indicates a straight line traced from one object to another—the connecting stroke which unites them. It expresses that which follows its laws, that which remains in its straight line, that which is in good order, in the way of salvation. May be generally similar in appearance to Gabriel.

3. The Empress

Attribution: Venus
Associated Godname: (יהוה צבאות) YHVH Tzabaoth
Archangel: (אנאל) Anael
Intelligence: (הגיאל) Hagiel

YHVH Tzabaoth: The divine name of the sephirah of Netzach as well as the planet Venus. It means "Lord of hosts (armies)" or "Lord of multitudes." It indicates the fourfold quality of the divine in its many aspects.

Anael[27]: The archangel of Venus and the ruler of Friday. Her name means "the glory of God" or "the grace of God." The root word of this name is *an,* which indicates the trials of the soul, the sphere of moral activity, and the body (or personality) of the individual.

Anael has appeared in many guises including a queen in a chariot drawn by doves or leopards, a sensual woman, a vast blooming rose, and a unicorn. She can be envisioned in robes of green ornamented in red with a hexagram containing the Venus symbol or the letter daleth. She may wear a girdle around her waist and a garland on her crown. Her symbols include a mirror, a necklace, a seashell, a rose, a torch, or a chalice. She may be visualized with great wings of muted green and red feathers.

Hagiel: The intelligence of Venus. The root of this name is *hag*, which indicates movement, activity, and pleasure. She is especially helpful in the consecration of Venusian talismans and the evocation of Venusian spirits. She may be generally similar in appearance to Anael.

4. The Emperor
Attribution: Aries
Associated Godname: (אלהים) Elohim
Archangel: (מלכידאל) Malkhidael
Angel: (שרהיאל) Sharahiel

Elohim: The divine name of the fire triplicity of the zodiac. It is one of the most important godnames and the third word to appear in the Book of Genesis. Generally translated as "God," it also means "gods." It is formed from the feminine noun *eloh*, or "goddess," and the masculine plural ending *im*. It signifies the creative principle formed from the perfect union of masculine and feminine principles. In the Western Magical Tradition the name of Elohim is especially related to the element of fire because of its association with the godname of the fiery sphere of Geburah (*Elohim* Gibor).

Malkhidael (alternative spellings: Melchidael, Melkejal): The archangel of Aries whose name means "the fullness of God." He is the governing angel of the month of March. Enoch referred to Malkhidiel as Melkejal saying, "He rises and rules in the beginning of the year." This archangel can be envisioned in robes of red trimmed with green and ornamented with the Aries symbol. The root word *mal* indicates continuity, plentitude, and continued movement from the beginning to the end of a thing.

Sharahiel (alternative spellings: Sharhiel): The angel of Aries. The root of this name is *shar*, which indicates that which liberates or emits; strength, domination, and power. Sharahiel may take on the form of a stocky, powerful bald man with piercing green eyes or he may be generally similar in appearance to Malkhidael.

5. The Hierophant
Attribution: Taurus
Associated Godname: (אדני) Adonai
Archangel: (אסמודאל) Asmodel
Angel: (ארזיאל) Eraziel

Adonai: The godname of the earth triplicity of the zodiac. Adonai is Hebrew for "Lord" or "my lord." In the Western Magical Tradition the name of Adonai is especially related to the element of earth because of its association with the godname of the earthy sphere of Malkuth (*Adonai ha-Aretz*).

Asmodel: The archangel of Taurus and of the month of April. The root word *as* indicates the idea of basis as well as the earth. Asmodel can be envisioned in robes of red-orange trimmed with blue-green and ornamented with the Taurus symbol.

Eraziel (alternative spelling: Araziel): The angel of Taurus. The root of this name is *ar,* which indicates ardor, productiveness, power, and strength. May be generally similar in appearance to Asmodel.

6. The Lovers

Attribution: Gemini
Associated Godname: (יהוה) YHVH
Archangel: (אמבריאל) Ambriel
Angel: (סראיאל) Serayel

YHVH: The divine name of the air triplicity of the zodiac (see the Fool).

Ambriel: The archangel of Gemini and the angel of the month of May. The name of Ambriel was found engraved upon a Hebrew amulet for warding off evil. The root word *am* indicates origin, source, mother, formative faculty, measure, and conditional possibility. Ambriel can be envisioned in robes of orange trimmed with blue and ornamented with the Gemini symbol.

Serayel (alternative spelling: Sarayel): The angel of Gemini. The root of this name is *ser,* which indicates that which is independent, disordered, rebellious, and refractory. May be similar in appearance to Ambriel.

7. The Chariot

Attribution: Cancer
Associated Godname: (אל) El
Archangel: (מוריאל) Muriel
Angel: (פכיאל) Pakhiel

El (alternative spelling: Al): The divine name of the water triplicity of the zodiac as well as the godname of the watery sephirah of Chesed. The Summerian origin of the name alludes to the meaning of "brightness" or "shining."[28] The Hebrews borrowed this name from the High God of the Canaanites. It means simply "God," but also implies "the divine one" or "the mighty one." El also refers to the primal feminine aspect of the deity.

Muriel: The archangel of Cancer and the angel of the month of June. The name of Muriel comes from the Greek "myrrh." The root word *mur* indicates variation or permutation. Muriel can be envisioned in robes of yellow-orange trimmed with blue-violet and ornamented with the Cancer symbol.

Pakhiel (alternative spelling: Pakiel): The angel of Cancer. May be generally similar in appearance to Muriel.

8. Strength
Attribution: Leo
Associated Godname: (אלהים) Elohim
Archangel: (ורכיאל) Verkhiel
Angel: (שרטיאל) Sheratiel

Elohim: The divine name of the fire triplicity of the zodiac (see the Emperor).

Verkhiel (alternative spelling: Verkiel): The archangel of Leo and the angel of the month of July. The root word *ver* indicates the noise of the wind, or that which is fanned. Verkhiel can be envisioned in robes of yellow trimmed with violet and ornamented with the Leo symbol.

Sheratiel (alternative spelling: Sharatiel): The angel of Leo. The root of this name is *shar* (see Sharahiel). May be generally similar in appearance to Verkhiel.

9. The Hermit
Attribution: Virgo
Associated Godname: (אדני) Adonai
Archangel: (המליאל) Hamaliel
Angel: (שלתיאל) Shelathiel

Adonai: The divine name of the earth triplicity of the zodiac (see the Hierophant).

Hamaliel: The archangel of Virgo and the angel of the month of August. The root word *ham* indicates effort, labor, activity, and contracting movement. Hamaliel can be envisioned in robes of yellow-green trimmed with red-violet and ornamented with the Virgo symbol.

Shelathiel: The angel of Virgo. The root of this name is *shel* (see Shelachel). May be generally similar in appearance to Hamaliel.

10. The Wheel of Fortune

Attribution: Jupiter
Associated Godname: (אל) El
Archangel: (סחיאל) Sachiel
Intelligence: (יהפיאל) Iophiel

El (alternative spelling: Al): The divine name of the sephirah of Chesed and of the planet Jupiter (see the Chariot).

Sachiel: The archangel of Jupiter and the ruler of Thursday. His name means "covering of God." The root word of this name is *sach*, which indicates pouring out, purifying, and cleansing.

  Sachiel has appeared in many guises including a king in a chariot drawn by eagles, a queen enthroned, a high priest standing atop a pyramid, and a mighty winged lion. He can be envisioned in robes of violet trimmed with yellow and ornamented in flashing colors with a hexagram containing the Jupiter symbol or the letter kaph. His implements include a royal scepter or a shepherd's staff, a lamp, an orb, a book, or a scroll.

Iophiel (alternative spelling: Yohphiel): The intelligence of Jupiter. His name means "the beauty of God." Iophiel is especially helpful in the consecration of Jovial talismans and the evocation of Jovial spirits. He may be generally similar in appearance to Sachiel.

11. Justice

Attribution: Libra
Associated Godname: (יהוה) YHVH
Archangel: (זוריאל) Zuriel
Angel: (חדקיאל) Chadaqiel

YHVH: The divine name of the air triplicity of the zodiac (see the Fool).

Zuriel: The archangel of Libra and angel of the month of September. The name of Zuriel means "my rock is God." The root word *zur* indicates the idea of dispersion, radiation, and dissemination, going out from the center, and manifesting light. One of the seventy childbed amulet angels, Zuriel is also said to cure foolishness in man. In the Hebrew scriptures, Zuriel is described as "chief of the house of the father of the families of Merari."[29] Zuriel can be envisioned in robes of green trimmed with red and ornamented with the Libra symbol.

Chadaqiel (alternative spelling: Chedeqiel): The angel of Libra. May be generally similar in appearance to Zuriel.

Figure 36: The Archangel Gabriel.

12. The Hanged Man

Attribution: Water
Associated Godname: (אל) El
Archangel: (גבריאל) Gabriel
Angel: (טליהד) Taliahad

El: The divine name of elemental water (see the Chariot).

Gabriel: The great winged archangel of elemental water, whose name means "strong one of God." She also bears the title of *Gabriel Maimel* or "Gabriel of Water." Stationed in the west, Gabriel is often visualized as a feminine archangel standing upon the waters of the sea wearing robes of blue trimmed with orange. She is the guardian of the Gates of the West Wind. She holds a chalice of water as a symbol of her creative, fertile powers of consciousness in all its forms.

Taliahad: The angel of elemental water. The root of this name is *tal*, which indicates a veil, something which covers or shelters. May be generally similar in appearance to Gabriel.

13. Death

Attribution: Scorpio
Associated Godname: (אל) El
Archangel: (ברכיאל) Barkhiel
Angel: (סאיציאל) Sayitziel

El: The godname of elemental water (see the Chariot).

Barkhiel (alternative spellings: Barkiel, Barchiel): The archangel of Scorpio and angel of the month of October. The name of Barkhiel means "lightning of God" and he is said to have dominion over lightning. The root word *bar* indicates the idea of production with power, potential emanation or creation, fruit, offspring, and movement that tends to manifest the creative force of being. Barkhiel is sometimes invoked to bring success in games of chance. He can be envisioned in robes of blue-green trimmed in red-orange and ornamented in flashing colors with the Scorpio symbol.

Sayitziel (alternative spellings: Saitziel, Saitzaiel): The angel of Scorpio. The root of this name is *sa,* which indicates circumference. May be generally similar in appearance to Barkhiel.

14. Temperance

Attribution: Sagittarius
Associated Godname: (אלהים) Elohim
Archangel: (אדנכיאל) Adnakhiel
Angel: (סריטיאל) Saritaiel

Elohim: The divine name of the fire triplicity of the zodiac (see the Emperor).

Adnakhiel: (alternative spellings: Adnakiel, Advakiel): The archangel of Sagittarius and angel of the month of November. The root word *ad* indicates the power of division, force, emanation, and individual distinction. Adnakhiel can be envisioned in robes of blue trimmed with orange and ornamented in flashing colors with the Sagittarius symbol.

Saritaiel (alternative spellings: Saritiel, Sairitaiel): The angel of Sagittarius. The root of this name is *shar* (see Sharahiel). May be generally similar in appearance to Adnakhiel.

15. The Devil

Attribution: Capricorn
Associated Godname: (אדני) Adonai
Archangel: (הניאל) Hanael
Angel: (סמקיאל) Samaqiel

Adonai: The deity name of the earth triplicity of the zodiac (see the Hierophant).

Hanael: An archangel of Capricorn and ruler of the month of December. The root word *han* indicates the idea of actual and present existence, realities, and anything that can be perceived by the senses. Hanael is invoked against evil. She can be envisioned in robes of blue-violet trimmed with yellow-orange and ornamented with the Capricorn symbol.

Samaqiel (alternative spellings: Sameqiel, Semaquiel, Samquiel): The angel of Capricorn. The root of this name is *sam,* which indicates that which is fragrant or aromatic. May be generally similar in appearance to Hanael.

16. The Tower

Attribution: Mars
Associated Godname: (אלהים גבור) Elohim Gibor
Archangel: (זמאל) Zamael
Intelligence: (גראפיאל) Graphiel

Elohim Gibor: The godname of the sephirah of Geburah as well as the planet Mars. It can be translated as "God of battles" or as "almighty God." This denotes that nothing can escape the might of the divine and universal law. The essence of Elohim Gibor is judgment that places the end before the means, striking quickly at the heart of a problem, even when the cure may be as harsh as the illness.

Zamael [30] *(alternative spelling: Zaumael):* The archangel of Mars and the angel of Tuesday. His name means "the severity of God." The root word of this name is *zam,* which indicates that which gives form or binds the many into the one. Zamael can be envisioned in robes and a helmet of red trimmed in green, ornamented with the symbol of Mars, and holding a sword, lance, or shield.

Zamael has appeared in many guises including a knight in a chariot drawn by wolves, a hawk-headed man, a cyclops, an Amazon, and a red and green dragon. He may be envisioned in red robes or armor ornamented in green with a hexagram containing the Mars symbol or the letter peh. His implements include a sword, a spear, a shield, an ax, or a chain. He may be visualized with great wings of green and red feathers.

Graphiel: The intelligence of Mars. His name means "the might of God." Graphiel is especially helpful in the consecration of Martial talismans and the evocation of Martial spirits. He may be generally similar in appearance to Zamael.

17. The Star

Attribution: Aquarius
Associated Godname: (יהוה) YHVH
Archangel: (כמבריאל) Kambriel
Angel: (צכמקיאל) Tzakmaqiel

YHVH: The deity name of the air triplicity of the zodiac (see the Fool).

Kambriel *(alternative spelling: Cambriel)*: The archangel of Aquarius and angel of the month of January. The root word *kam* indicates the desire for assimilation. Kambriel can be envisioned in robes of violet trimmed with yellow and ornamented with the Aquarius symbol.

Tzakmaqiel *(alternative spellings: Tzakmiqiel, Tzakamquiel)*: The angel of Aquarius. He may be generally similar in appearance to Kambriel.

18. The Moon

Attribution: Pisces
Associated Godname: (אל) El
Archangel: (אמניציאל) Amnitziel
Angel: (וכביאל) Vakhabiel

El: The godname of elemental water (see the Chariot).

Amnitziel *(alternative spellings: Amnitzial, Amnixiel)*: The archangel of Pisces and angel of the month of February. He is associated with the idea of reflected light. Amnitziel can be envisioned in robes of red-violet trimmed with yellow-green and ornamented with the Pisces symbol.

Vakhabiel *(alternative spellings: Vakabiel, Vacabiel)*: The angel of Pisces. May be generally similar in appearance to Amnitziel.

19. The Sun

Attribution: Sol, the sun
Associated Godname: (יהוה אלוה ודעת) YHVH Eloah ve-Daath
Archangel: (מיכאל) Michael
Intelligence: (נכיאל) Nakhiel

YHVH Eloah ve-Daath: The deity name of Tiphareth which means "Lord God of knowledge," but which might also be interpreted as "God made manifest in the sphere of the mind." Once again we have the combined title of *YHVH Eloah*, indicating a perfect balance of masculine and feminine polarities. In addition, we have the idea that knowledge is power. YHVH Eloah ve-Daath is the divine mind within us that comprehends its own divinity. In modern terms, it is the Universal Mind—that mind which encompasses all minds.

Michael (alternative spelling: Mikhael): The archangel of Sol and the ruler of Sunday. His name means "one who is as God." He also bears the title of *Mikhael Shemeshel* or "Michael of Sol." He is chief among the seven archangels of the planets. Michael can be envisioned in robes of orange trimmed with blue and ornamented with the symbol of Sol, wearing a sunburst diadem and breastplate.

Mikhael Shemeshel has appeared in many guises including a king in a chariot drawn by lions, a rooster-headed king, and a lion-headed angel. He may be envisioned in robes of orange or gold trimmed with blue, and ornamented with a hexagram containing the Solar symbol or the letter resh in blue. His implements include a scepter, a book or scroll, an orb, or a seven-branched candlestick. He may be visualized with great wings of pastel orange and blue feathers.

Nakhiel (alternative spellings: Nachiel, Nakiel): The intelligence of Sol. The root of the name is *na,* which means youth, beauty, and grace. It is also related to the root word *nak,* which denotes innocence and purity. Nakhiel is especially helpful in the consecration of Solar talismans and the evocation of Solar spirits. He may be generally similar in appearance to Michael.

20a. Judgement
Attribution: Fire
Associated Godname: (אלהים) Elohim
Archangel: (מיכאל) Michael
Angel: (אריאל) Ariel

Elohim: The godname of elemental fire (see the Emperor).

Michael (alternative spelling: Mikhael): The great winged archangel of elemental Fire, whose name means "one who is as God." He is sometimes called the "perfect one of God," the "house of God," and the "power of God." This archangel is also known by the title *Michael Ashel* or "Michael of Fire." He is the guardian of the Gates of the South Wind. Michael is visualized as a masculine archangel dressed in robes or armor of red trimmed with green. He stands in the attitude of a warrior amid flames with great wings of red and green feathers. Bearing a sword or spear as a weapon and a symbol of masculine fire energy, Michael is the vanquisher of evil and protector of humanity.

Figure 37: The Archangel Michael.

Ariel [31] *(alternative spelling: Aeriel):* The angel of elemental fire whose name means "lion of God." He is said to cure diseases, control harmful spirits, and mete out punishment in the lower worlds. The name of Ariel was used by Jewish mystics as a poetic name for Jerusalem. Ariel appears in many forms, including a winged man with the head of a lion, and a lion with a mane of fire. He may also be generally similar in appearance to Michael Ashel.

20b. Judgement

Attribution: Spirit
Associated Godnames: (אהיה) Eheieh, (אגלא) Agla
Archangels: (מטטרון) Metatron, (סנדלפון) Sandalphon
Angel: (נוריאל) Nuriel

Eheieh: The divine name of active or masculine spirit is *Eheieh* or "I am." This is also the godname of the sephirah of Kether. It indicates the inhaling and exhaling of the breath, alluding to the idea that spirit is the root from which all begins and to which all returns. The letters of the name, aleph heh yod heh, yield further meanings: aleph indicates the beginning or initial outpouring of force, heh is the stabilizing factor or receptacle, yod symbolizes the fertilizing principle, and the final heh is the stabilizing factor and resulting manifestation. The whole word encompasses the idea of increasing manifestation. It is the first and the last—the heart of everything—the first living breath of God and the last breath of being.

Agla: The godname of passive or feminine spirit is Agla, which is a Hebrew notariqon or acronym for the phrase "Atah Gibor Le-Olahm Adonai," meaning "Thou art great forever, my Lord."

Metatron: The archangel of Kether is Metatron who may also be employed as the archangel of active spirit. In this function he is known by the title *Metatron Ethiel*[32] or "Metatron of Spirit." His name has no clear etymological base and may in fact be a channeled or skryed name. The root word *met* may indicate downward communicated movement. Some authors have tried to provide a Greek etymology for it and have translated the name as *meta ton thronos* or "near thy throne."

Metatron is described as "the angel of the divine presence" and "the world-prince." He presides over the whole Tree of Life and is considered the right-hand masculine kerub of the Ark of the Covenant. Tradition has it that Metatron communicated the Qabalah to humankind. He has the additional titles of "the lesser YHVH," "the king of angels," "the great scribe," "the prince of the countenance," and the name *Ioel*—"I am God." Some sources identify him with the patriarch Enoch and the god Thoth-Hermes. Metatron is responsible for presenting God and human to each other. He is the link between the human and the divine, and is responsible for increasing the flow of light to the initiate.

Metatron has manifested in many forms, including a sphere of glory, a white lotus, a rose of light, the eye of God, and an infinite number of white-robed figures arrayed in an endless fractal pattern and speaking with one collective, melodious voice. He may be envisioned in robes of the purest white with great white wings containing the shimmering colors of the rainbow. He does not often appear with implements, but may occasionally be envisioned with a crown, a lamp, and a white rose.

Sandalphon: The archangel of Malkuth is Sandalphon, who may also be employed as the archangel of passive spirit. In this function she is known by the title *Sandalphon Ethiel* or "Sandalphon of Spirit." Her name has no clear etymological base and may in fact be a channeled or skryed name. The root word *san* may indicate something that is luminous. Some authors have tried to provide a Greek etymology for her name—and have translated it variously as "co-brother," "lord of the extent of height," or "the sound of sandals."

Sandalphon is the twin of Metatron and the left-hand feminine kerub of the Ark. She is the life-transforming archangel of initiation, and she presides over equilibrium and the Middle Pillar of the Tree of Life. As the *anima mundi* or "soul of the world," she conveys the power and beauty of the natural world to the souls of humanity. Sandalphon is the peculiar guardian of the evolving human race and she radiates a sense of profound and all-embracing love.

Sandalphon has manifested in many forms including a shepherdess and a queen. She may be envisioned as a beautiful mature woman of grace and power, dressed in robes of black or the four colors of Malkuth,[33] ornamented with a white Greek cross. A white halo containing the form of the sacred hexagram can be seen around her head. Her symbols include a monolith, a lamp, a key, a stone circle which surrounds her, a horn of plenty, and a crown of grape leaves.

Nuriel: The name of the angel of spirit is Nuriel, which means "light of the divine." His name can be found in the acronym of the Hebrew word *argaman,* which means "purple," a color that has long been associated with royalty and with the holy day of Pentecost, commemorating the descent of the Holy Spirit. The word *argaman* is spelled from the Hebrew letters aleph, resh, gimel, mem, and nun, which stand for Uriel (or Auriel—earth), Raphael (air), Gabriel (water), Michael (fire), and Nuriel (spirit).

Nuriel is seen in Jewish lore as one of the great angels who is a "spell-binding power" and protector against evil. In his harsh aspect he manifests as a hailstorm, but when issuing from the side of Chesed (mercy) he takes on the form of an eagle.

21a. The Universe

Attribution: Saturn
Associated Godname: (יהוה אלהים) YHVH Elohim
Archangel: (כסיאל) Kassiel
Intelligence: (אגיאל) Agiel

YHVH Elohim: The divine name of Binah and Saturn which has been translated as "the Lord God." However, the word "Elohim" is a feminine noun (*eloh*) with a masculine plural ending, implying a dual polarity of masculine and feminine. Since YHVH can be considered the action of the divine in the four Qabalistic Worlds, YHVH Elohim presents the idea of the polarity principle—the perfect balance of masculine and feminine operating on all planes of existence—as the creator and foundation of all form.

Kassiel: The archangel of Saturn and ruler of Saturday. He is said to be the archangel of solitude and tears who "shows forth the unity of the eternal kingdom." Kassiel is sometimes called the Angel of Temperance and his name means "speed of God." The root word of this name is *kas,* which indicates sum, accumulation, pinnacle, or throne.

Kassiel has appeared in many guises including a wise crone in a chariot drawn by dragons, an angel with a raven's head and wings, a giant winged skeleton, and a man who passes through the life phases of youth, maturity, and age, while on his robe the seasons pass in endless rotation. He may be envisioned in a hooded robe of blue-violet trimmed with yellow-orange and ornamented with a hexagram containing the symbol of Saturn or the letter tau.

Figure 38: The Archangel Uriel.

His implements may include a sickle, a scythe, an hourglass, a book or scroll, an astrolabe, or a compass.

Agiel: The intelligence of Saturn. The root of this name is *ag*, which indicates ignition and intense excitement. Agiel is especially helpful in the consecration of Saturnian talismans and the evocation of Saturnian spirits. May be generally similar in appearance to Kassiel.

21b. The Universe

Attribution: Earth
Associated Godname: (אדני) Adonai
Archangel: (אוריאל) Uriel
Angel: (פורלאך) Phorlakh

Adonai: The divine name of the earth triplicity of the zodiac (see the Hierophant).

Uriel (alternative spelling: Auriel): The great winged archangel of elemental earth, whose name means "the light of God." This archangel is also known by the title *Uriel Aretzel* or

"Uriel of Earth." He is the guardian of the Gates of the North Wind. Uriel is visualized as rising up from the vegetation of the earth holding stems of ripened wheat and wearing robes of citrine, russet, olive, and black.

Phorlakh: The angel of elemental earth. The root of this word is *phor,* which indicates that which appears or bursts forth. May be generally similar in appearance to Uriel.

Additional Godnames

We have introduced most of the important Hebrew godnames associated with the tarot trumps. However, there are two other important godnames that must be mentioned. Although these names are not associated with any trump card, they do play a significant role in the attributions of some of the minor cards.

Yah (יה): The godname of Chokmah which has been translated as "the Lord." It is half of the Tetragrammaton, although some authors ascribe the full name YHVH to the second sephirah. The name Yah implies explosive masculine power and fertilizing force (Yod). It is the great initiator of all action.

Adonai Ha Aretz (אדני הארץ): The godname of Malkuth, which means "the Lord of Earth." This signifies that in Malkuth, we confront the creator of all matter as the supreme ruler thereof. Like Eheieh, El, and YHVH, the name Adonai ("Lord") is considered a holy emanation of God. Therefore Malkuth is every bit as exalted as Kether, for both are holy aspects of the divine. An additional deity name of Malkuth is *Adonai Melekh* or "the Lord and King," which stresses these same ideas.

---

1 Ramsay MacMullen, *Christianity & Paganism in the Fourth to Eighth Centuries* (New Haven, CT: Yale University Press, 1997), 125.

2 Hans Dieter Betz, *The Greek Magical Papyri in Translation: Including the Demotic Spells* (Chicago: The University of Chicago Press, 1992), 22.

3 MacGregor Mathers quoted in Regardie's *The Golden Dawn,* 488.

4 A hymn of thanksgiving addressed to Apollo. It is also an epithet of the god.

5 Betz, *The Greek Magical Papyri in Translation: Including the Demotic Spells,* 11.

6 The so-called "forgotten books of the Bible," which were not included in either the Old or New Testaments.

7 See Henry Cornelius Agrippa, *Three Books of Occult Philosophy* (St. Paul, MN: Llewellyn Publications, 1993), 532–537. This list can be found in earlier sources such as *Of the Heavenly Intelligences* by Johannes Trithemius (1462–1516). Also see Gustav Davidson's *A Dictionary of Angels* (New York: The Free Press, A Division of Macmillan, Inc., 1992), 342.

8 S. Liddell MacGregor Mathers, *The Key of Solomon the King* (York Beach, ME: Samuel Weiser, Inc., 1974), 74.

9 See Agrippa, 320–328.

10 See Israel Regardie, *The Complete Golden Dawn System of Magic,* vol. 3, (Phoenix, AZ: Falcon Press, 1984), 21–26. Also see Regardie, *The Golden Dawn,* 85–86.

11 See Eliphas Levi, *The Magical Ritual of the Sanctum Regnum* (Kila, MT: Kessinger Publishing Company, n.d. [originally 1896]), 31.

12 See Eliphas Levi, *Transcendental Magic* (York Beach, ME: Samuel Weiser, Inc., 1972), 337–338.

13 See Agrippa, *Three Books of Occult Philosophy,* 320–328. It is possible that Agrippa used the term "intelligence" because the origins of the qameoth system are probably non-Judeo-Christian and he wished to avoid the term "angel" in describing them.

14 Many of these various angelic hierarchy lists can be found in Gustav Davidson's *A Dictionary of Angels* (New York: The Free Press, A Division of Macmillan, Inc., 1992).

15 Shelachel is the name of a lunar intelligence developed from the qameoth system by Adam P. Forrest. See "Mysteria Geomantica" in *The Golden Dawn Journal, Book I: Divination*, Chic Cicero and Sandra Tabatha Cicero, editors, (St. Paul, MN: Llewellyn Publications, 1994), page 190, and our book *Self-Initiation into the Golden Dawn Tradition* (St. Paul, MN: Llewellyn Publications, 1998), pages 163–164. The name of Shelachel is a far more manageable form than the commonly listed tongue-twister *Malka be-Tarshism voEd Ruachoth Shechalim*.

16 Anael, the archangel of Venus, has often been wrongly given as Hanael through confusion with Haniel, the archangel of Netzach. See Adam Forrest's "Mysteria Geomantica," *The Golden Dawn Journal, Book I: Divination,* 190.

17 Adnakhiel, the name of the archangel of Sagittarius, has been frequently misspelled as Advakhiel, through a scribal mistake switching the Hebrew letter nun for vav. The same error often occurred in Renaissance Latin typesetting, where the *n* of Ad*n*achiel could easily be set upside-down as a *u*, producing Ad*u*achiel.

18 These godnames, as well as the corresponding archangels and angels of spirit, can also be used for the "Genesis" card of *The Babylonian Tarot*.

19 The correct name of the angel of elemental fire is Ariel, not Aral. An error in Agrippa, which has been repeated in countless books, switched the two names. This long-lived confusion is due to the fact that the four angels of the elements have not been recognized as the names of angelic orders: seraph, cherub, tharsis, and aral (erel) are simply the singular forms of seraphim, kerubim, tarshishim, and erelim.

20 Bernhard Lang, "Why God Has So Many Names" (*Bible Review*, August 2003), 54.

21 R. H. Charles, *The Book of Enoch the Prophet* (York Beach, ME: Weiser Books, 2003), 32.

22 Adam Forrest, *The Rhodostauroticon: The Angels & Spirits of the Hermetic Qabalah of the Golden Dawn* (Unpublished manuscript, 1997).

23 Lang, "Why God Has So Many Names," 52.

24 Malcolm Godwin, *Angels, an Endangered Species* (New York: Simon and Schuster, 1990), 43.

25 Forrest, *The Rhodostauroticon*.

26 See endnote 15.

27 See endnote 16.

28 Malcolm Godwin, *Angels, an Endangered Species.* (Simon and Schuster, 1990), page 36.

29 Numbers 3:35.

30 There has been much confusion regarding the names Zamael, Khamael, and Samael. According to Adam P. Forrest, the original archangel of Mars was Samael—a name that MacGregor Mathers changed to Zamael in order to avoid confusion with the qlippothic Samael. When the Qabalists began to assign archangels to the sephiroth, someone attributed a list of planetary archangels to their corresponding sephiroth, and the martial Samael was naturally assigned to Geburah. At some point this list was copied into Greek. In late Greek writing, the letter sigma (the first letter in Samael) came to be drawn in the shape of a "C." Still later, when the Greek list was copied into Latin, the copyist made the error of transliterating the Greek name of CAMAHL as "Camael" rather than "Samael." Even later, someone (perhaps a member of the Golden Dawn) back-transliterated Camael as כמאל and thus was Khamael born. And although it originated as an error in transliteration, it does help magicians distinguish between *Samael* the archangel of evil, *Zamael* the archangel of Mars, and *Khamael* the archangel of Geburah.

31 See endnote 19.

32 The title of *Ethiel* is formed from the letters aleph and tau, the first and last letters of the Hebrew alphabet, which together signify essence or spirit, and the angelic suffix "al."

33 Citrine, olive, russet, and black.

5
THE ANGELS OF THE MINOR ARCANA

The tarot trumps contain a wealth of information that can be used in the creation of talismans. So much so, that some people use the major arcana exclusively in their tarot meditations and ritual work. But to focus solely on the trump cards is to neglect the largest section of the tarot—one that is replete with a vast array of magical correspondences that can be used for very detailed and nuanced talismans. And one of the most important attributions of the minor arcana is a complete listing of angels that can be invoked for added power in tarot talisman consecration rituals.

As far as the angels of the tarot are concerned, the pip cards of the minor arcana are unique. This is because each pip card from the Twos through the Tens has two angels exclusively associated with it. Why? Because these thirty-six pip cards correspond exactly to the thirty-six decanates of the zodiac.

A *decanate* or *decan* is one of thirty-six divisions of ten degrees on a zodiacal chart. Each of the twelve signs contains thirty degrees that are divided into three decanates. Each decanate contains two *quinances* or two five-degree divisions of a zodiacal sign. To summarize, there are thirty-six decanates and seventy-two quinances in a 360-degree wheel we call the zodiacal chart, and these correspond to the numbered cards of the minor arcana (see figure 39).

You will notice that the thirty-six decanates do not include the four Aces of the tarot. This is because the Aces are assigned to pure element.

The tarot angels of the minor arcana are those of the thirty-six decanates, which are derived from a Qabalistic teaching known as the *Shem ha-Mephoresh*.[1]

THE SHEM HA-MEPHORESH

The *Shem ha-Mephoresh* (שם המפרש), the "name of brilliant fire" or the "divided name," refers to the seventy-two-fold name of God, or to be exact, the seventy-two names of the expounded name of the Tetragrammaton, YHVH. The Shem ha-Mephoresh is sometimes referred to as the "seventy-two leaves of the Tree of Life," or the "healing leaves."

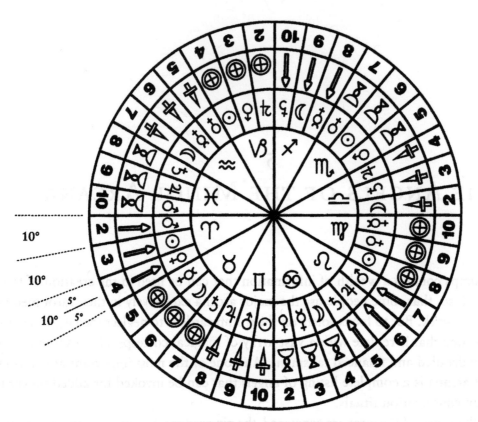

Figure 39: The Decanates and the Tarot Pips.

What the Shem ha-Mephoresh refers to is a divine name of 216 letters derived from the Book of Exodus 14:19–21. Each of these three verses from Exodus contains seventy-two letters which are then organized to generate the seventy-two syllables of the expounded name. The Shem ha-Mephoresh was then attributed to the letters of the Tetragrammaton (see figures 40 and 41).

The verses involved read as follows:

Exodus 14:19: And the Angel of the Elohim, that went before the camp of Israel, removed and went behind them; and the pillar of cloud removed from before them and stood behind them.

Exodus 14:20: And it came between the camp of the Egyptians and the camp of Israel; and it was a cloud and darkness (to the first) but it gave light by night (to these); and the one came not near unto the other all the night.

Exodus 14:21: And Moses stretched out his hand over the sea, and the Lord drove back the sea with a strong east wind all that night and made the sea dry land, and the waters divided.

The names are obtained by writing these three verses in Hebrew, with alternating lines written in opposite directions. In other words, the verses are to be written out one above the other, the first verse from right to left, the second verse from left to right, and the third verse from right to left. The result is seventy-two columns of three letters apiece, each of which is considered a holy name—a *trigram* or "three-lettered" name. The seventy-two names are thought of as expansions of YHVH; they are separated under four groupings of eighteen letters. Each group (read from top to bottom) corresponds to one of the four letters of the Tetragrammaton.

From the seventy-two names of God, the names of seventy-two mighty angels are formed by adding the suffix *yod heh* (ה'—iah) or the suffix *aleph lamed* (אל—el) to the end of the name. *Iah* signifies mercy and beneficence, whereas *el* embodies severity and judgment. Each deity name contains three letters, while each angelic name formed therefrom has five letters.

Each one of these seventy-two angels also rules over one of the seventy-two quinances (5°) of the zodiac. Therefore, two angels rule over each of the thirty-six decanates as well as the thirty-six pip cards that correspond to these decanates. Every zodiacal sign has six of these decanate angels assigned to it.

These angels are also separated into different "choirs" of angels and further classified into four groupings under the four elemental divisions of the Tetragrammaton. The charts that follow list many of the correspondences of these angels. Bear in mind, however, that these charts are only provided as a helpful reference. You will not need to know all of this information in order to charge a tarot talisman.

Readers may notice that these attributions are based on a fixed sidereal system of astrology, wherein the signs coincide with the constellations after which they are named. Using this method the star called Regulus, said to correspond with 0° Leo, was selected as the beginning point of the zodiacal chart.[2]

The meanings of the holy trigrams and the angelic names formed from them are derived from the Book of Psalms—those Biblical verses in which the name of Tetragrammaton appears.[3] You can invoke these angels whenever you are consecrating a tarot talisman of a given pip card by reciting their respective Psalms.[4]

The pip cards also correspond to the ten sephiroth on the Tree of Life, and so we have provided two godnames for each card listed here—the godname of the card's sephirah as well as its elemental triplicity. The ruling archangels are those of the zodiacal signs described in the previous chapter.

The Aces

Since the Aces are not attributed to decanates, they are not included in this list. The sephirah godname for all Aces is Eheieh. The elemental godnames, archangels, and angels would be: Ace of Wands—Elohim, Michael, Ariel; Ace of Cups—El, Gabriel, Taliahad; Ace of Swords—YHVH, Raphael, Chassan; Ace of Pentacles—Adonai, Uriel, Phorlakh.

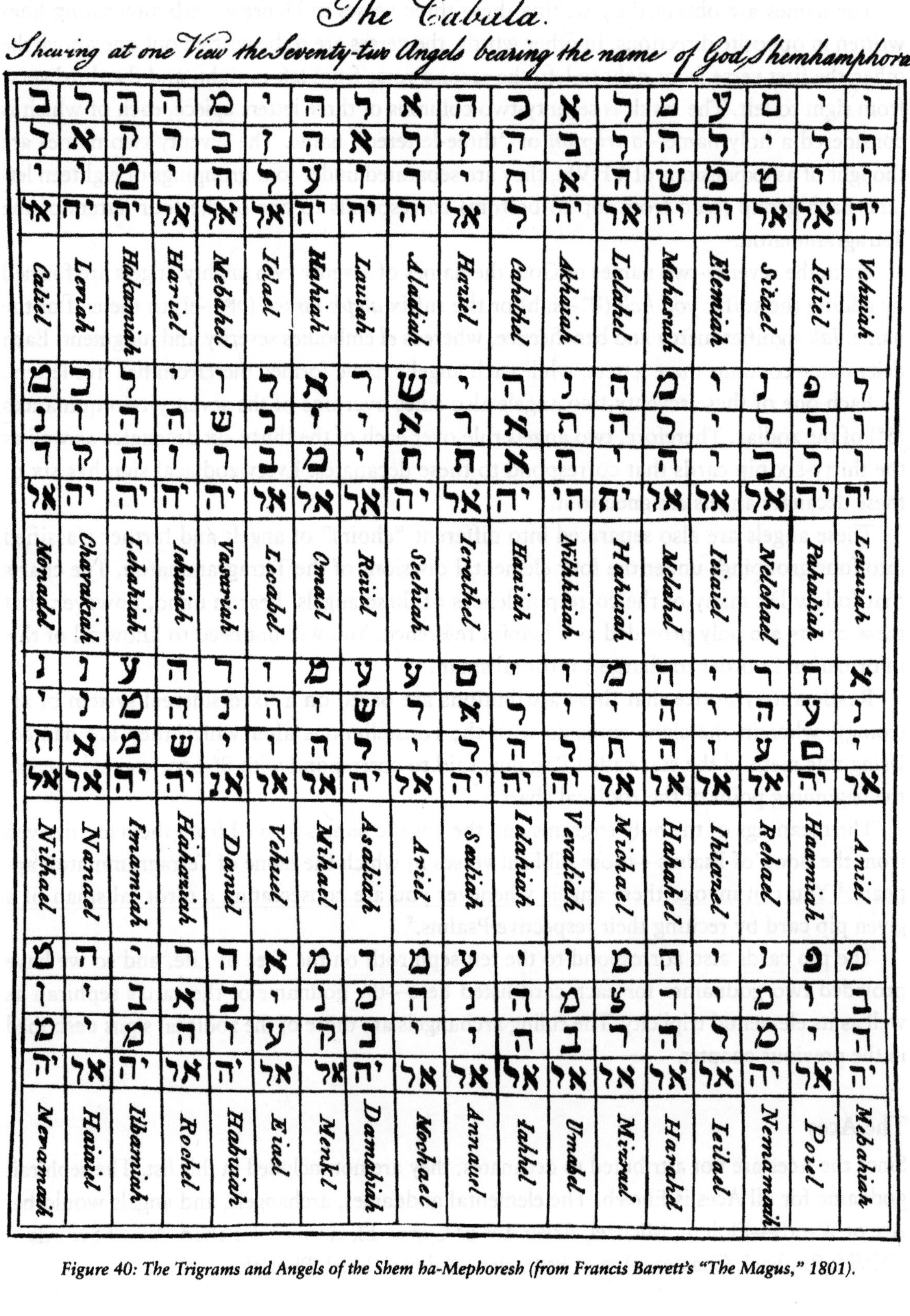

The Cabula.

Shewing at one View the Seventy-two Angels bearing the name of God, Shemhamphora.

Figure 40: The Trigrams and Angels of the Shem ha-Mephoresh (from Francis Barrett's "The Magus," 1801).

					♎︎						♍︎						♌︎
18	17	16	15	14	13	12	11	10	9	8	7	6	5	4	3	2	1

	K	L	H	H	M	Y	H	L	A	H	K	A	L	M	O	S	Y	V
Y	L	A	Q	R	B	Z	H	A	L	Z	H	K	L	H	L	Y	L	H
	Y	V	M	Y	H	L	O	V	D	Y	Th	A	H	Sh	M	T	Y	V

					♑︎						♐︎						♏︎
36	35	34	33	32	31	30	29	28	27	26	25	24	23	22	21 .	20	19

	M	K	L	Y	V	L	A	R	Sh	Y	H	N	Ch	M	Y	N	P	L
H	N	V	H	Ch	Sh	K	V	Y	A	R	A	Th	H	L	Y	L	H	V
	D	Q	Ch	V	R	B	M	Y	H	Th	A	H	V	H	Y	K	L	V

					♈︎						♓︎						♒︎
54	53	52	51	50	49	48	47	46	45	44	43	42	41	40	39	38	37

	N	N	O	H	D	V	M	O	O	S	Y	V	M	H	Y	R	Ch	A
V	Y	N	M	Ch	N	H	Y	Sh	R	A	L	V	Y	H	Y	H	O	N
	Th	A	M	Sh	Y	V	H	L	Y	L	H	L	K	H	Z	O	M	Y

					♋︎						♊︎						♉︎
72	71	70	69	68	67	66	65	64	63	62	61	60	59	58	57	56	55

	M	H	Y	R	Ch	A	M	D	M	O	Y	V	M	H	Y	N	P	M
H	V	Y	B	A	B	Y	N	M	Ch	N	H	M	Tz	R	Y	M	V	B
	M	Y	M	H	V	O	Q	B	Y	V	H	B	R	Ch	L	M	Y	H

Figure 41: The Trigrams Assigned to the Zodiacal Signs and the Four Letters of the Tetragrammaton.

The 72 Names of the Shem ha-Mephoresh

No.	Holy Trigram	Angel	Title derived from Psalm	Sign	Decan	Angel of	YHVH Letter	Angelic Choir	Tarot Card	Card Keyword
1	VHV	Vahaviah	God the Exalter	♌	♄	Day	Y	Seraphim	5 of Wands	Strife
2	YLY	Yelayel	Strength	♌	♄	Night	Y			
3	SYT	Sitael	Refuge, fortress	♌	♃	Day	Y	Seraphim	6 of Wands	Victory
4	OLM	Almiah	Concealed, strong	♌	♃	Night	Y			
5	MHSh	Mahashiah	Seeking safety	♌	♂	Day	Y	Seraphim	7 of Wands	Valor
6	LLH	Lelahel	Praiseworthy, declaring his works	♌	♂	Night	Y			
7	AKA	Akayah	Long-suffering	♍	☉	Day	Y	Seraphim	8 of Pent.	Prudence
8	KHTh	Kehethel	Adorable	♍	☉	Night	Y			
9	HZY	Haziel	Merciful	♍	♀	Day	Y	Kerubim	9 of Pent.	Material Gain
10	ALD	Eldayah	Profitable	♍	♀	Night	Y			
11	LAV	Laviah	To be exalted	♍	☿	Day	Y	Kerubim	10 of Pent.	Wealth
12	HHO	Hihaayah	Refuge	♍	☿	Night	Y			
13	YZL	Yezalel	Rejoicing over	♎	☽	Day	Y	Kerubim	2 of Swords	Peace Restored
14	MBH	Mebahel	Guardian, preserver	♎	☽	Night	Y			
15	HRY	Hariel	Aid	♎	♄	Day	Y	Kerubim	3 of Swords	Sorrow
16	HQM	Haqamiah	Raise up, praying day and night	♎	♄	Night	Y			
17	LAW	Levayah	Wonderful	♎	♃	Day	Y	Kerubim	4 of Swords	Rest from Strife
18	KLY	Keliel	Worthy to be invoked	♎	♃	Night	Y			
19	LVV	Luvayah	Hastening to hear	♏	♂	Day	H	Thrones	5 of Cups	Loss in Pleasure
20	PHL	Phaheliah	Redeemer, liberator	♏	♂	Night	H			
21	NLK	Nelakhel	Thou alone	♏	☉	Day	H	Thrones	6 of Cups	Pleasure
22	YYY	Yeyayel	Thy right hand	♏	☉	Night	H			
23	MLH	Melohel	Turning away evil	♏	♀	Day	H	Thrones	7 of Cups	Illusionary Success
24	ChHV	Chahaviah	Goodness in himself	♏	♀	Night	H			
25	NThH	Nethahiah	Wide in extent, the enlarger, wonderful	♐	☿	Day	H	Dominations	8 of Wands	Swiftness
26	HAA	Haayah	Heaven in Secret	♐	☿	Night	H			
27	YRTh	Yerathel	Deliverer	♐	☽	Day	H	Dominations	9 of Wands	Great Strength
28	ShAH	Saahiah	Taker-away of evils	♐	☽	Night	H			
29	RYY	Reyayel	Expectation	♐	♄	Day	H	Dominations	10 of Wands	Oppression
30	AVM	Umael	Patient	♐	♄	Night	H			
31	LKB	Lekhabel	Teacher, instructor	♑	♃	Day	H	Dominations	2 of Pent.	Harmonious Change
32	VShR	Veshiriah	Upright	♑	♃	Night	H			
33	YChV	Yechaviah	Knower of all things	♑	♂	Day	H	Powers	3 of Pent.	Material Works
34	LHCh	Lehachiah	Clement, merciful	♑	♂	Night	H			
35	KVQ	Kuqiah	To be rejoiced in	♑	☉	Day	H	Powers	4 of Pent.	Earthly Power
36	MND	Menadel	Honorable	♑	☉	Night	H			
37	ANY	Eniel	Lord of Virtues	♒	♀	Day	V	Powers	5 of Swords	Defeat
38	ChOM	Chaamiah	The hope of all the ends of the earth	♒	♀	Night	V			

The 72 Names of the Shem ha-Mephoresh (*continued*)

No.	*Holy Trigram*	*Angel*	*Title derived from Psalm*	*Sign*	*Decan*	*Angel of*	*YHVH Letter*	*Angelic Choir*	*Tarot Card*	*Card Keyword*
39	RHO	Rehael	Swift to condone	♒	☿	Day	V	Powers	6 of Swords	Earned Success
40	YYZ	Yeyezel	Making joyful	♒	☿	Night	V			
41	HHH	Hehahel	Triune	♒	☽	Day	V	Virtues	7 of Swords	Unstable Effort
42	MYK	Mayakhel	Who is like unto him	♒	☽	Night	V			
43	VVL	Vuliah	King and ruler	♓	♄	Day	V	Virtues	8 of Cups	Abandoned Success
44	YLH	Yelahiah	Abiding forever	♓	♄	Night	V			
45	SAL	Saaliah	Mover of all things	♓	♃	Day	V	Virtues	9 of Cups	Material Happiness
46	ORY	Eriel	Revealer	♓	♃	Night	V			
47	OShL	Esheliah	Just judge	♓	♂	Day	V	Virtues	10 of Cups	Perfected Success
48	MYH	Mayahel	Sending forth as a father	♓	♂	Night	V			
49	VHV	Vehuel	Great and Lofty	♈	♂	Day	V	Principalities	2 of Wands	Dominion
50	DNY	Deniel	Merciful	♈	♂	Night	V			
51	HChSh	Hechashiah	Secret and impenetrable	♈	☉	Day	V	Principalities	3 of Wands	Established Strength
52	OMM	Amemiah	Covered in darkness	♈	☉	Night	V			
53	NNA	Nanael	Caster-down of the proud	♈	♀	Day	V	Principalities	4 of Wands	Perfected Work
54	NYTh	Nithael	Celestial King	♈	♀	Night	V			
55	MBH	Mibahayah	Eternal	♉	☿	Day	Hs	Principalities	5 of Pent.	Material Trouble
56	PVY	Puyael	Supporting all things	♉	☿	Night	Hs			
57	NMM	Nemamiah	Lovable	♉	☽	Day	Hs	Archangels	6 of Pent.	Material Success
58	YYL	Yeyelel	Hearer of cries	♉	☽	Night	Hs			
59	HRCh	Herachel	Permeating all things	♉	♄	Day	Hs	Archangels	7 of Pent.	Success Unfulfilled
60	MTzR	Mitzrael	Raising up the oppressed	♉	♄	Night	Hs			
61	VMB	Vembael	The name which is over all	♊	♃	Day	Hs	Archangels	8 of Swords	Shortened Force
62	YHH	Yahohel	The supreme ens, or essence	♊	♃	Night	Hs			
63	ONV	Anuel	Rejoicing	♊	♂	Day	Hs	Archangels	9 of Swords	Cruelty
64	MChY	Machiel	Vivifying	♊	♂	Night	Hs			
65	DMB	Dambayah	Fountain of wisdom	♊	☉	Day	Hs	Angels	10 of Swords	Ruin
66	MNQ	Meneqel	Nourishing all	♊	☉	Night	Hs			
67	AYO	Ayael	Delights of the sons of men	♋	♀	Day	Hs	Angels	2 of Cups	Love
68	ChBW	Chavuyah	Most liberal giver	♋	♀	Night	Hs			
69	RAH	Raahel	Beholding all	♋	☿	Day	Hs	Angels	3 of Cups	Abundance
70	YBM	Yebemiah	Producing by his word	♋	☿	Night	Hs			
71	HYY	Hayayel	Lord of the universe	♋	☽	Day	Hs	Angels	4 of Cups	Blended Pleasure
72	MVM	Mumiah	End of the universe	♋	☽	Night	Hs			

THE DECANATE ANGELS OF THE MINOR ARCANA

Two of Wands

Card Keyword: Dominion
Decan: Mars in Aries, 1°–10°
Sephirah Godname: Yah
Element Godname: Elohim
Archangel: Malkhidael
First Trigram: והו (VHV) Vaho
Second Trigram: דני (DVY) Deni
Angels: Vehuel (והואל) and Deniel (דניאל)

Vehuel (alternative spellings: Vehooel, Uhauel): The forty-ninth angel of the Shem ha-Mephoresh is *Vehuel,* whose title is "God the great and lofty" or "great and high God." Associated with the first decanate and first quinance of Aries (1°–5°), Vehuel is the angel by day of the Two of Wands.

Invocation: Psalms 145:3: "Great is Tetragrammaton and greatly to be praised; and unto his greatness there is not an end."

Function: Vehuel helps find peace, protects against trouble and affliction, dominates great personalities, and influences humility. He also helps to overcome chagrin, unease, and disappointment. He can be invoked to combat a contrary spirit. This angel orients one toward God, to bless and glorify the divine. He rules over great individuals who distinguish themselves by their talents and virtues. The entire Psalm may be recited to invoke this angel.

Deniel (alternative spellings: Deneyal, Deneyael, Daniel): The fiftieth angel of the Shem ha-Mephoresh is *Deniel,* whose titles include "the merciful judge," "sign of mercy," and "giver of mercies." Associated with the first decanate and second quinance of Aries (6°–10°), Deniel is the angel by night of the Two of Wands.

Invocation: Psalms 103:8: "Tetragrammaton is merciful and gracious; slow to anger and abounding in mercy."

Function: Deniel protects and consoles, inspires decisions, dominates justice and law, and influences judges, courts, counsels, magistrates, and lawyers. Deniel is the angel of confession who is invoked to obtain the mercy of God and to receive consolation. This angel also gives inspiration to those who are indecisive.

Three of Wands

Card Keywords: Established Strength, Virtue, Achievement
Decan: Sun in Aries, 10°–20°
Sephirah Godname: YHVH Elohim

Element Godname: Elohim
Archangel: Malkhidael
First Trigram: החש (HChSh) Hachash
Second Trigram: עמם (OMM) Amem
Angels: Hechashiah (החשיה) and Amemiah (עממיה)

Hechashiah (*alternative spellings: Ha-Hashiah, Hechasheiah, Hahaziah*): The fifty-first angel of the Shem ha-Mephoresh is *Hechashiah*, whose titles include "the secret and impenetrable" and "God concealed." Associated with the second decanate and third quinance of Aries (11°–15°), Hechashiah is the angel by day of the Three of Wands.

Invocation: Psalms 104:31: "The glory of Tetragrammaton shall endure forever; Tetragrammaton shall rejoice in his works."

Function: Hechashiah helps those who wish to know the occult mysteries and arcane wisdom. He dominates chemistry and physics, and influences the abstract sciences. He raises the soul to the contemplation of all things divine, and reveals the greatest secrets of nature—especially the Philosopher's Stone and the universal medicine of alchemy.

Amemiah (*alternative spellings: Amamiah, Aumemiah, A'amamiah, Imamiah*): The fifty-second angel of the Shem ha-Mephoresh is *Amemiah*, whose titles include "he who is covered in darkness" and "God elevated above all things." Associated with the second decanate and fourth quinance of Aries (16°–20°), Amemiah is the angel by night of the Three of Wands.

Invocation: Psalms 7:17: "I will praise Tetragrammaton according to his righteousness; and I will sing praise unto the name of Tetragrammaton most high."

Function: Amemiah helps to destroy the power of one's enemies and thereby humiliate them. Amemiah also protects prisoners who turn to the angel for aid, inspiring them with the means of obtaining liberty. This angel dominates vigor, influences research, rules all journeys in general, and influences all who renounce their errors to turn back toward God—seeking truth in good faith.

Four of Wands
Card Keywords: Perfected Work, Completion, Reward
Decan: Venus in Aries, 20°–30°
Sephirah Godname: El
Element Godname: Elohim
Archangel: Malkhidael
First Trigram: ננא (NNA) Nena
Second Trigram: ניח (NYTh) Nith
Angels: Nanael (ננאאל) and Nithael (ניטאל)

Nanael (alternative spelling: Nenael): The fifty-third angel of the Shem ha-Mephoresh is *Nanael*, whose titles include "the caster-down of the proud" and "God who abases the proud." Associated with the third decanate and fifth quinance of Aries (21°–25°), Nanael is the angel by day of the Four of Wands.

Invocation: Psalms 119:75: "I know, O Tetragrammaton, that thy judgments are righteous, and in faithfulness hast thou humbled me."

Function: Nanael serves to obtain enlightenment and dominates the higher sciences including chemistry, physics, and medicine. He also rules over ecclesiastics, teachers, professors, judges, magistrates, and men of law. This angel influences health and long life. He gives success in all things and brings experience to completion.

Nithael (alternative spelling: Nithal): The fifty-fourth angel of the Shem ha-Mephoresh is *Nithael*, whose title is "the celestial king" or "king of the heavens." Associated with the third decanate and sixth quinance of Aries (26°–30°), Nithael is the angel by night of the Four of Wands.

Invocation: Psalms 103:19: "Tetragrammaton hath established his throne in Heaven, and his kingdom ruleth over all."

Function: Nithael serves to obtain mercy and longevity. This angel dominates legitimate dynasties (emperors, kings, and princes) as well as all civil and ecclesiastical dignitaries. Nithael controls the stability of empires and gives a long and peaceful reign to sovereigns and princes, and protects those who wish to remain in their employ.

Five of Wands

Card Keywords: Strife, Conflict
Decan: Saturn in Leo, 1°–10°
Sephirah Godname: Elohim Gibor
Element Godname: Elohim
Archangel: Verkhiel
First Trigram: והו (VHV) Vehu
Second Trigram: ילי (YLY) Yeli
Angels: Vahaviah (והויה) and Yelayel (יליאל)

Vahaviah (alternative spellings: Vehuiah, Vahuaih): The first angel of the Shem ha-Mephoresh is *Vahaviah*, whose titles include "God the exalter" and "God raised and exalted above all things." Associated with the first decanate and first quinance of Leo (1°–5°), Vahaviah is the angel by day of the Five of Wands.

Invocation: Psalms 3:3: "But Thou, O Tetragrammaton, art a shield about me: my glory; and he who lifteth up mine head."

Function: Vahaviah is endowed with great wisdom and energy. This angel can help a person to receive enlightenment, expand the consciousness, and accomplish the most difficult things. Vahaviah dominates the arts and sciences, fulfills prayers, and influences the shrewd.

Yelayel (alternative spellings: Yelauiel, Jeliel, Ieliel): The second angel of the Shem ha-Mephoresh is *Yelayel*, whose titles include "my strength" and "helpful God." Associated with the first decanate and second quinance of Leo (6°–10°), Yelayel is the angel by night of the Five of Wands.

Invocation: Psalms 22:19: "Be not far off, O Tetragrammaton, O my strength: to my help make haste."

Function: Yelayel helps repress sedition and unjust revolts; he establishes peace between spouses, maintains conjugal fidelity, dominates kings and princes, and influences all generations. He helps to obtain victory over those who would attack a person unjustly.

Six of Wands

Card Keyword: Victory
Decan: Jupiter in Leo, 10°–20°
Sephirah Godname: YHVH Eloah ve-Daath
Element Godname: Elohim
Archangel: Verkhiel
First Trigram: סיט (SYT) Sit
Second Trigram: עלם (OLM) Alem
Angels: Sitael (סיטאל) and Almiah (עלמיה)

Sitael (alternative spellings: Saitel, Satiel): The third angel of the Shem ha-Mephoresh is *Sitael*, whose titles include "my refuge, fortress, and confidence" and "God, hope of all creatures." Associated with the second decanate and third quinance of Leo (11°–15°), Sitael is the angel by day of the Six of Wands.

Invocation: Psalms 91:2: "I will say of Tetragrammaton, he is my refuge, my fortress, my God; in him will I trust."

Function: Sitael protects against weapons, adversity, calamity, and ferocious beasts. He is associated with magnanimity (i.e., those with great influence), great undertakings, and nobility. This angel rules mobility and influences lovers of truth.

Almiah (alternative spellings: Elemiah, Olmiah, Nghelamiah): The fourth angel of the Shem ha-Mephoresh is *Almiah*, whose titles include "the concealed and strong," "the concealed and saving," and "hidden God." Associated with the second decanate and fourth quinance of Leo (16°–20°), Almiah is the angel by night of the Six of Wands.

Invocation: Psalms 6:4: "Return, O Tetragrammaton, deliver my soul; save me for thy mercies' sake."

Function: Almiah protects against spiritual torment and reveals traitors. He dominates travel, sea voyages and maritime expeditions, and brings useful discoveries.

Seven of Wands

Card Keywords: Valor, Courage
Decan: Mars in Leo, 20°–30°
Sephirah Godname: YHVH Tzabaoth
Element Godname: Elohim
Archangel: Verkhiel
First Trigram: מהש (MHSh) Mahash
Second Trigram: ללה (LLH) Lelah
Angels: Mahashiah (מהשׁיה) and Lelahel (ללהאל)

Mahashiah (alternative spelling: Mahasiah): The fifth angel of the Shem ha-Mephoresh is *Mahashiah,* whose titles include "seeking safety from trouble" and "God the savior." Associated with the third decanate and fifth quinance of Leo (21°–25°), Mahashiah is the angel by day of the Seven of Wands.

Invocation: Psalms 34:4: "I sought Tetragrammaton and he answered me; and out of all my fears he delivered me."

Function: Mahashiah helps a person to live in peace with everyone. He dominates high science, occult philosophy, magic, theology, and the liberal arts, and influences learning.

Lelahel (alternative spelling: Lecahel): The sixth angel of the Shem ha-Mephoresh is *Lelahel,* whose titles include "Praiseworthy, declaring his works" and "praiseworthy God." Associated with the third decanate and sixth quinance of Leo (26°–30°), Lelahel is the angel by night of the Seven of Wands.

Invocation: Psalms 9:11: "Sing praises unto Tetragrammaton, who dwelleth in Zion; declare among the nations his deeds."

Function: Lelahel serves to acquire knowledge and "light," and to cure contagious diseases. This angel governs love, fame, and fortune, and influences the arts and sciences.

Eight of Wands

Card Keywords: Swiftness, Swift Action
Decan: Mercury in Sagittarius, 1°–10°
Sephirah Godname: Elohim Tzabaoth
Element Godname: Elohim

Archangel: Adnakhiel
First Trigram: נתה (NThH) Nethah
Second Trigram: האא (HAA) Haa
Angels: Nethahiah (נתהיה) and Haayah (האאיה)

Nethahiah (alternative spellings: Nithahiah, Nithhaiah, Nethhiah, Nilaihah): The twenty-fifth angel of the Shem ha-Mephoresh is *Nethahiah*, whose titles include "wide in extent," "the enlarger," "wonderful," and "God who gives wisdom." Associated with the first decanate and first quinance of Sagittarius (1°–5°), Nethahiah is the angel by day of the Eight of Wands.

Invocation: Psalms 9:1: "I will give thanks unto Tetragrammaton with all my heart; I will tell of all thy wondrous works."

Function: Nethahiah serves to obtain wisdom, to discover the truth of hidden mysteries, and provides revelations in dreams, particularly to those born on the day over which he presides. He dominates the occult sciences and influences those who practice the magic of the sages—those wise men who love peace and solitude. Said to be a poet-angel, Nethahiah delivers prophecies in rhyme.

Haayah (alternative spellings: Haaiah, Heeiah): The twenty-sixth angel of the Shem ha-Mephoresh is *Haayah*, whose titles include "hearer in secret" and "hidden God." Associated with the first decanate and second quinance of Sagittarius (6°–10°), Haayah is the angel by night of the Eight of Wands.

Invocation: Psalms 119:145: "I have called out with all my heart; answer me, O Tetragrammaton: I will preserve thy statutes."

Function: Haayah leads men to the contemplation of things divine and protects all those who seek truth and the True Light. This angel helps to win in lawsuits and renders judges favorable. Haayah rules politics, peace treaties, diplomats, ambassadors, commerce, and all conventions; and generally influences through couriers, dispatches, agents, and secret expeditions.

Nine of Wands

Card Keywords: Great Strength, Power
Decan: Moon in Sagittarius, 10°–20°
Sephirah Godname: Shaddai El Chai
Element Godname: Elohim
Archangel: Adnakhiel
First Trigram: ירת (YRTh) Yereth
Second Trigram: שאה (ShAH) Shaah
Angels: Yerathel (ירתאל) and Saahiah (שאהיה)

Yerathel (alternative spellings: Yirthiel, Ierathel, Irthel): The twenty-seventh angel of the Shem ha-Mephoresh is *Yerathel*, whose titles include "the deliverer," and "God who punishes the wicked." Associated with the second decanate and third quinance of Sagittarius (11°–15°), Yerathel is the angel by day of the Nine of Wands.

Invocation: Psalms 140:1: "Deliver me, O Tetragrammaton from the evil man; preserve me from the violent man."

Function: Yerathel protects against those who provoke and attack one unjustly. He acts to confound the wicked and delivers people from their enemies. Yerathel dominates civilization and liberty, and works to influence peace and propagate light.

Saahiah (alternative spellings: Seehiah, Seheiah, Sehaiah, Sahiah): The twenty-eighth angel of the Shem ha-Mephoresh is *Saahiah*, whose titles include "the taker-away of evils" and "God who heals the sick." Associated with the second decanate and fourth quinance of Sagittarius (16°–20°), Saahiah is the angel by night of the Nine of Wands.

Invocation: Psalms 71:12: "O Elohim be not far from me, O my God, O Tetragrammaton; make haste for my help."

Function: Saahiah protects against fire, incendiaries, lightning, ruin, falls, infirmities, and maladies. This angel also protects against the collapse of battlements, fortifications, and structural supports. Saahiah dominates health and longevity and influences prudence.

Ten of Wands

Card Keyword: Oppression
Decan: Saturn in Sagittarius, 20°–30°
Sephirah Godname: Adonai ha-Aretz
Element Godname: Elohim
Archangel: Adnakhiel
First Trigram: ריי (RYY) Riyi
Second Trigram: אום (AVM) Aum
Angels: Reyayel (רייאל) and Umael (אומאל)

Reyayel (alternative spellings: Rayayel, Reiiel): The twenty-ninth angel of the Shem ha-Mephoresh is *Reyayel*, whose titles include "my expectation" and "God prompt to aid." Associated with the third decanate and fifth quinance of Sagittarius (21°–25°), Reyayel is the angel by day of the Ten of Wands.

Invocation: Psalms 54:4: "Behold Elohim ḥelpeth me; and Tetragrammaton is with them who uphold my soul."

Function: Reyayel aids and protects a person from all enemies visible and invisible, and defends against the impious and the enemies of religion. He dominates religious sentiment, mystical feeling, meditation, and sacred philosophy.

Umael (alternative spellings: Avamel, Omael, Evamel): The thirtieth angel of the Shem ha-Mephoresh is *Umael*, whose title is "the patient." Associated with the third decanate and sixth quinance of Sagittarius (26°–30°), Umael is the angel by night of the Ten of Wands.

Invocation: Psalms 71:5: "For thou art my hope, O Tetragrammaton; O Adonai, thou art my trust from my youth."

Function: Umael aids against desperation, chagrin, and trouble, and strengthens patience. This angel influences chemists, doctors, and surgeons. He dominates the generation of men and animals, perpetuates races, and multiplies species.

Two of Cups

Card Keyword: Love
Decan: Venus in Cancer, 1°–10°
Sephirah Godname: Yah
Element Godname: El
Archangel: Muriel
First Trigram: איע (AYO) Aya
Second Trigram: חבו (ChBW) Chevo
Angels: Ayael (איעאל) and Chavuyah (חבויה)

Ayael (alternative spellings: Ayoel, Aiael, Aiaual, Eiael): The sixty-seventh angel of the Shem ha-Mephoresh is *Ayael*, whose titles are "delights of the sons of men" or "God, delight of the children of men." Associated with the first decanate and first quinance of Cancer (1°–5°), Ayael is the angel by day of the Two of Cups.

Invocation: Psalms 37:4: "Delight in Tetragrammaton; and he shall give thee the desire of thine heart."

Function: Ayael rules over change, longevity, and the preservation of monuments. He helps and consoles in adversity, helps to obtain wisdom, influences the occult sciences, and brings knowledge and truth to those who have recourse to him in their works.

Chavuyah (alternative spellings: Chabuyah, Chabooyah, Chabeoiah, Habuhiah, Habuiah): The sixty-eighth angel of the Shem ha-Mephoresh is *Chavuyah*, whose titles are "the most liberal giver" or "God who gives freely." Associated with the first decanate and second quinance of Cancer (6°–10°), Chavuyah is the angel by night of the Two of Cups.

Invocation: Psalms 107:1: "O give thanks unto Tetragrammaton, for he is good; for his mercy endureth forever."

Function: Chavuyah helps maintain health and cure disease. He dominates fertility and agriculture, and rules over the earth.

Three of Cups

Card Keyword: Abundance
Decan: Mercury in Cancer, 10°–20°
Sephirah Godname: YHVH Elohim
Element Godname: El
Archangel: Muriel
First Trigram: ראה (RAH) Raah
Second Trigram: יבם (YBM) Yebem
Angels: Raahel (ראהאל) and Yebemiah (יבמיה)

Raahel (alternative spellings: Raahal, Rahael, Rochel, Rohael): The sixty-ninth angel of the Shem ha-Mephoresh is *Raahel,* whose titles include "beholding all" and "God who sees all." Associated with the second decanate and third quinance of Cancer (11°–15°), Raahel is the angel by day of the Three of Cups.

Invocation: Psalms 16:5: "Tetragrammaton is the portion of mine inheritance and my cup. Thou maintainest my lot."

Function: Raahel helps to find lost or stolen objects and to discover the person who took them. He rules fame, renown, fortune, succession, and inheritance, and dominates laws, judges, jurists, magistrates, barristers, advocates, and notaries.

Yebemiah (alternative spellings: Yebamiah, Yebamaiah, Yebomayah, Jabamiah, Iibamiah): The seventieth angel of the Shem ha-Mephoresh is *Yebemiah,* whose titles are "producing by his word" or "word which produces all things." Associated with the second decanate and fourth quinance of Cancer (16°–20°), Yebemiah is the angel by night of the Three of Cups.

Invocation: Genesis 1:1: "In the beginning Elohim created the substance of the Heavens and the substance of the earth." (The name signifies eternal fecundity.)

Function: Yebemiah protects those who wish to regenerate themselves and establish within themselves the inner harmony and elemental equilibration of the soul/psyche that existed before the Fall from Eden. This angel rules the generation of beings, dominates philosophical knowledge, and influences the phenomena of nature.

Four of Cups

Card Keywords: Blended Pleasure, Luxury, Mixed Blessing
Decan: Moon in Cancer, 20°–30°
Sephirah Godname: El
Element Godname: El
Archangel: Muriel
First Trigram: היי (HYY) Hayeya

Second Trigram: מום (MVM) Mum
Angels: Hayayel (הייאל) and Mumiah (מומיה)

Hayayel (alternative spellings: Haiaiel, Haiael, Heyaiel): The seventy-first angel of the Shem ha-Mephoresh is *Hayayel,* whose titles include "the lord of the universe" and "God, master of the universe." Associated with the third decanate and fifth quinance of Cancer (21°–25°), Hayayel is the angel by day of the Four of Cups.

Invocation: Psalms 109:30: "I will greatly praise unto Tetragrammaton with my mouth; and in the midst of many will I praise him."

Function: Hayayel confounds evil, grants release from enemies, gives victory and peace, dominates weapons and soldiers, and influences iron, arsenals, fortresses, and all things relating to warfare. This angel protects all who call upon him.

Mumiah (alternative spellings: Mevamiah, Mevamayah, Mevamaih): The seventy-second angel of the Shem ha-Mephoresh is *Mumiah,* whose title is "the end of the universe." Associated with the third decanate and sixth quinance of Cancer (26°–30°), Mumiah is the angel by night of the Four of Cups.

Invocation: Psalms 116:7: "Turn unto thy rest, O my soul; for Tetragrammaton hath rewarded thee."

Function: Mumiah brings every experience to a happy conclusion and grants success in all things. This angel provides protection in mysterious operations, dominates chemistry, physics, and medicine, and influences health and longevity.

Five of Cups

Card Keywords: Loss in Pleasure, Disappointment, Loss
Decan: Mars in Scorpio, 1°–10°
Sephirah Godname: Elohim Gibor
Element Godname: El
Archangel: Barkhiel
First Trigram: לוו (LVV) Levo
Second Trigram: פהל (PHL) Pahel
Angels: Luvayah (לוואה) and Phaheliah (פהליה)

Luvayah (alternative spellings: Luviah, Livayah, Leuuiah, Leuviah, Levoiah, Livoih): The nineteenth angel of the Shem ha-Mephoresh is *Luvayah,* whose titles include "hastening to hear," "God who takes away sins," and "God who forgives sinners." Associated with the first decanate and first quinance of Scorpio (1°–5°), Luvayah is the angel by day of the Five of Cups.

Invocation: Psalms 40:1: "I waited patiently for Tetragrammaton; and he inclined unto me and heard my cry."

Function: Luvayah aids and protects, and helps a person obtain the grace of God. He dominates the memory, intelligence, and joviality.

Phaheliah (alternative spellings: Palaliah, Pehilyah, Pheheliah): The twentieth angel of the Shem ha-Mephoresh is *Phaheliah*, whose titles include "the redeemer," and "the liberator." Associated with the first decanate and second quinance of Scorpio (6°–10°), Phaheliah is the angel by night of the Five of Cups.

Invocation: Psalms 120:1-2: "In my distress I cried unto Tetragrammaton and he heard me: O Tetragrammaton, deliver my soul."

Function: Phaheliah aids in religious conversions, dominates theology and religion, and influences chastity, piety, and morals in those who are attracted to the priesthood.

Six of Cups

Card Keywords: Pleasure
Decan: Sun in Scorpio, 10°–20°
Sephirah Godname: YHVH Eloah ve-Daath
Element Godname: El
Archangel: Barkhiel
First Trigram: נלך (NLK) Nelak
Second Trigram: ייי (YYY) Yeyaya
Angels: Nelakhel (נלכאל) and Yeyayel (ייאל)

Nelakhel (alternative spellings: Nelakiel, Nelokhiel, or Nelchael): The twenty-first angel of the Shem ha-Mephoresh is *Nelakhel*, whose titles include "Thou alone," "God unique and alone," and "God, one and alone." Associated with the second decanate and third quinance of Scorpio (11°–15°), Nelakhel is the angel by day of the Six of Cups.

Invocation: Psalms 31:14: "And in thee have I trusted, O Tetragrammaton; I have said, thou art my God. My times are in thy hands."

Function: Nelakhel rules over mathematics, astronomy, geometry, geography, and all abstract sciences. He protects a person against slanderers, liars, and harmful magic, and destroys the power of evil spirits. He influences the wise and philosophers.

Yeyayel (alternative spellings: Yeiael, Yiaial, Ieiaiel, Ieaiel): The twenty-second angel of the Shem ha-Mephoresh is *Yeyayel*, whose titles include "thy right hand" and "the right of God." Associated with the second decanate and fourth quinance of Scorpio (16°–20°), Yeyayel is the angel by night of the Six of Cups.

Invocation: Psalms 121:5: "Tetragrammaton is thy protector; Tetragrammaton is thy shadow upon thy right hand."

Function: Yeyayel protects maritime expeditions against storms and shipwrecks. This angel foretells the future, dominates fame, diplomacy, fortune in business and commercial ventures, and influences business trips and voyages.

Seven of Cups

Card Keywords: Illusionary Success, Debauch, Seduction
Decan: Venus in Scorpio, 20°–30°
Sephirah Godname: YHVH Tzabaoth
Element Godname: El
Archangel: Barkhiel
First Trigram: מלה (MLH) Melah
Second Trigram: חהו (ChHV) Chaho
Angels: Melohel (מלהאל) and Chahaviah (חהויה)

Melohel (alternative spellings: Melahel, Malahel, Melchal): The twenty-third angel of the Shem ha-Mephoresh is *Melohel,* whose titles include "turning away evil" and "God who delivers from evil." Associated with the third decanate and fifth quinance of Scorpio (21°–25°), Melohel is the angel by day of the Seven of Cups.

Invocation: Psalms 121:8: "Tetragrammaton will preserve thy going out and thy coming in, from this time forth, and even for evermore."

Function: Melohel protects against weapons and the perils of travel. He rules the produce of the earth, especially medicinal herbs used to cure illness, and water.

Chahaviah (alternative spellings: Hahuiah, Hahiuiah, Hahauiah): The twenty-fourth angel of the Shem ha-Mephoresh is *Chahaviah,* whose titles include "goodness in himself" and "trust in mercy." Associated with the third decanate and sixth quinance of Scorpio (26°–30°), Chahaviah is the angel by night of the Seven of Cups.

Invocation: Psalms: 33:18: "From Tetragrammaton is a blessing upon those that fear him; and upon those who trust in his mercy."

Function: Chahaviah serves to obtain the grace and mercy of God. This angel governs exiles, fugitives, and defaulters. Chahaviah protects a person against thieves, murderers, assassins, and dangerous animals.

Eight of Cups

Card Keywords: Abandoned Success, Indolence, Neglect
Decan: Saturn in Pisces, 1°–10°
Sephirah Godname: Elohim Tzabaoth

Element Godname: El
Archangel: Amnitziel
First Trigram: וול (VVL) Vaval
Second Trigram: ילה (YLH) Yelah
Angels: Vuliah (ווליה) and Yelahiah (ילהיה)

Vuliah (alternative spellings: Vavaliah, Veualiah, Vevaliah): The forty-third angel of the Shem ha-Mephoresh is *Vuliah*, whose titles include "king and ruler" and "dominating king." Associated with the first decanate and first quinance of Pisces (1°–5°), Vuliah is the angel by day of the Eight of Cups.

Invocation: Psalms 88:13: "And unto thee, O Tetragrammaton, have I cried; and in the morning my prayer shall come before thee."

Function: Vuliah rules peace and influences prosperity, especially the prosperity of empires—strengthening the power of weakened kings. He helps defeat enemies and liberates people from slavery.

Yelahiah (alternative spellings: Ielahiah, Ilhaiah): The forty-fourth angel of the Shem ha-Mephoresh is *Yelahiah*, whose titles are "abiding forever" and "eternal God." Associated with the first decanate and second quinance of Pisces (6°–10°), Yelahiah is the angel by night of the Eight of Cups.

Invocation: Psalms 119:108: "Let the free will offerings of my mouth please thee, O Tetragrammaton; and teach me thy judgments."

Function: Yelahiah protects against weapons and gives courage and victory in battle. This angel offers protection to magistrates and helps to win a lawsuit or trial. He is invoked to obtain success in a useful enterprise.

Nine of Cups

Card Keywords: Material Happiness, Contentment
Decan: Jupiter in Pisces, 10°–20°
Sephirah Godname: Shaddai El Chai
Element Godname: El
Archangel: Amnitziel
First Trigram: סאל (SAL) Sael
Second Trigram: ערי (ORY) Eri
Angels: Saaliah (סאליה) and Eriel (עריאל)

Saaliah (alternative spellings: Saliah, Sealiah, Saelaih): The forty-fifth angel of the Shem ha-Mephoresh is *Saaliah*, whose title is "the mover of all things." Associated with the second decanate and third quinance of Pisces (11°–15°), Saaliah is the angel by day of the Nine of Cups.

Invocation: Psalms 94:18: "When I said, My foot slippeth, thy mercy, O Tetragrammaton, held me up."

Function: Saaliah helps confound the evil and the arrogant. He influences through the principal agencies of nature, rules vegetation, and brings life and health to all who breathe. Saaliah influences education and relieves those who are humble. He lifts up all those who are humiliated and fallen.

Eriel (alternative spellings: Ariel, Airiel, A'ariel, Aurial, Ngharaiel): The forty-sixth angel of the Shem ha-Mephoresh is *Eriel*, whose title is "God the revealer." Associated with the second decanate and fourth quinance of Pisces (16°–20°), Eriel is the angel by night of the Nine of Cups.

Invocation: Psalms 145:9: "Tetragrammaton is good to all; and his tender mercies are over all his works."

Function: Eriel helps one discover hidden treasures and have revelations. This angel dominates night-time visions, reveals the greatest secrets of nature, influences difficult solutions, and enables people to obtain their heart's desire in dreams. Also helps a person to give thanks to God for the good he sends them.

Ten of Cups

Card Keywords: Perfected Success, Satiety, Success
Decan: Mars in Pisces, 20°–30°
Sephirah Godname: Adonai ha-Aretz
Element Godname: El
Archangel: Amnitziel
First Trigram: עשל (OShL) Ashel
Second Trigram: מיה (MYH) Miah
Angels: Esheliah (עשליה) and Mayahel (מיהאל)

Esheliah (alternative spellings: Asaliah, Aslaiah, A'asliah): The forty-seventh angel of the Shem ha-Mephoresh is *Esheliah*, whose titles include "the just judge" or "just God who indicates truth." Associated with the third decanate and fifth quinance of Pisces (21°–25°), Esheliah is the angel by day of the Ten of Cups.

Invocation: Psalms 92:5: "How great are thy works, O Tetragrammaton; and thy thoughts are very deep."[5]

Function: Esheliah helps those who wish to raise themselves spiritually—helping them to praise God and to lift themselves toward the contemplation of the divine when God grants them illumination. Esheliah rules justice and makes the truth known in lawsuits. He influences contemplation and rules over persons of integrity and goodness.

Mayahel (alternative spellings: Mihael, Mihal, Mihel): The forty-eighth angel of the Shem ha-Mephoresh is *Mayahel,* whose title is "sending forth as a father." Associated with the third decanate and sixth quinance of Pisces (26°–30°), Mayahel is the angel by night of the Ten of Cups.

Invocation: Psalms 98:2: "Tetragrammaton hath made known his salvation; in the sight of the nations hath he revealed his justice."

Function: Mayahel helps preserve harmony, fidelity, and union between spouses. This angel dominates the generation of beings, fertility, and influences love. He protects and inspires those who turn to him.

Two of Swords

Card Keywords: Peace Restored, Peace
Decan: Moon in Libra, 1°–10°
Sephirah Godname: Yah
Element Godname: YHVH
Archangel: Zuriel
First Trigram: יזל (YZL) Yezel
Second Trigram: מבה (MBH) Mebah
Angels: Yezalel (יזלאל) and Mebahel (מבהאל)

Yezalel (alternative spellings: Iezalel, Yezeliah, Ielael): The thirteenth angel of the Shem ha-Mephoresh is *Yezalel,* whose titles are "rejoicing over all things" and "God glorified by all things." Associated with the first decanate and first quinance of Libra (1°–5°), Yezalel is the angel by day of the Two of Swords.

Invocation: Psalms 98:4: "Make a joyful noise unto Tetragrammaton, all the earth; break ye forth and rejoice and sing praise."

Function: Yezalel helps to gain amity, reconciliation, and conjugal faithfulness. He dominates friendship and affability, and influences memory and shrewdness.

Mebahel (alternative spellings: Mebehel, Mebahal, Mebahael): The fourteenth angel of the Shem ha-Mephoresh is *Mebahel,* whose titles include "the guardian and preserver," and "conservative God." Associated with the first decanate and second quinance of Libra (6°–10°), Mebahel is the angel by night of the Two of Swords.

Invocation: Psalms 9:9: "And Tetragrammaton shall be a refuge for the oppressed; a refuge of times of trouble."

Function: Mebahel protects the innocent and guards against those wishing to usurp the fortunes of others. This angel dominates justice and liberty. He delivers the oppressed and protects the truth, allowing truth to be known.

Three of Swords

Card Keyword: Sorrow
Decan: Saturn in Libra, 10°–20°
Sephirah Godname: YHVH Elohim
Element Godname: YHVH
Archangel: Zuriel
First Trigram: הרי (HRY) Hari
Second Trigram: הקם (HQM) Haqem
Angels: Hariel (הריאל) and Haqamiah (הקמיה)

Hariel (alternative spellings: Harael, Harayel): The fifteenth angel of the Shem ha-Mephoresh is *Hariel*, whose titles include "my aid," "God is my aid," and "creator God." Associated with the second decanate and third quinance of Libra (11°–15°), Hariel is the angel by day of the Three of Swords.

Invocation: Psalms 94:22: "But Tetragrammaton has become my fortress; and my God is the rock in whom I take refuge."

Function: Hariel gives aid against the disrespectful and the defilists, and guards against impieties. He dominates the arts and sciences, influences discoveries and new methodologies, and also rules over livestock and domestic animals.

Haqamiah (alternative spellings: Haqmiah, Hoqmiah, Hoqamiah, Hakamiah): The sixteenth angel of the Shem ha-Mephoresh is *Haqamiah*, whose titles include "the raiser-up," "God who erects the universe," and "praying day and night." Associated with the second decanate and fourth quinance of Libra (16°–20°), Haqamiah is the angel by night of the Three of Swords.

Invocation: Psalms 88:1: "O Tetragrammaton, God of my salvation, I have cried day and night before thee."

Function: Haqamiah aids against traitors, gives victory over enemies, warns of sedition, dominates arsenals, governs great captains and sovereigns, and influences honesty. He is associated with fire, arsenals, and all things connected with the genie of war.

Four of Swords

Card Keywords: Rest from Strife, Truce, Rest
Decan: Jupiter in Libra, 20°–30°
Sephirah Godname: El
Element Godname: YHVH
Archangel: Zuriel
First Trigram: לאו (LAW) Lau

Second Trigram: כלי (KLY) Keli
Angels: Levayah (לאויה) and Keliel (כליאל)

Levayah (alternative spellings: Laviah, Lauiah, Lauviah, Leviah): The seventeenth angel of the Shem ha-Mephoresh is *Levayah*, whose titles are "the wonderful" and "admirable God." Associated with the third decanate and fifth quinance of Libra (21°–25°), Levayah is the angel by day of the Four of Swords.

Invocation: Psalms 8:1: "O Tetragrammaton, our Lord, how excellent is thy name in all the earth; who hast set thy glory above the heavens."

Function: Levayah dominates the high sciences, marvelous discoveries, literature, philosophy, musicians, and poets. He gives revelations in dreams, protects against spiritual torment and sadness, and aids in obtaining restful sleep at night.

Keliel (alternative spellings: Kaliel, Kelial, Caliel): The eighteenth angel of the Shem ha-Mephoresh is *Keliel*, whose titles include "worthy to be invoked" and "God prompts to fulfill." Associated with the third decanate and sixth quinance of Libra (26°–30°), Keliel is the angel by night of the Four of Swords.

Invocation: Psalms 35:24: "Judge me according to thy righteousness, O Tetragrammaton, my God; and let them not rejoice over me."[6]

Function: Keliel is invoked to give prompt aid in the face of adversity. This angel serves to make known the truth, especially in lawsuits, aids the triumph of innocence, dominates courts and trials, and influences witnesses. He confounds the guilty and false testimony.

Five of Swords

Card Keywords: Defeat
Decan: Venus in Aquarius, 1°–10°
Sephirah Godname: Elohim Gibor
Element Godname: YHVH
Archangel: Kambriel
First Trigram: אני (ANY) Ani
Second Trigram: חעם (ChOM) Cham
Angels: Eniel (אניאל) and Chaamiah (חעמיה)

Eniel (alternative spellings: Aniel, Anaiel): The thirty-seventh angel of the Shem ha-Mephoresh is *Eniel*, whose titles are "lord of virtues" and "God of virtues." Associated with the first decanate and first quinance of Aquarius (1°–5°), Eniel is the angel by day of the Five of Swords.

Invocation: Psalms 80:19: "O Tetragrammaton, Elohim Tzabaoth, turn us and cause thy face to shine upon us; and we shall be saved."[7]

Function: Eniel helps to conquer, win victory, and obtain the release from siege (especially of a city). He dominates the sciences and arts, reveals the secrets of nature, and inspires wise philosophers in their meditations.

Chaamiah (alternative spellings: Chamiah, Cha'amiah, Haamiah): The thirty-eighth angel of the Shem ha-Mephoresh is *Chaamiah*, whose titles include "the hope of all the ends of the earth" and "God the hope of all the children of earth." Associated with the first decanate and second quinance of Aquarius (6°–10°), Chaamiah is the angel by night of the Five of Swords.

Invocation: Psalms 91:9: "Because thou, O Tetragrammaton, art my refuge; thou hast thy refuge in the most high."

Function: Chaamiah protects against lightning, fever, weapons, infernal spirits, and ferocious animals. He is invoked to acquire all the treasures in heaven and earth. This angel dominates all religions and creeds that pertain to God, and protects those who seek the truth.

Six of Swords

Card Keywords: Earned Success, Science, Relief
Decan: Mercury in Aquarius, 10°–20°
Sephirah Godname: YHVH Eloah ve-Daath
Element Godname: YHVH
Archangel: Kambriel
First Trigram: רהע (RHO) Reha
Second Trigram: ייז (YYZ) Yeyaz
Angels: Rehael (רהעאל) and Yeyezel (ייזאל)

Rehael (alternative spellings: Reheael, Reha'ayel): The thirty-ninth angel of the Shem ha-Mephoresh is *Rehael*, whose titles include "swift to condone" and "God who receives sinners." Associated with the second decanate and third quinance of Aquarius (11°–15°), Rehael is the angel by day of the Six of Swords.

Invocation: Psalms 30:10: "Hear, O Tetragrammaton and be merciful to me, O Tetragrammaton; be thou my helper."

Function: Rehael governs health and longevity and is invoked for the healing of the sick. He cures diseases and influences paternal and filial love, granting parents the respect of their children. He helps to obtain the mercy of God.

Yeyezel (alternative spellings: Yeyazel, Yeyeziel, Yeizael, Ieiazel, Ihiazel): The fortieth angel of the Shem ha-Mephoresh is *Yeyezel*, whose titles include "making joyful as wine" and "God who rejoices." Associated with the second decanate and fourth quinance of Aquarius (16°–20°), Yeyezel is the angel by night of the Six of Swords.

Invocation: Psalms 88:14: "O Tetragrammaton, why castest thou off my soul; and why hidest thy face from me?"

Function: Yeyezel gives consolation, helps release prisoners, and delivers people from their enemies. This angel rules printing, the press, libraries, and books. He influences artists and people of letters.

Seven of Swords

Card Keywords: Unstable Effort, Futility, Stealth
Decan: Moon in Aquarius, 20°–30°
Sephirah Godname: YHVH Tzabaoth
Element Godname: YHVH
Archangel: Kambriel
First Trigram: ההה (HHH) Hehah
Second Trigram: מיך (MYK) Mik
Angels: Hehahel (הההאל) and Mayakhel (מיכאל)

Hehahel (alternative spellings: Hahahel, Hahihel, Hehihel): The forty-first angel of the Shem ha-Mephoresh is *Hehahel*, whose titles include "the triune" and "God in three persons." Associated with the third decanate and fifth quinance of Aquarius (21°–25°), Hehahel is the angel by day of the Seven of Swords.

Invocation: Psalms 120:2: "O Tetragrammaton, deliver my soul from lying lips, and from a deceitful tongue."

Function: Hehahel protects missionaries and influences priests, prelates, and all things related to the priesthood. He is invoked to protect against slanderers, liars, and the wicked.

Mayakhel (alternative spellings: Michael, Mikhael): The forty-second angel of the Shem ha-Mephoresh is *Mayakhel*, whose titles include "Who is like unto him," "virtue of God," and "house of God." Associated with the third decanate and sixth quinance of Aquarius (26°–30°), Mayakhel is the angel by night of the Seven of Swords.

Invocation: Psalms 121:7: "Tetragrammaton shall keep thee from all evil; he shall preserve thy soul."

Function: Mayakhel is invoked for safety in travel. This angel dominates the powerful, monarchs, and princes, and keeps their subjects happy. He uncovers conspiracies and all those who seek to cause harm to governments. Mayakhel influences curiosity and politics.

Eight of Swords

Card Keywords: Shortened Force, Interference, Restriction
Decan: Jupiter in Gemini, 1°–10°
Sephirah Godname: Elohim Tzabaoth

Element Godname: YHVH
Archangel: Ambriel
First Trigram: ומב (VMB) Vameb
Second Trigram: יהה (YHH) Yehah
Angels: Vembael (ומבאל) and Yahohel (יההאל)

Vembael (alternative spellings: Vemibael, Vamibael, Umabel): The sixty-first angel of the Shem ha-Mephoresh is *Vembael,* whose titles are "the name which is over all" or "God above all things." Associated with the first decanate and first quinance of Gemini (1°–5°), Vembael is the angel by day of the Eight of Swords.

Invocation: Psalms 118:2: "Let Israel now say that the name of Tetragrammaton be praised; from this time forth for evermore."[8]

Function: Vembael serves to obtain the friendship of a given person, and dominates astronomy and physics and all who distinguish themselves in these fields. He influences the sensitivity of the heart.

Yahohel (alternative spellings: Yehohel, Iahhel, Iahahel): The sixty-second angel of the Shem ha-Mephoresh is *Yahohel,* whose titles include "yah is God," "supreme being," and "the supreme ENS (essence)." Associated with the first decanate and second quinance of Gemini (6°–10°), Yahohel is the angel by night of the Eight of Swords.

Invocation: Psalms 119:159: "See how I have loved thy precepts, O Tetragrammaton; quicken me according to thy loving kindness."

Function: Yahohel helps to obtain wisdom and knowledge, and influences virtue and solitude. This angel rules philosophers, the enlightened, and those who wish to retire from the world.

Nine of Swords

Card Keywords: Cruelty
Decan: Mars in Gemini, 10°–20°
Sephirah Godname: Shaddai El Chai
Element Godname: YHVH
Archangel: Ambriel
First Trigram: ענו (ONV) Anu
Second Trigram: מחי (MChY) Mechi
Angels: Anuel (ענואל) and Machiel (מחיאל)

Anuel (alternative spellings: Anevel, A'aneval, Annauel, Anauel, Nghaneauel): The sixty-third angel of the Shem ha-Mephoresh is *Anuel,* whose titles include "the rejoicing" and

"God, infinitely good." Associated with the second decanate and third quinance of Gemini (11°–15°), Anuel is the angel by day of the Nine of Swords.

Invocation: Psalms 100:2: "Serve Tetragrammaton with joy; enter into his presence with exultation."[9]

Function: Anuel protects against accidents, maintains health, and heals the sick. He dominates trade, commerce, businessmen, and clerks, influences business, and rules over religious conversions.

Machiel (alternative spellings: Mochayel, Mochael, Mechial, Mehiel, Mochaiel): The sixty-fourth angel of the Shem ha-Mephoresh is *Machiel*, whose titles are "the vivifying" and "God who vivifies all things." Associated with the second decanate and fourth quinance of Gemini (16°–20°), Machiel is the angel by night of the Nine of Swords.

Invocation: Psalms 33:18: "Behold the eye of Tetragrammaton is upon those who fear him; upon those who hope in his mercy."

Function: Machiel is associated with adversities, including rage, fierce animals, and rabies. This angel rules over the wise, savants, professors, orators, and authors, and influences the press, books, bookshops, libraries, and all those established in the book trade. He grants the prayers and wishes of those who hope in the mercy of God.

Ten of Swords

Card Keywords: Ruin
Decan: Sun in Gemini, 20°–30°
Sephirah Godname: Adonai ha-Aretz
Element Godname: YHVH
Archangel: Ambriel
First Trigram: דמב (DMB) Dameb
Second Trigram: מנק (MNQ) Menaq
Angels: Dambayah (דמביה) and Meneqel (מנקאל)

Dambayah (alternative spellings: Damabiah, Damabaiah, Dambayah): The sixty-fifth angel of the Shem ha-Mephoresh is *Dambayah*, whose titles are "fountain of wisdom" and "God, fountain of wisdom." Associated with the third decanate and fifth quinance of Gemini (21°–25°), Dambayah is the angel by day of the Ten of Swords.

Invocation: Psalms 90:13: "Return, O Tetragrammaton, how long? And repent thee concerning thy servants."

Function: Dambayah aids against sorcery and helps to obtain wisdom. He grants success in useful enterprises. Dambayah dominates the waters (rivers, seas, springs), as well as maritime expeditions, and naval constructions. He influences sailors, pilots, fishermen, and all those engaged in this type of commerce.

Meneqel (alternative spellings: Menqel, Manakel, Menkl): The sixty-sixth angel of the Shem ha-Mephoresh is *Meneqel,* whose titles include "nourishing all" or "God who supports and maintains all things." Associated with the third decanate and sixth quinance of Gemini (26°–30°), Meneqel is the angel by night of the Ten of Swords.

Invocation: Psalms 38:21: "Forsake me not, O Tetragrammaton, my God; be not thou far from me."

Function: Meneqel serves to appease the anger of God, calms anger in general, and heals epilepsy. This angel rules vegetation and aquatic animals, and influences sleep and dreams.

Two of Pentacles

Card Keywords: Harmonius Change, Change
Decan: Jupiter in Capricorn, 1°–10°
Sephirah Godname: Yah
Element Godname: Adonai
Archangel: Hanael
First Trigram: לכב (LKB) Lekab
Second Trigram: ושר (VShR) Vesher
Angels: Lekhabel (לכבאל) and Veshiriah (ושריה)

Lekhabel (alternative spellings: Lekabel, Lecabel): The thirty-first angel of the Shem ha-Mephoresh is *Lekhabel,* whose titles include "the teacher," "instructor," and "God who inspires." Associated with the first decanate and first quinance of Capricorn (1°–5°), Lekhabel is the angel by day of the Two of Pentacles.

Invocation: Psalms 71:16: "I will go forth in the might of Tetragrammaton Elohim; I will cause to remember thy justice alone."

Function: Lekhabel rules the acquisition of knowledge and serves to cast light on one's job. He grants useful advantages in one's profession. He governs vegetation, agriculture, astrology, astronomy, mathematics, and geometry.

Veshiriah (alternative spellings: Veshriah, Vesheriah, Vasiariah, Vasariah): The thirty-second angel of the Shem ha-Mephoresh is *Veshiriah,* whose titles include "the upright" and "God the just." Associated with the first decanate and second quinance of Capricorn (6°–10°), Veshiriah is the angel by night of the Two of Pentacles.

Invocation: Psalms 33:4: "For the word of Tetragrammaton is right; and all his works are done in truth."

Function: Veshiriah rules nobility, justice, judges, jurists, magistrates, and advocates. He softens the hearts of those who attack others unjustly in court, causing them to repent. He helps to obtain the grace of those who have recourse to the clemency of the powerful. This angel protects against false and unjust accusations, and influences the spoken word.

Three of Pentacles

Card Keywords: Material Works, Work
Decan: Mars in Capricorn, 10°–20°
Sephirah Godname: YHVH Elohim
Element Godname: Adonai
Archangel: Hanael
First Trigram: יחו (YChV) Yecho
Second Trigram: להח (LHCh) Lehach
Angels: Yechaviah (יחויה) and Lehachiah (להחיה)

Yechaviah (alternative spellings: Yechavah, Yechuiah, Yechoiah, Iehuiah): The thirty-third angel of the Shem ha-Mephoresh is *Yechaviah*, whose titles are "the knower of all things," or "God who knows all things." Associated with the second decanate and third quinance of Capricorn (11°–15°), Yechaviah is the angel by day of the Three of Pentacles.

Invocation: Psalms 94:11: "Tetragrammaton knoweth the thoughts of man; that they are vain."

Function: Yechaviah serves to uncover plots and traitors, undoing their plans. He dominates and influences just rulers and keeps their subjects happy.

Lehachiah (alternative spellings: Lehahiah, Lehahaih): The thirty-fourth angel of the Shem ha-Mephoresh is *Lehachiah*, whose titles include "the merciful" and "God the clement." Associated with the second decanate and fourth quinance of Capricorn (16°–20°), Lehachiah is the angel by night of the Three of Pentacles.

Invocation: Psalms 131:3: "Let Israel trust in Tetragrammaton; now and forever."

Function: Lehachiah helps maintain peace, understanding, and harmony between countries. He dominates faithfulness, respect, obedience, and devotion.

Four of Pentacles

Card Keywords: Earthly Power, Power, Security
Decan: Sun in Capricorn, 20°–30°
Sephirah Godname: El
Element Godname: Adonai
Archangel: Hanael
First Trigram: כוק (KVQ) Keveq
Second Trigram: מנד (MND) Menad
Angels: Kuqiah (כוקיה) and Menadel (מנדאל)

Kuqiah (alternative spellings: Keveqiah, Keveqaiah, Chavakiah): The thirty-fifth angel of the Shem ha-Mephoresh is *Kuqiah*, whose titles include "to be rejoiced in" or "God who gives joy." Associated with the third decanate and fifth quinance of Capricorn (21°–25°), Kuqiah is the angel by day of the Four of Pentacles.

Invocation: Psalms 116:1: "I rejoice in Tetragrammaton because he hath heard my voice and my supplications."

Function: Kuqiah helps recover the friendship of those we have offended, and favors peace and harmony in family life. He governs wills, testaments, successions, inheritance, friendly distribution, and all things which are based on friendship.

Menadel (alternative spellings: Mendal, Mendial, Mendiel, Monadel): The thirty-sixth angel of the Shem ha-Mephoresh is *Menadel,* whose titles include "the honorable" and "God adorable." Associated with the third decanate and sixth quinance of Capricorn (26°–30°), Menadel is the angel by night of the Four of Pentacles.

Invocation: Psalms 26:8: "O Tetragrammaton, I have loved the habitation of thy house; and the place where thine honor dwelleth."

Function: Menadel is invoked to maintain one's employment and to preserve the means of existence which one possesses. This angel protects against slander, works to release prisoners, and rules the return of the exiled to their native land.

Five of Pentacles

Card Keywords: Material Trouble, Worry, Trouble
Decan: Mercury in Taurus, 1°–10°
Sephirah Godname: Elohim Gibor
Element Godname: Adonai
Archangel: Asmodel
First Trigram: מבה (MBH) Mabeh
Second Trigram: פוי (PVY) Poi
Angels: Mibahayah (מבהיה) and Puyael (פויאל)

Mibahayah (alternative spellings: Mebahiah, Mibahiah, Mibahaih): The fifty-fifth angel of the Shem ha-Mephoresh is *Mibahayah,* whose titles are "the eternal" or "God eternal." Associated with the first decanate and first quinance of Taurus (1°–5°), Mibahayah is the angel by day of the Five of Pentacles.

Invocation: Psalms 102:12: "But thou, O Tetragrammaton, shalt endure forever; and thy memorial from generation to generation."

Function: Mibahayah helps one receive consolation, and aids those who wish to have children. He rules over morals, religion, and piety, and grants protection in one's spiritual endeavors—making their undertakings prosperous through all possible means.

Puyael (alternative spellings: Poyel, Payiel, Pooyal, Poiel, Poial, Puiael): The fifty-sixth angel of the Shem ha-Mephoresh is *Puyael,* whose titles include "supporting all things" and "God who sustains the universe." Associated with the first decanate and second quinance of Taurus (6°–10°), Puyael is the angel by night of the Five of Pentacles.

Invocation: Psalms 145:14: "Tetragrammaton upholdeth all those who fall; and lifteth up all those who are down."

Function: Puyael serves to obtain what is asked for, or what one requires. This angel rules renown, fame, success, fortune, and philosophy, and influences moderation.

Six of Pentacles

Card Keywords: Material Success, Success, Assistance
Decan: Moon in Taurus, 10°–20°
Sephirah Godname: YHVH Eloah ve-Daath
Element Godname: Adonai
Archangel: Asmodel
First Trigram: נמם (NMM) Nemem
Second Trigram: ייל (YYL) Yeyal
Angels: Nemamiah (נממיה) and Yeyelel (יילאל)

Nemamiah (alternative spellings: Nemamaiah, Nemamaih): The fifty-seventh angel of the Shem ha-Mephoresh is *Nemamiah,* whose titles are "the lovable" and "praiseworthy God." Associated with the second decanate and third quinance of Taurus (11°–15°), Nemamiah is the angel by day of the Six of Pentacles.

Invocation: Psalms 115:11: "Ye who fear Tetragrammaton, trust in Tetragrammaton; he is their help and their shield."

Function: Nemamiah is invoked for prosperity in all things. He helps release prisoners, influences combatants, and rules over generals, admirals, and all those who fight for a just cause.

Yeyelel (alternative spellings: Yeyalel, Yeyelal, Yeileel, Yeilial, Ieialel, Ieilael): The fifty-eighth angel of the Shem ha-Mephoresh is *Yeyelel,* whose titles are "the hearer of cries," and "God who hears the generations." Associated with the second decanate and fourth quinance of Taurus (16°–20°), Yeyelel is the angel by night of the Six of Pentacles.

Invocation: Psalms 6:3: "And my soul hath been greatly troubled; but thou, O Tetragrammaton, how long?"

Function: Yeyelel helps against trouble and heals illnesses, particularly eye diseases. He dominates fire, iron, armorers, metalworkers, locksmiths, and knife-grinders, as well as those involved in commerce.

Seven of Pentacles

Card Keywords: Success Unfulfilled, Failure, Inertia
Decan: Saturn in Taurus, 20°–30°
Sephirah Godname: YHVH Tzabaoth
Element Godname: Adonai
Archangel: Asmodel
First Trigram: הרח (HRCh) Herach
Second Trigram: מצר (MTzR) Metzer
Angels: Herachel (הרחאל) and Mitzrael (מצראל)

Herachel (alternative spellings: Herachiel, Harachal, Herachael, Herochiel, Harahel): The fifty-ninth angel of the Shem ha-Mephoresh is *Herachel,* whose titles are "permeating all things," and "God who knows all things." Associated with the third decanate and fifth quinance of Taurus (21°–25°), Herachel is the angel by day of the Seven of Pentacles.

Invocation: Psalms 113:3: "From the rising of the sun unto the going down of the same; let the name of Tetragrammaton be praised."

Function: Herachel protects against sterility in women and causes rebellious children to be respectful toward their parents. He rules over all who are engaged in commerce, agents of change, treasurers, public funds, archives, libraries, the press, and all rare and precious connections. He influences printing and all involved in the book trade.

Mitzrael (alternative spellings: Mizrael, Metzrael): The sixtieth angel of the Shem ha-Mephoresh is *Mitzrael,* whose titles include "raising up the oppressed" and "God who comforts the oppressed." Associated with the third decanate and sixth quinance of Taurus (26°–30°), Mitzrael is the angel by night of the Seven of Pentacles.

Invocation: Psalms 145:17: "Righteous is Tetragrammaton in all his ways; and holy in all his works."

Function: Mitzrael helps heal the ills of the spirit, releases a person from persecutors, dominates people of virtue and industriousness, and influences faithfulness and obedience.

Eight of Pentacles

Card Keywords: Prudence, Skill
Decan: Sun in Virgo, 1°–10°
Sephirah Godname: Elohim Tzabaoth
Element Godname: Adonai
Archangel: Hamaliel
First Trigram: אכא (AKA) Aka
Second Trigram: כהת (KHTh) Kahath
Angels: Akayah (אכאיה) and Kehethel (כהתאל)

Akayah (alternative spellings: Akaiah, Achaiah, Akhaiah): The seventh angel of the Shem ha-Mephoresh is *Akayah*, whose titles include "long-suffering" and "God good and patient." Associated with the first decanate and first quinance of Virgo (1°–5°), Akayah is the angel by day of the Eight of Pentacles.

Invocation: Psalms 103:8: "Tetragrammaton is merciful and gracious; slow to anger, and plenteous in mercy."

Function: Akayah helps discover the secrets of nature, rules patience and temperance, influences the spread of knowledge and enlightenment, and aids industry.

Kehethel (alternative spellings: Kehethal, Kahathal, Cahethel): The eighth angel of the Shem ha-Mephoresh is *Kehethel*, whose titles are "the adorable" or "God adorable." Associated with the first decanate and second quinance of Virgo (6°–10°), Kehethel is the angel by night of the Eight of Pentacles.

Invocation: Psalms 95:6: "O come, let us bow down; let us kneel before Tetragrammaton; who hath made us."

Function: Kehethel serves to bring one closer to God, to obtain divine blessings, and to protect against evil spirits. This angel influences the hunt and dominates agricultural production, especially those aspects necessary to the existence of humans and animals.

Nine of Pentacles

Card Keywords: Material Gain, Gain
Decan: Venus in Virgo, 10°–20°
Sephirah Godname: Shaddai El Chai
Element Godname: Adonai
Archangel: Hamaliel
First Trigram: הזי (HZY) Hezi
Second Trigram: אלד (ALD) Elad
Angels: Haziel (הזיאל) and Eldayah (אלדיה)

Haziel (alternative spellings: Hazayel, Hazeyael): The ninth angel of the Shem ha-Mephoresh is *Haziel*, whose titles are "the merciful" and "God of mercy." Associated with the second decanate and third quinance of Virgo (11°–15°), Haziel is the angel by day of the Nine of Pentacles.

Invocation: Psalms 25:6: "Remember Thy tender mercies, O Tetragrammaton, and thy loving kindness; for they have been ever of old."

Function: Haziel helps obtain the friendship and favors of the great. He rules over good faith, and influences sincerity, reconciliation, and faith in general. He helps one obtain divine mercy and pardon. He oversees promises made by a person and ensures that they are carried out.

Eldayah (alternative spellings: Aldiah, Aladiah, Eldiah): The tenth angel of the Shem ha-Mephoresh is *Eldayah*, whose titles are "the profitable" and "God the propitious." Associated with the second decanate and fourth quinance of Virgo (16°–20°), Eldayah is the angel by night of the Nine of Pentacles.

Invocation: Psalms 33:22: "Let thy mercy, O Tetragrammaton, be upon us, in proportion to our hope in thee."

Function: Eldayah helps to hide secrets or that which one does not wish to reveal. This angel protects against pestilence, plagues, and rabies. He influences healing and recovery from sickness.

Ten of Pentacles

Card Keywords: Wealth, Completion
Decan: Mercury in Virgo, 20°–30°
Sephirah Godname: Adonai ha-Aretz
Element Godname: Adonai
Archangel: Hamaliel
First Trigram: לאו (LAV) Lav
Second Trigram: ההע (HHO) Hahau
Angels: Laviah (לאויה) and Hihaayah (ההעיה)

Laviah (alternative spellings: Leviah, Lauviah, Lauiah): The eleventh angel of the Shem ha-Mephoresh is *Laviah*, whose title is "to be exalted." Associated with the third decanate and fifth quinance of Virgo (21°–25°), Laviah is the angel by day of the Ten of Pentacles.

Invocation: Psalms 18:46: "Tetragrammaton liveth; and blessed be my rock; and let the God of my salvation be exalted."

Function: Laviah protects against lightning, sudden unwanted emotions, and serves to obtain victory. He rules over fame and renown through great personages, and influences the wise who have become famous or who win celebrity through their talents.

Hihaayah (alternative spellings: Hihayah, Hihaiah, Hiha'ayah, Hahaiah, Hahiah): The twelfth angel of the Shem ha-Mephoresh is *Hihaayah*, whose titles are "my refuge" or "God is refuge." Associated with the third decanate and sixth quinance of Virgo (26°–30°), Hihaayah is the angel by night of the Ten of Pentacles.

Invocation: Psalms 10:1: "Why standest thou afar off, O Tetragrammaton? Why hidest thyself in time of trouble?"

Function: Hihaayah protects against adversity and provides help in times of need. This angel rules over dreams and reveals mysteries hidden from mortals. He influences wise, discrete, and spiritual people.

DIVINE FORCES OF THE COURT CARDS

In addition to their primary elemental affiliation, the four "royal" figures of the tarot court are each assigned to a sephirah on the Qabalistic Tree of Life: Kings to Chokmah, Queens to Binah, Princes to Tiphareth, and Princesses to Malkuth.[10] Therefore each of these cards have two godnames associated with them—one sephirotic and one elemental. The archangels and angels associated with the court cards are the same as those of the elements.

Godnames, Archangels, and Angels of the Court Cards

Card Name	Sub-Element	Sephirah	Sephirah Godname	Element Godname	Element Archangel	Element Angel
King of Wands	Fire of Fire	Chokmah	Yah	Elohim	Michael	Ariel
Queen of Wands	Water of Fire	Binah	YHVH Elohim	Elohim	Michael	Ariel
Prince of Wands	Air of Fire	Tiphareth	YHVH Eloah ve-Daath	Elohim	Michael	Ariel
Princess of Wands	Earth of Fire	Malkuth	Adonai ha-Aretz	Elohim	Michael	Ariel
King of Cups	Fire of Water	Chokmah	Yah	El	Gabriel	Taliahad
Queen of Cups	Water of Water	Binah	YHVH Elohim	El	Gabriel	Taliahad
Prince of Cups	Air of Water	Tiphareth	YHVH Eloah ve-Daath	El	Gabriel	Taliahad
Princess of Cups	Earth of Water	Malkuth	Adonai ha-Aretz	El	Gabriel	Taliahad
King of Swords	Fire of Air	Chokmah	Yah	YHVH	Raphael	Chassan
Queen of Swords	Water of Air	Binah	YHVH Elohim	YHVH	Raphael	Chassan
Prince of Swords	Air of Air	Tiphareth	YHVH Eloah ve-Daath	YHVH	Raphael	Chassan
Princess of Swords	Earth of Air	Malkuth	Adonai ha-Aretz	YHVH	Raphael	Chassan
King of Pentacles	Fire of Earth	Chokmah	Yah	Adonai	Uriel	Phorlakh
Queen of Pentacles	Water of Earth	Binah	YHVH Elohim	Adonai	Uriel	Phorlakh
Prince of Pentacles	Air of Earth	Tiphareth	YHVH Eloah ve-Daath	Adonai	Uriel	Phorlakh
Princess of Pentacles	Earth of Earth	Malkuth	Adonai ha-Aretz	Adonai	Uriel	Phorlakh

1 See Agrippa, *Three Books of Occult Philosophy*, 538–540.

2 The star that is also called *Cor Leonis,* "the heart of the lion." *Regulus* means "star of the prince." Regulus is one of four very bright fixed stars that the Persians called "royal stars" and "guardians of the heavens." There is evidence to support the view that in parts of ancient Egypt this astrological method (beginning with 0° Leo) was employed. "The oldest version of the zodiac was without doubt measured from the fixed stars." —Rupert Gleadow, *The Origins of the Zodiac,* 28.

3 With the exception of the seventieth trigram which is assigned to Genesis 1:1.

4 These Psalms can be recited in Hebrew or Latin if desired. Different editions of the Bible also give subtle variations of these verses; at times the numeration of these verses varies as well. "YHVH" can be substituted for "Tetragrammaton."

5 An alternative invocation given is Psalm 104:24: "Oh Tetragrammaton, how manifold are thy works! In wisdom hast thou made them. All the earth is full of thy riches."

6 An alternative invocation given is Psalm 7:8: "Judge me, O Tetragrammaton, according to my righteousness, and according to mine integrity that is in me."

7 An alternative invocation given is Psalm 80:7: "Turn us again, O Elohim Tzabaoth, and cause thy face to shine; and we shall be saved."

8 An alternative invocation given is Psalm 113:2: "Blessed be the name of Tetragrammaton, from this time forth and for evermore."

9 An alternative invocation given is Psalm 2:11: "Serve Tetragrammaton with fear, and rejoice with trembling."

10 The sixteen court cards are also attributed to the sixteen tetragrams of geomancy or "earth divination." However, these associations are not vital to the creation of tarot talismans as presented here.

6

WORKING WITH THE TAROT ANGELS

In our sacred universe, angels perform a multitude of tasks. Their first responsibility is to carry out divine directives from the One Source. They are also holy messengers who carry communications from the divine to humanity. But many assist human beings directly, acting as protectors, guides, counselors, and advisors. They command hierarchies of lesser angels and spirits who are directly responsible for cosmic mechanics—for causing change to occur on the many planes of existence, including the material world. When conditions are favorable, angels respond to properly performed invocations by magicians and other ritualists.

Herein lies the main distinction between the mystic and the magician, who employ different means to arrive at the same goal of union with the divine. While the mystic tries to transcend the physical world and separate himself from its enticements . . .

> The Magician, through his Quest is oriented clearly toward the One, is by vocation a Pilgrim, a dedicated Traveler who values the rich diversity of the realms through which the Path leads, commencing with this physical world where his Quest begins. The Magician strives to fully encompass both the outer and inner worlds in a sacramental relationship by which his experience of both the world and himself is made holy. The Angels are the inhabitants of the realms through which the Pilgrim travels on his Path.[1]

Angels and humans exist on different planes or levels. Our two species are normally "out of phase" with each other. In order for contact between the two to occur, humans must raise their vibrational rate and angelic beings must lower theirs. Thus for brief periods when the two are in alignment, angelic communication and visions are possible. Angels are our link to the divine in the eternal chain of consciousness. Therefore, connecting with the angelic forces of the tarot will give additional strength and potency to the consecration of tarot talismans. One way to make this connection is to use your ability to visualize these angels and build them up in your imagination.

VISUALIZATION AND IMAGINATION

One of the meanings of the word *visualize* is "to make visible." This involves creating a mental image or envisaging something, especially as a future possibility. The magical use of the term refers to *making something visible on the astral plane.*

Some of the archangels and angels that are used to invoke the energies of the tarot cards are easy for us to visualize because they've been described many times in rituals such as the Lesser Banishing Ritual of the Pentagram. The archangels of the four elements—Raphael, Gabriel, Michael, and Uriel—are well known to most Western magicians. Through repeated practice of rituals such as the LBRP, many readers already know what colors and symbols are associated with these angels. However, other angels, including many of the planetary and zodiacal angels and archangels, are more obscure and not so well known. These angels are not so easy for us to visualize because there is quite simply no visual description of them anywhere. For many of these angels, such as Adnakhiel, the archangel of Sagittarius, or Nakhiel, the intelligence of Sol, all we know about them is their name, the numerology of their name, and their basic function. No grimoire tells us what they look like. To resolve this problem we must turn to the imagination.

The faculty of imagination has gotten a bad rap over the years. Too often people encourage the faculty of imagination in children as a welcome process of mental growth, only to inexplicably discourage and stifle this vital ability in adults. It is important to realize that the imagination is much more than mere daydreaming or fantasizing. Envisioning something is pure inspiration—it is the crucial first step in the process of creation. In the art and science of magic we will not refer to this process as *imaginary,* a word that has the connotation of being "childish" or unreal. Instead we will use the term *imaginal,* which celebrates the creative process of the imagination as a valuable tool for magic and growth.

Since the "laws" of magic suggest that the magician's imaginal ability is an essential factor in successful ritual magic, it is vital to develop your capacity for visualization on the astral plane. For some lucky individuals this ability comes quite easily. For many others it is a skill that must be slowly nurtured and developed by magical training, and by encouraging what some have called the *transconscious self*[2] or the human psyche's creative and intuitive imagination.

The transconscious self is a reconciling intelligence, a connecting link between all parts of human consciousness. Composed of the processes of imagination, intuition, and will, the transconscious has the ability to move through, communicate with, and cause change on all levels of the psyche. It is inclusive of a wide range of powers associated with communication and transformation. Operating as a single organized mechanism, the transconscious purposefully flows between all portions of the psyche with a unifying objective. Its vast creative resources are a primary influence in the development of music, dance, literature, and art. Properly used, the imaginative faculties can activate one's latent psychic abilities and make the practice of ritual magic much easier and more effective.

Making a viable connection with an angel you wish to invoke is an important step in the ritual consecration of tarot talismans. One way to do this is to utilize your faculty of imagination to create magical images and sigils of the angels.

Magical Images of the Tarot Angels

Now you must know that angelic spirits, seeing that they are of a pure intellect, and altogether incorporeal, are not marked with any marks or characters, and pingible (coarse) figures, or any other human signs; but we not knowing their essence, or quality, do from their names, or works, or otherwise, according to our fancies devote and consecrate to them figures, and marks, by which we cannot any way compel them to us, *but by which we rise up to them* . . . we calling upon them in spirit, and truth, by true names and characters do obtain from them that virtue or power which we desire.[3]

In scriptural texts, angels are often described as taking on the form of geometric shapes, fireballs, or great pillars of fire and light. When assuming these forms, angels display their breathtaking power and are viewed with awe by the Biblical authors:

And I saw another mighty angel come down from heaven, clothed with a cloud: and a rainbow was upon his head, and his face was as if it were the sun, and his feet as pillars of fire. And he had in his hand a little book open: and he set his right foot upon the sea, and his left foot on the earth. And he cried out with a loud voice, as when a lion roareth: and when he cried, seven thunders uttered their voices.[4]

Some Islamic traditions describe the archangel Michael in marvelous form:

Wings the color of green emerald . . . covered with saffron hairs, each of them containing a million faces and mouths and as many tongues which, in a million dialects, implore the pardon of Allah.[5]

Angels certainly can and do present themselves to us in human form for our better understanding. This is evidenced by numerous encounters between humans and angels as recounted in religious texts from various traditions. The Book of Tobit describes one incident where the archangel Raphael was mistaken for a human:

Tobiah went to look for someone acquainted with the roads who would travel with him to Media. As soon as he went out, he found the angel Raphael standing before him, though he did not know this was an angel of God. Tobiah said to him, "Who are you, young man?"[6]

Figure 42: The Seventh Angel from the Book of Revelations.

Many angelic representations are classified as *mantic* or dream images. These are forms that angels and archangels assume spontaneously without any conscious effort on the part of the magician, priest, or priestess viewing them.

Unfortunately, visual representations of angels are few and far between, and they do not begin to cover the various angels specified in talismanic magic.

If no written descriptions of particular angels and archangels exist, how can we know what they look like? How can we get a firm picture in our minds in order to connect with them? What can we do to visualize them in our magical work? One approach to tackling this problem is to use *telesmatic images*.

TELESMATIC MAGIC

All of the work that goes into the planning of a talisman consecration ritual is a crucial part of the ceremony. Preparation helps the ritualist focus on the goal of the ceremony, rather than worrying about ad-lib speeches or unrehearsed movements. Telesmatic magic, a system of magic developed by the Golden Dawn, is all about correspondences, preparation, and visualization.

The word *telesmata* is a Greek term which means "talismans." A *telesmatic image* is an image of a deity or angel that is consciously constructed by the magician. The energy that is put into the telesmatic image is known as *telesma*. It is the force used to activate and charge the image.

A telesmatic image is an illustration constructed according to a predetermined set of correspondences. This image is then consecrated and charged to achieve a specific purpose. The charged image becomes a sacred icon—a powerful living symbol of the force it represents. The image of the angel may be drawn or painted to serve as a physical talisman in its own right, or it may be simply envisioned on the astral plane to give power and energy to a talisman consecration ritual.

General Telesmatic Images

A *general telesmatic image* is a coherent, logically constructed image of a deity or angel that is formulated in accordance with a standard set of colors, symbols, and other correspondences employed by Western magicians. The chart on the next page gives a breakdown of the color correspondences used to create these magical images.

In the color attributions chart, the *main* color and the *complementary* color of a given sephirah or Hebrew letter are known as *flashing colors*. These are colors that are opposite each other on a standard artist's color wheel. Used together they appear to "flash" or "vibrate," providing an optical effect that is important in magical work. The main color is sometimes referred to as the *field* or *ground* color. This is the principal color of a magical image. The complementary color is sometimes called the *charge* color. This is a secondary color that is often used to ornament the main color in a magical image. By utilizing these basic color attributions as well as other symbolism, anyone can create a general telesmatic image of a given angel.

For example, the archangel of Mars and the Tower card is Zamael. This entity can be pictured as a mighty warrior angel, dressed in robes of red ornamented with green, with flaming red hair and wings composed of red and green feathers. He may have the symbol of Mars or the Hebrew letter peh (the letter assigned to Mars) emblazoned on his chest. Zamael might also be visualized with a sword and a shield—implements that are well suited to a Martial temperament (see figure 43).

In another example, the archangel of Saturn and the Universe card is Kassiel. This entity could be pictured as a mighty winged angel dressed in a hooded robe of indigo (blue-violet) ornamented with yellow-orange. He might appear to be surrounded by a halo of rings, as is the planet Saturn. The symbol of Saturn or the Hebrew letter tau could be emblazoned on the front of Kassiel's robe. He might carry the symbol of an hourglass, a scythe, or an astrolabe—all symbols associated with the planet Saturn.

Color Attributions

Attribution[7]	Hebrew Letter	Main Color	Complementary Color
Kether	—	white	black
Chokmah	—	gray	white
Binah	—	black	white
Chesed	—	blue	orange
Geburah	—	red	green
Tiphareth	—	yellow	violet
Netzach	—	green	red
Hod	—	orange	blue
Yesod	—	violet	yellow
Malkuth	—	citrine, olive, russet, black	white
△ Air	aleph א	yellow	violet
☿ Mercury	beth ב	yellow	violet
☽ Luna	gimel ג	blue	orange
♀ Venus	daleth ד	green	red
♈ Aries	heh ה	red	green
♉ Taurus	vav ו	red-orange	blue-green
♊ Gemini	zayin ז	orange	blue
♋ Cancer	cheth ח	yellow-orange	blue-violet
♌ Leo	teth ט	yellow	violet
♍ Virgo	yod י	yellow-green	red-violet
♃ Jupiter	kaph כ	violet	yellow
♎ Libra	lamed ל	green	red
▽ Water	mem מ	blue	orange
♏ Scorpio	nun נ	blue-green	red-orange
♐ Sagittarius	samekh ס	blue	orange
♑ Capricorn	ayin ע	blue-violet	yellow-orange
♂ Mars	peh פ	red	green
♒ Aquarius	tzaddi צ	violet	yellow
♓ Pisces	qoph ק	red-violet	yellow-green
☉ Sol	resh ר	orange	blue
△ Fire ⊕ Spirit	shin ש	red white[8]	green black
♄ Saturn ▽ Earth	tau ת	blue-violet citrine, olive, russet, black	yellow-orange white

Figure 43: General Telesmatic Image of Zamael.

Finally, Ambriel, the archangel of Gemini, could be envisioned as a mighty angel dressed in orange robes ornamented on the chest with the symbol of Gemini in blue. He might carry a book, a scroll, or a writing stylus and tablet—emblems associated with the sign of Gemini. The feathers of his wings may be pictured in pastel orange and blue.

Any of the tarot angels can be visualized in this fashion, using their own correspondences to build them up in the imagination.

It may be somewhat more difficult for readers to create general telesmatic images of the angels of the thirty-six decanate cards, since these angels are derived from the Shem ha-Mephoresh and each card has *two* angels attributed to it. However, this can also be accomplished with a little effort.

Let's take, for example, the Two of Pentacles, which corresponds to the first decanate of Capricorn (Jupiter in Capricorn 1°–10°). The two angels who correspond to this card are Lekabel and Veshiriah. It would be logical to visualize one of these angels as male and the other female. But which one is which?

One school of thought says that angels whose names end in the suffix "iah" are masculine and those that end in "el" are feminine, since these are the respective masculine and feminine names of God on the male and female Pillars of the Qabalistic Tree of Life.[9] However, this rule of thumb is not helpful in all cases. In the Hebrew language, names that end in "ah"

Figure 44: General Telesmatic Image of Veshiriah and Lekabel.

are usually considered feminine. Also, some pip cards have two angels whose names both end in "el" or both end in "iah".

In the previous chapter, we found that Lekabel is listed as Shem ha-Mephoresh angel number thirty-one while Veshiriah is angel number thirty-two. We also found that the first angel of any decanate card is called the "day" angel while the second angel is known as the "night" angel. For millennia, day and night have been assigned respectively to male (solar) and female (lunar). Therefore, in our current example it would be a natural conclusion to make Lekabel appear male and Veshiriah to appear female.

One simple way to visualize this pair of angels is to apply to them the correspondences of their card's decanate. The Two of Pentacles corresponds to the first decanate of Capricorn—specifically, Jupiter in Capricorn. You could relate the first angel of the pair (Lekabel) to Jupiter and the second angel (Veshiriah) to Capricorn. Using this method, Lekabel could be imagined as a male angel wearing violet-colored robes emblazoned with the symbol of the planet Jupiter in yellow. Veshiriah could be visualized as a female angel dressed in robes of blue-violet ornamented with the symbol of Capricorn in yellow-orange. Both angels would have wings in the appropriate colors and they could hold a single pentacle between them, the symbol of this card's suit. Following the symbolism of the Pillars on the Tree of Life, Lekabel would stand on the right or masculine side, and Veshiriah would be on the left or feminine side.

For another example, we will pick the Ten of Cups. This card is attributed to the second decanate of Pisces—Mars in Pisces, 20°–30°. The two angels assigned to this card are Ashiliah (angel number forty-seven) and Mayahel (angel number forty-eight). The first angel, Ashiliah, could be visualized dressed in robes of red, emblazoned with the symbol of Mars. The second angel, Mayahel, could be imagined in red-violet robes ornamented with the symbol of Pisces. The two angels could hold a large cup between them.

You could envision the day angel Ashiliah as male and the night angel Mayahel as female. Or, if you tend to think of angels whose names end in "iah" as feminine and those whose names end in "el" as masculine, go right ahead and reverse the gender for your magical image of these two beings. Remember that angels can appear to us in any form that they choose. In many instances, *we* choose the manner in which angels will appear, because they will take on whatever form is needed in order to communicate with us.

Literal Telesmatic Images

A *literal telesmatic image* is an image of a deity or angel that is constructed from its name, letter by letter. In other words, the Hebrew name of a spiritual entity is first analyzed. The various correspondences of each Hebrew letter are then used to construct the image of the being.

To create a literal telesmatic image of an angel, you must first have its name transliterated into Hebrew letters. Next you would construct the image of the angel so that the first letter of the name represents its head and the last letter represents its feet. All the remaining letters would represent the rest of the body, in order from head to foot. There will be as many body parts as there are letters in the name.

For example, suppose you were working with the tarot trump of the Hierophant and wanted to make a literal telesmatic image of the archangel Asmodel. The Hebrew letters of this angel's name are aleph, samekh, mem, vav, daleth, aleph, and lamed. The first letter Aleph will represent the head and the last letter lamed will represent the feet, with all the middle letters comprising the body parts in between:

א	aleph	=	crown of head
ס	samekh	=	face and neck
מ	mem	=	shoulders and arms
ו	vav	=	chest and stomach
ד	daleth	=	hips and thighs
א	aleph	=	legs
ל	lamed	=	feet

Once you have determined the letters of the angel's name, refer to the following chart:

Correspondences and Traditional Telesmatic Attributions of the Hebrew Alphabet

Letter	Meaning	Attribution	Sound	Value[10]	Traditional (Golden Dawn) Telesmatic Attribution
א aleph	ox	△ Air	a	1	Generally hermaphroditic but leaning more toward masculine. Spiritual. Winged. Slender.
ב beth	house	☿ Mercury	b, v	2	Masculine. Active. Slender.
ג gimel	camel	☽ Luna	g, gh	3	Feminine. Gray. Beautiful, yet changeable. Full face and body.
ד daleth	door	♀ Venus	d, dh	4	Feminine. Beautiful. Attractive. Full face and body.
ה heh	window	♈ Aries	h	5	Feminine. Fiery. Strong. Fierce.
ו vav	nail, hook, pin	♉ Taurus	o, u, w	6	Masculine. Steady. Strong. Heavy. Clumsy.
ז zayin	sword	♊ Gemini	z	7	Masculine. Thin. Intelligent.
ח cheth	fence, enclosure	♋ Cancer	ch	8	Feminine. Full face without expression.
ט teth	serpent	♌ Leo	t	9	Feminine. Strong and Fiery.
י yod	hand	♍ Virgo	y, i, j	10	Feminine. White. Delicate.
כ kaph	fist, palm of hand	♃ Jupiter	k, kh	20	Masculine. Big and strong.
ל lamed	ox goad	♎ Libra	l	30	Feminine. Well-proportioned.
מ mem	water	▽ Water	m	40	Generally hermaphroditic but leaning more toward feminine. Reflective. Dreamlike.
נ nun	fish	♏ Scorpio	n	50	Masculine. Square, determined face. Full. Dark. Sinewy.
ס samekh	prop	♐ Sagittarius	s	60	Masculine. Thin. Expressive face. Active.
ע ayin	eye	♑ Capricorn	aa	70	Masculine. Mechanical.
פ peh	mouth	♂ Mars	p, ph	80	Feminine. Fierce. Strong, full, and resolute.
צ tzaddi	fishhook	♒ Aquarius	tz, ts	90	Feminine. Thoughtful and intellectual.
ק qoph	back of head	♓ Pisces	q	100	Masculine. Full face.
ר resh	head	☉ Sol	r	200	Masculine. Proud and dominant.
ש shin	tooth	△ Fire / ⊛ Spirit	s, sh	300	Generally hermaphroditic but leaning more toward masculine. Fierce and active.
ת tau	cross	♄ Saturn / ▽ Earth	t, th	400	Generally hermaphroditic but leaning more toward feminine. Dark and gray.

From this chart you can determine the telesmatic attributions of each letter of the name Asmodel and build up the figure of the angel thus:

א aleph	crown of head	yellow	Generally hermaphroditic but leaning more toward masculine. Spiritual. Winged. Slender.
ס samekh	face and neck	blue	Masculine. Thin. Expressive face. Active.
מ mem	shoulders and arms	blue	Generally hermaphroditic but leaning more toward feminine. Reflective. Dreamlike.
ו vav	chest and stomach	red-orange	Masculine. Steady. Strong. Heavy. Clumsy.
ד daleth	hips and thighs	green	Feminine. Beautiful. Attractive. Full face and body.
א aleph	legs	yellow	Generally hermaphroditic but leaning more toward masculine. Spiritual. Winged. Slender.
ל lamed	feet	green	Feminine. Well-proportioned.

Each letter is also assigned a color—the main color as listed in the color attributions chart on page 182. These colors would be blended together to get the overall color of the image. This color could be used on the figure's clothing, or as an aura of light that surrounds the being.

The gender of the figure is determined by the predominance of the gender of the letters. When we talk about the gender of an angelic being, we are not talking about sex in human terms. In higher divine beings, gender can be described more in terms of movement and stability. Activity and movement are considered masculine traits. Stability and composure are feminine traits. So when we talk about the sex of a telesmatic image or a Hebrew letter, we are really talking about its gender in terms of energetic forces.

These classifications are merely for our convenience. They are not meant to imply that each letter is strictly male or strictly female. As is the case with each sephirah, each Hebrew letter also has a dual nature containing both feminine and masculine traits. However, each letter has a gender quality that dominates it. In this sense, both genders are seen as equal in strength, although different. They are complements of each other.

Most of the letters that make up the name of Asmodel are masculine or leaning toward masculine, so the telesmatic image of the archangel would portray him as male. Thus, his head would be winged with long, golden hair framing an expressive face. His body would be slender but well-proportioned and very strong. He would wear a red-orange robe. His skin color might be blue or blue-green, or he might simply be surrounded by a bluish halo.

In a traditional telesmatic image, any angel whose name ends in "el" will have golden wings that may partially cover the lower part of the figure. The figure may also have the symbols of justice—the scales of Libra and the sword of justice in green. These implements may be held in the angel's hands or lying at his or her feet.

Also, in many telesmatic images the figure wears a wide belt engraved with the name of the entity in Hebrew letters.

TELESMATIC IMAGES OF GODNAMES

The Qabalah teaches that there are four distinct levels or planes of existence. These are known as the four Qabalistic Worlds. Each world emanates from the one before it, progressively becoming more solid as the divine energy manifests from pure spirit into dense, physical form. These four worlds are *Atziluth, Briah, Yetzirah,* and *Assiah,* and their attributions are given in the following chart:

World	Description	Holy Letter	Element	Contains Sephiroth
Atziluth	Divine, Archetypal	yod '	Fire	Kether
Briah	Archangelic, Creative	heh ה	Water	Chokmah and Binah
Yetzirah	Angelic, Formative	vav ו	Air	All six from Chesed through Yesod
Assiah	Material, Active	heh ה	Earth	Malkuth

In telesmatic magic the highest divine Hebrew godnames are assigned to the world of Atziluth. The names of archangels are assigned to Briah. The lesser angels and groups of angels correspond to Yetzirah. Elementals, lower spirits, and human beings are all attributed to the material world of Assiah.[11]

It would be difficult to apply a telesmatic image to a divine Atziluthic name, for in reality all telesmatic images belong to the world of Yetzirah, the formative world. This is because the magician astrally formulates the image from symbols, creating them from visual correspondences found in the astral world of Yetzirah, the so-called "treasure house of images."

The telesmatic image of a Hebrew godname such as Shaddai El Chai or Adonai ha-Aretz therefore could not really represent that force in the divine world of Atziluth, because such a holy name cannot be accurately portrayed in telesmatic fashion. Instead, any godname constructed in a telesmatic manner would represent the counterpart of that name in Yetzirah. Telesmatic images of the mighty archangels would also portray the Yetziratic image of a Briatic name. However, the magicians of the Golden Dawn, as well as its offshoot orders the Stella Matutina and the Alpha et Omega, certainly did make telesmatic images from the highest godnames and archangels as evidenced by the following description and accompanying drawing:

The name ADONAI will represent the figure from the head to the waist; and HA-ARETZ from the waist to the feet, This is the Divine Name of the Zelator Grade, answering to MALKUTH and the material Universe. ALEPH: winged: white brilliant radiating crown. DALETH: Beautiful Woman's head and neck with a stern and fixed expression. Hair long, dark and very waving. The hair is dark to represent Malkuth, which derives its radiance from the Spiritual force of Kether which

Figure 45: Telesmatic Image of Adonai ha-Aretz from Flying Roll No. XII (dated December 18, 1921).

crowns it. NUN: Arms and hands bare and strong, extended in the form of a cross, holding a golden cup in the left hand and in the right ears of ripe corn bound together. Large, dark and spreading wings. YOD: Deep yellow-green robe, covering the strong chest, on which is a square gold Lamen with a scarlet Greek Cross occupying the centre thereof. This does not quite touch the borders of the Lamen. In the angles are 4 small red Greek Crosses. A broad gold belt surrounds the waist; and thereon is written in scarlet, thus, in the Theban Characters:

৪	৸	๗	٦	⅄	Ʊ	৸ₘ	๗	٦
ץ	T[12]	ר	א	ה	י	נ	ד	א

The feet are shown flesh-colored with golden sandals. Long yellow-green drapery, rayed with olive, reaches down to the feet. Beneath are black and rolling clouds with lurid patches of colour. Around the figure are red flashings of lightning. Sword is girt to the right side of the figure. It is a terrific form which stretches through the Universe, the crown being in Yetzirah and the clouds bordering on the Qlippoth.[13]

Figure 46: Flaming Cross Image of Shaddai El Chai.

However, the magicians of the Golden Dawn also created Atziluthic images of godnames by drawing the letters of the name in the formation of a cross. The name would be written twice—from right to left and from top to bottom. A flaming aura would be drawn around the figure. This cross formation was considered a more accurate representation of the holy power of a godname such as Adonai ha-Aretz or Shaddai El Chai on the level of Atziluth.

Suppose you wanted to create a telesmatic image of the twenty-eighth decanate angel, Saahiah, who is associated with the Nine of Wands. The Hebrew letters of this angel's name are shin, aleph, heh, yod, heh. The letters would form the body of the angel thus:

ש	shin	head	red	Generally hermaphroditic but leaning more toward masculine. Fierce and active.
א	aleph	neck and shoulders	yellow	Generally hermaphroditic but leaning more toward masculine. Spiritual. Winged. Slender.
ה	heh	chest and arms	red	Feminine. Fiery. Strong. Fierce.
י	yod	hips and legs	yellow-green	Feminine. White. Delicate.
ה	heh	feet	red	Feminine. Fiery. Strong. Fierce.

Most of the letters that make up the name of Saahiah are feminine, so the telesmatic image of the archangel would portray her as female, but fierce and strong. She would wear a red robe and might have red skin or be surrounded by a red halo. She would have large golden wings on her shoulders.

In a traditional telesmatic image, any angel whose name ends in "yah" may look like a king or queen sitting on a throne with a brilliant aura around his or her feet.

As with most things, there are exceptions to the rules in creating telesmatic images. One such exception is the great archangel Sandalphon, who is employed as the archangel of spirit passive for the trump card of Judgement (when used for shin's spirit attribution). The letters of Sandalphon's name are samekh, nun, daleth, lamed, peh, vav, nun. These break down as:

ס samekh	crown of head	blue	Masculine. Thin. Expressive face. Active.
נ nun	face and neck	blue-green	Masculine. Square, determined face. Full. Dark. Sinewy.
ד daleth	shoulders and arms	green	Feminine. Beautiful. Attractive. Full face and body.
ל lamed	chest and stomach	green	Feminine. Well-proportioned.
פ peh	hips and thighs	red	Feminine. Fierce. Strong, full, and resolute.
ו vav	legs	red-orange	Masculine. Steady. Strong. Heavy. Clumsy.
נ nun	feet	blue-green	Masculine. Square, determined face. Full. Dark. Sinewy.

The name is predominantly composed of masculine letters. However, Sandalphon is no ordinary name—it is the name of the great feminine kerub of the Tree of Life, and therefore she is almost always envisioned as female. The traditional telesmatic image depicts Sandalphon as having a beautiful, thin, and active face, a full neck, the shoulders of a beautiful woman, a well-proportioned chest, strong and full hips, massive legs, and sinewy winged feet.

In another example, suppose you were working with the tarot trump of the Hanged Man and you wanted to make a telesmatic image of the angel Taliahad. The Hebrew letters of this angel's name are teth, lamed, yod, heh, and daleth. The first letter, teth, will represent the head and the last letter, daleth, will represent the feet with all the middle letters making up the body parts in between:

ט teth	head	yellow	Feminine. Strong and fiery.
ל lamed	neck and shoulders	green	Feminine. Well-proportioned.
י yod	chest and arms	yellow-green	Feminine. White. Delicate.
ה heh	hips and legs	red	Feminine. Fiery. Strong. Fierce.
ד daleth	feet	green	Feminine. Beautiful. Attractive. Full face and body.

All of the letters that make up this name are feminine, therefore in the telesmatic image the angel Taliahad would be female. She would be beautiful and well-proportioned. She might have a golden-yellow halo around her head and be surrounded by a greenish aura.

This image of Taliahad, however, points out some of the limitations of the traditional telesmatic attributions. There simply is not enough information given to form anything other than a very general description of the angel. The Golden Dawn manuscripts state that these attributions are supplied only as a convenient guide—they are not carved in stone. It is for this reason that we have decided to provide readers with our own modified attributions for creating literal telesmatic figures.

A DIFFERENT LIST OF TELESMATIC ATTRIBUTIONS

The following list shows the traditional gender attributions of the Hebrew letters taken from the chart on page 186. Next to this is our own amended list of Hebrew letter gender attributions. Why have we revised the genders of some of the letters? We will explain.

Letter	Traditional (GD) Gender Attribution	Amended (Cicero) Gender Attribution
א aleph	H/M	H/M
ב beth	M	M
ג gimel	F	F
ד daleth	F	F
ה heh	F	F
ו vav	M	M
ז zayin	M	M
ח cheth	F	F
ט teth	F	M
י yod	F	M
כ kaph	M	M
ל lamed	F	F
מ mem	H/F	H/F
נ nun	M	F
ס samekh	M	F
ע ayin	M	M
פ peh	F	M
צ tzaddi	F	F
ק qoph	M	F
ר resh	M	M
ש shin	H/M	H/M
ת tau	H/F	H/F

When developing the list for telesmatic attributions, the Golden Dawn originally divided up the Hebrew letters into two groups, eleven male and eleven female, based on their sound. They postulated that some letters had a prolonged or active sound, while others had an arrested or stable sound. This seems to be particularly true of the twelve simple letters assigned to the zodiacal signs. These twelve letters were divided up into two groups, six male and six female. This classification was based on the sounds of the letters—and whether they were "prolonged" (male) or "arrested" (female).

The Hebrew letters that represent the elements—aleph, mem, shin, and tau—were thought to be gender-neutral or hermaphroditic. But of these, the gender of the element influences the gender of the letter. Therefore aleph-air and shin-fire are more masculine (H/M).[14] Mem-water and tau-earth are more feminine (H/F).[15]

The letters assigned to the planets were described as alternately masculine and feminine. This classification appears to have been derived not so much from the sound of the letters, but primarily from each planet's correspondence to the sephiroth in a descending progression on the Tree of Life.

♄	Saturn	(Binah)	tau	=	feminine
♃	Jupiter	(Chesed)	kaph	=	masculine
♂	Mars	(Geburah)	peh	=	feminine
☉	Sol	(Tiphareth)	resh	=	masculine
♀	Venus	(Netzach)	daleth	=	feminine
☿	Mercury	(Hod)	beth	=	masculine
☽	Luna	(Yesod)	gimel	=	feminine

It appears that no single method was used to produce the traditional gender attributions of the twenty-two letters. The original teachings on telesmatic magic affirm that each letter contains *both* masculine and feminine natures, although one tendency will appear to be dominant.

We decided to change some of the telesmatic gender attributions for our own use, because we felt there were a few problems with the traditional list that created some glaring inconsistencies with other characteristics of the Hebrew letters.

The major problem we had with the traditional telesmatic attribution list was the letter yod being listed as a feminine letter. In the Tetragrammaton, yod is always described as masculine—it represents the paternal element of fire. It is the archetypal "father" letter and a prominent symbol for male energy.

Hebrew has no letters that are considered vowels,[16] although Western magicians use certain Hebrew letters (aleph, vav, ayin, and yod) to stand in for and to be transliterated as vowels. Since vowel sounds are the only letters that can truly be "prolonged" in human speech,[17] it is unclear to us why yod, a vowel stand-in, should be considered "arrested" and "feminine" while a consonant such as qoph should be regarded as "prolonged" and "masculine."

It is possible that the zodiacal attribution of yod (Virgo) was also being considered when the traditional list was composed. The visual telesmatic attribution for the letter yod (feminine, white, and delicate) would seem to suggest an overriding "virginal" quality that took precedence over all other considerations. However, outside of the four letters that directly represent the elements (aleph, mem, shin, and tau), the elemental attributions of the zodiacal signs seem to play no part in the gender attributions of the Hebrew letters. For example, the letter heh is assigned to Aries, a fiery, masculine sign. But heh is a letter that is traditionally associated with the Great Mother, the second letter of Tetragrammaton, and with water. Thus the letter heh is regarded as feminine.

Another problem was the letter peh, the letter of Mars, being described as feminine. Mars is traditionally considered a planet of masculine energy. Changing the gender of the Martial letter from male to female based on an alternating list of secondary sephirotic correspondences simply did not seem justified to us.

Therefore we have changed the genders of six of the twenty-two letters in our amended list. The result is eleven masculine and eleven feminine letters.[18]

Whereas the traditional list is rather sparse in its visual imagery, appearing to rely primarily upon the astrological imagery associated with each letter, the amended list incorporates the root essences and literal meanings of the Hebrew letters, in addition to their astrological imagery, to develop the visual descriptions and symbolism used to create powerful telesmatic images.

We must stress that both lists are valid and effective in the creation of telesmatic images. Some readers will naturally wish to use the traditional Golden Dawn correspondences and gender attributions. Others will not. Since angels will appear in whatever form is needed, it does not ultimately matter from which list you choose. Keep in mind that a telesmatic image is meant to be a *personal* magical creation. Any list of correspondences is meant to be used merely as a guideline. You may find that a particular angel you are working with appears to have a different symbol than the one our list provides. If this is the case, then make the appropriate changes to your image based on what seems right to you.

AMENDED TELESMATIC ATTRIBUTIONS
OF THE HEBREW ALPHABET

א Aleph

Correspondence: △ Air
Gender: Generally hermaphrodite tending toward male (H/M)
Telesmatic Attributions: Spiritual. Energetic, yet serene. Silent. Winged. Slender. Athletic. Having the horns of an ox. Fair hair and eyes. Standing upon clouds. Holds a rose and a fan. Lamen (badge) can be either a spiral, whorl, or the fylfot cross (the swastika—whirling creation of the universe).

ב Beth

Correspondence: ☿ Mercury
Gender: Male
Telesmatic Attributions: Blessed. Parental. Courageous. Intelligent. Quick. Agile. Active. Slender. Fair hair and eyes. Stands upon clouds. Holds the Caduceus Wand of Hermes. Lamen (badge) can be either the caduceus, the triskelion (three-legged fylfot—speed), or an octogram.

ג Gimel

Correspondence: ☽ Luna
Gender: Female
Telesmatic Attributions: Beautiful. Veiled. Mysterious. Kindly. Compassionate. Full face and body. Dark hair and eyes. In motion. Stepping forward. Crowned with the lunar crescent. Stands upon waves of water. Holds bow and arrow. Lamen (badge) can be either a crescent or a lunate cross (equal-armed cross with arms formed by lunar crescents).

ד Daleth

Correspondence: ♀ Venus

Gender: Female

Telesmatic Attributions: Radiant and beautiful. Maternal. Nurturing. Humble. Full face and body. Dark hair and eyes. Standing on water and earth, or in a doorway. Holds a rose, or a scepter topped by a heptagram or a fleur-de-lis. Wears a magic girdle adorned with letters or symbols. Lamen (badge) can be either a vesica, a rosette, a cross patonce, or a heptagram.

ה Heh

Correspondence: ♈ Aries

Gender: Female

Telesmatic Attributions: Vibrant. Fiery and active. Strong and fierce. Contemplative. Ram-like or ram-horned. Red hair and eyes. Standing upon flames. One hand holds either a phoenix wand (*uas*) or the royal orb scepter of dominion, the other holds a royal orb. Lamen (badge) can be either a simplified royal orb (a circle containing a tau and a dot) a cross moline (with four Aries symbols), or a pyramidal cross (descent of divine forces).

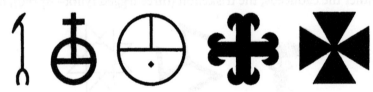

ו Vav

Correspondence: ♉ Taurus

Gender: Male

Telesmatic Attributions: Reconciling. Mediating. Strong and sturdy. Fixed. Heavy-set. Slow-moving. Dark hair and eyes. Bull-like or bull-horned. Wears the *skhenet* crown (unification). Standing tall. Feet on the ground. Hands holding either a crook and a scourge (majesty and balance) or a pastoral staff (bishop's staff). Lamen (badge) can be either a Coptic cross with four nails, or a square heraldic knot (binding).

ז Zayin

Correspondence: ♊ Gemini

Gender: Male

Telesmatic Attributions: Intelligent. Thin. Light hair and eyes. Dualistic. Mercurial. Armored. Wears a crown. Hands holding a sword and a shield. Stands upon clouds. Lamen (badge) can be either the cross fitche (pointed cross), the crux decussata (the x-cross, a barrier), or the flaming sword (lightning bolt).

ח Cheth

Correspondence: ♋ Cancer

Gender: Female

Telesmatic Attributions: Enclosed. Parental. Protective. Vibrant. Full face without expression. Sphinx-like. Dark hair and eyes. Crowned with a laurel wreath. Stands on waves of water. Holds a cup or a wand surmounted by a cube or a triple enclosure (three concentric squares bisected with a cross—the containment and foundation of the triad). Lamen (badge) can be either a scarab or a triple enclosure.

ט Teth

Correspondence: ♌ Leo

Gender: Male

Telesmatic Attributions: Dramatic. Long and serpentine. Lion-like. Fiery and strong. Brilliant and pure. Protective and sheltering. Red hair and eyes. Stands on flames. Holds either a phoenix wand (*uas*) or a staff surmounted by the serpent-entwined orphic egg. Lamen (badge) can be either the orphic egg, a winged cobra (*uraeus*), or a snake biting its own tail (*oroboros*).

' Yod

Correspondence: ♍ Virgo

Gender: Male

Telesmatic Attributions: Empathetic. Humble. Slender. Fair-colored hair and eyes. Extended hands hold a lamp, sheaves of grain, a plain staff, the lotus flower (*sesen*), or lotus wand (the *uadj* or papyrus scepter—youth, virility, and growth). Feet on the ground. May give the Sign of Isis Mourning. Lamen (badge) can be either a stylized hand (such as the *hamsa*) or the cartouche (*ren* or *shenu*—the name amulet).

⊃ Kaph

Correspondence: ♃ Jupiter

Gender: Male

Telesmatic Attributions: Exuberant. Large and expansive. Strong. Humble. Eagle-like. Dark hair and eyes. Wears a crown. One hand is open and extended; the other holds a scepter topped with either a royal orb, a *sekhem* (staff of authority) or a *djed*[19] (stability). Stands upon flames or waves of water. Lamen (badge) is a square, *nefer*[20] (luck and happiness), or a *djed*.

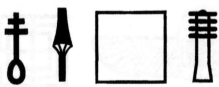

ל Lamed

Correspondence: ♎ Libra

Gender: Female

Telesmatic Attributions: Poised. Graceful. Righteous. Humble. Intelligent. Well-proportioned. Winged. Crowned with a laurel wreath. Fair hair and eyes. Hands holding the scales and the sword of justice, the crook and scourge, or an ox-goad. Stands elevated above clouds. Lamen (badge) can be either the Feather of Maat (justice and truth), a Greek cross (equal-armed cross) or a cross crosslet (arms that end in crosses).

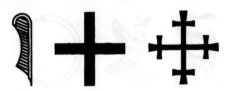

מ Mem

Correspondence: ▽ Water
Gender: Generally hermaphrodite tending toward female (H/F)
Telesmatic Attributions: Watery. Wise. Pure. Dreamlike. Sensitive. Reflective. Loving. Parental. Eagle-like. Dark hair and eyes. Wears the *menat* necklace[21] of generation and fertility. Hands holding a cup, a lotus flower, a lotus wand, or a sistrum.[22] Stands on waves of water. Lamen (badge) can be either an anchor cross (anchor ankh) or a *tet* (Knot of Isis—fertility).

נ Nun

Correspondence: ♏ Scorpio
Gender: Female
Telesmatic Attributions: Transforming. Powerful. Intense. Prophesying. Humble. Full face and body. Square, determined face. Dark hair and eyes. Sinewy. Fish-like or eagle-like. Holds a scythe, a flaming torch crowned with a laurel wreath (life and victory after death), an ankh wand, a jackal-headed wand (*usr*), or a cup. Gives either the Sign of Apophis, or the Sign of Osiris Slain. Stands on water. Lamen (badge) can be either an ankh (eternal life) or the ladder of transmigration (from earth to heaven).

ס Samekh

Correspondence: ♐ Sagittarius
Gender: Female
Telesmatic Attributions: Exalted. Protective. Supportive. Encircling. Active. Thin, expressive face. Red hair and eyes. Horse-like or centaur-like. Hands holding a bow and arrow. Encircled by a flaming glory of light. Stands upon flames. Lamen (badge) can be either the *sema*[23] (union), the strut (support), an arrow cross, or a Maltese cross (swift arrow-like impact of the divine).

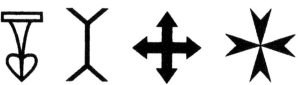

ע Ayin

Correspondence: ♑ Capricorn
Gender: Male
Telesmatic Attributions: Insightful. Watchful. All-seeing. Industrious. Strong. Sturdy. Mechanical. Goat-like or goat-horned. Full face. Dark hair and eyes. Hands holding a flaming torch and a horn of water. Feet on the Earth. Lamen (badge) can be either the *udjat* (Eye of Horus) or the all-seeing eye in the triangle.

פ Peh

Correspondence: ♂ Mars
Gender: Male
Telesmatic Attributions: Communicative. Vocal. Ferocious. Fierce. Strong. Resolute. Full face. Red hair and eyes. Warrior-like. Armored. Wears a helmet or the *khepresh* (Egyptian war crown). Hands holding a flaming sword (lightning bolt). Stands upon flames or on waves of water. Lamen (badge) can be either the *er* (Egyptian symbol for "mouth"), the embattled cross (an armored cross), or the fivefold Jerusalem cross (Crusader cross).

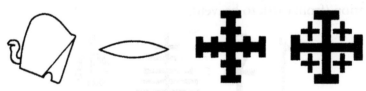

צ Tzaddi

Correspondence: ♒ Aquarius
Gender: Female
Telesmatic Attributions: Righteous. Radiant. Compassionate. Comforting. Intelligent. Thoughtful. Meditative. Wears the *shuti* crown (double-feathered). Thin. Fair hair and eyes. Hands holding two vases, or a censer and a cup (or a*spergillum*: a sprinkler for holy water). Stands upon clouds. Lamen (badge) can be either the crux stellata (star cross), the *shuti* (two feathers of light and air), or the cross of invocation (God's blessing).

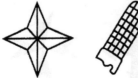

ק Qoph

Correspondence: ♓ Pisces

Gender: Female

Telesmatic Attributions: Transcendent. Sanctifying. Dreamy. Jackal-like. Fish-like. Dolphin-like. Full face. Dark hair and eyes. Eyes may be closed. Holds a jackal-headed scepter (*usr*), a mirror, or a trident. Stands on waves of water. Lamen (badge) can be either an *urs* (head-rest), a mirror, or a trident.

ר Resh

Correspondence: ☉ Sol

Gender: Male

Telesmatic Attributions: Fiery and active, yet balanced. Proud. Authoritative. Commanding. Thoughtful. Illuminating. Life-giving. Healing. Tranquil. Glowing. Well-proportioned. Fair hair and eyes. Stands upon flaming clouds. Holds either a crosier staff (topped by a calvary cross) or an *ur-uatchti* (a wand topped with the winged sun disk). Gives the Sign of Osiris Risen. Lamen (badge) can be either a six-squared cross, a hexagram, a winged sun disk, a rose cross, or the *shen* (a circle on the horizon—solar power).

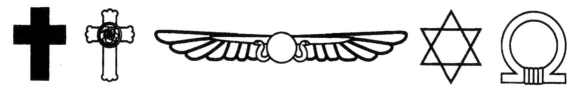

ש Shin

Correspondence: △ Fire

Gender: Generally hermaphrodite tending toward male (H/M)

Telesmatic Attributions: Fierce and active. Penetrating. Initiating. Glowing. Purifying. Flaming. Lion-like or phoenix-like. Red hair and eyes. Winged. Red. Stands upon flames. Hands holding a pyramid or a phoenix wand (*uas*). Lamen (badge) can be either the triangle of flame, the flaming heart, or the eye of fire (a diamond with a cross in the center).

♈ Shin

Correspondence: ✳ Spirit

Gender: Generally hermaphrodite tending toward male (H/M)

Telesmatic Attributions: Joyful. Graceful. Transforming. Illuminating. Gloried. Surrounded by an aura. Penetrating. Pale. White. Dove-like. Winged. Holds an olive branch and a palm frond, or an *ur-uatchti*. Lamen (badge) can be either a pentagram, a triquetra (three linked vesicas), a trefoil (three linked circles—the triad), or a triangle and trefoil united.

♊ Tau

Correspondence: ♄ Saturn

Gender: Generally hermaphrodite tending toward female (H/F)

Telesmatic Attributions: Impressive. Memorable. Features are hidden from view by dark gray swirling clouds and lightning. Hands holding a scythe, a notched palm branch (Egyptian tool for measuring time), a winged hourglass, or a chalice. Feet in the stars. Lamen (badge) can be either a tau cross (a "t" cross), a triple tau, the infinity sign, or the cross of infinity (eternity).

♊ Tau

Correspondence: ▽ Earth

Gender: Generally hermaphrodite tending toward female (H/F)

Telesmatic Attributions: Impressive. Memorable. Having horns. Bull-like. Winged. Massive. Dark hair and eyes. Full face and body. Hands holding sheaves of grain. Feet on the earth. Lamen (badge) can be either a tau cross, a triangle of manifestation, a cross potent (four taus), or a wheel cross.

CREATING TELESMATIC IMAGES
FROM THE AMENDED LIST

Whatever letter is used to represent the chest of the figure also indicates the symbol for the *lamen,* or badge, worn on the chest. The lamen may include one of the symbols given in our list, or it may include the sigil of the figure. More information on sigils is given later in this chapter. Alternatively, the lamen of any angel may simply be the Hebrew letter or astrological symbol associated with its corresponding energy.

You may choose to represent the telesmatic image of a godname as wearing a brilliant crown, whereas an archangel might be represented as wearing a *strophion,* or headband, with a symbol on the brow.

If you intend to draw or paint the figure, the image must be constructed as purely and as beautifully as possible. Remember that these are sacred forces. An impure image means a faulty construction. All angelic figures created in this way should have a human head and natural skin-color.

Which Correspondences to Use?

Our amended list gives the reader much more choice in picking symbolism for the creation of telesmatic images. Choosing the appropriate correspondences from the amended list is not difficult at all—it depends on where the letters fall in the angelic name. For example, if ayin was the first letter in the angel's name, use the correspondences that describe the face and head. In this case, the face would be full with dark hair and eyes. It would have features and attitudes that reflect the sign of Capricorn, which is assigned to this letter. Therefore the face would have an industrious, no-nonsense expression. The symbol given on the list for ayin is the Eye of Horus, which could be attached to the brow of the figure by a headband.

If the letter ayin falls in the middle of a name, it would represent the body of the figure. With the earthy influence of Capricorn, the body would be short, stocky, and strong. In this case, the Eye of Horus would be displayed on a lamen and worn on the chest.

If the letter ayin described the arms of the angel, then the figure would hold a flaming torch and a horn of water.

If ayin was at the end of the name, then it would describe the legs and feet. They would be stocky and muscular, with the feet firmly planted on the earth.

It might be useful to look for other correspondences when analyzing a name. For example, let's say a certain name contained the letters resh and teth. The archangel Metatron—spelled mem, teth, teth, resh, vav, nun—is a perfect example of this. Resh is attributed to the sun and teth corresponds to the sign of Leo, which is ruled by the sun. Therefore we could conclude that there was a strong underlying current of solar energy in the name of Metatron.

Examples of Images from the Amended List

Suppose you wanted to make a telesmatic image of the godname Shaddai El Chai. To create a Yetziratic version of the name, you would follow the same method as before. In this case, the name is formed from two names—*Shaddai* (spelled shin, daleth, yod) and *El Chai* (aleph, lamed, cheth, yod). The word Shaddai would form the upper part of the body and El Chai would form the lower part:

ש shin	head	red	(*Spirit Attribution*)[23] Joyful. Graceful. Transforming, illuminating, gloried, surrounded by an aura. Penetrating. Pale. White. Dove-like. Winged. Holds an olive branch and a palm frond, or an *ur-uatchti*. Lamen (badge) can be either a pentagram, a triquetra (three linked vesicas), a trefoil (three linked circles—the triad), or a triangle and trefoil united.
ד daleth	neck and shoulders	green	Radiant and beautiful. Maternal. Nurturing. Humble. Full face and body. Dark hair and eyes. Standing on water and earth, or in a doorway. Holds a rose, or a scepter topped by a heptagram or a fleur-de-lis. Wears a magic girdle adorned with letters or symbols. Lamen (badge) can be either a vesica, a rosette, a cross patonce, or a heptagram.
י yod	chest	yellow-green	Empathetic. Humble. Slender. Fair-colored hair and eyes. Extended hands hold a lamp, sheaves of grain, a plain staff, the lotus flower (*sesen*), or lotus wand (the *uadj* or papyrus scepter—youth, virility, and growth). Feet on the ground. May give the Sign of Isis Mourning. Lamen (badge) can be either a stylized hand (such as the *hamsa*) or the cartouche (*ren* or *shenu*—the name amulet).
א aleph	arms	yellow	Spiritual. Energetic, yet serene. Silent. Winged. Slender. Athletic. Having the horns of an ox. Fair hair and eyes. Standing on clouds. Holds a rose and a fan. Lamen (badge) can be either a spiral, a whorl, or a fylfot cross (the swastika—whirling creation of the universe).
ל lamed	hips and thighs	green	Poised. Graceful. Righteous. Humble. Intelligent. Well-proportioned. Winged. Crowned with a laurel wreath. Fair hair and eyes. Hands holding the scales and the sword of justice, the crook and scourge, or an ox-goad. Stands elevated above clouds. Lamen (badge) can be either the Feather of Maat (justice and truth), a Greek cross (equal-armed cross), or a cross crosslet (arms that end in crosses).
ח cheth	legs	yellow-orange	Enclosed. Parental. Protective. Vibrant. Full face without expression. Sphinx-like. Dark hair and eyes. Crowned with a laurel wreath. Stands on waves of water. Holds a cup or a wand surmounted by a cube or a triple enclosure (three concentric squares bisected with a cross—the containment and foundation of the triad). Lamen can be either a scarab or a triple enclosure.
י yod	feet	yellow-green	Empathetic. Humble. Slender. Fair-colored hair and eyes. Extended hands hold a lamp, sheaves of grain, a plain staff, the lotus flower (*sesen*), or lotus wand (the *uadj* or papyrus scepter—youth, virility, and growth). Feet on the ground. May give the Sign of Isis Mourning. Lamen can be either a stylized hand (such as the *hamsa*) or the cartouche (*ren* or *shenu*—the name amulet).

Your Yetziratic image of Shaddai El Chai could look like this: the figure would have a white winged crown upon which is a triangle and trefoil united. The figure itself would be hermaphroditic with a slight masculine leaning, and light hair and eyes. The face would be peaceful but active. The neck and shoulders would be graceful and well-formed. The chest would be slender. The lamen would be a stylized hand. One hand would hold a rose, the

Figure 47: Literal Telesmatic Image of Shaddai El Chai.

other a fan. The figure might be dressed in a yellow-green robe, while a golden winged belt could surround the waist—on it could be the name Shaddai El Chai written in violet letters. A sword might hang from the belt. The lower part of the body would be well-proportioned. The feet would stand upon the ground. The figure might be surrounded by a yellow-green aura, the synthesis of all the corresponding colors.

Suppose you wanted to create a telesmatic image of Shelachel, the intelligence of Luna associated with the trump card of the High Priestess. The Hebrew letters of this angel's name are shin, lamed, cheth, aleph, lamed. The letters would form the body of the angel thus:

ש shin	head and neck	red	(*Spirit Attribution*) Joyful. Graceful. Transforming, illuminating, gloried, surrounded by an aura. Penetrating. Pale. White. Dove-like. Winged. Holds an olive branch and a palm frond, or an *ur-uatchti*. Lamen (badge) can be either a pentagram, a triquetra (three linked vesicas), a trefoil (three linked circles—the triad), or a triangle and trefoil united.
ל lamed	shoulders and chest	green	Poised. Graceful. Righteous. Humble. Intelligent. Well-proportioned. Winged. Crowned with a laurel wreath. Fair hair and eyes. Hands holding the scales and the sword of justice, the crook and scourge, or an ox-goad. Stands elevated above clouds. Lamen (badge) can be either the Feather of Maat (justice and truth), a Greek cross (equal-armed cross), or a cross crosslet (arms that end in crosses).
ח cheth	arms and torso	yellow-orange	Enclosed. Parental. Protective. Vibrant. Full face without expression. Sphinx-like. Dark hair and eyes. Crowned with a laurel wreath. Stands on waves of water. Holds a cup or a wand surmounted by a cube or a triple enclosure (three concentric squares bisected with a cross—the containment and foundation of the triad). Lamen can be either a scarab or a triple enclosure.
א aleph	hips and legs	yellow	Spiritual. Energetic, yet serene. Silent. Winged. Slender. Athletic. Having the horns of an ox. Fair hair and eyes. Standing upon clouds. Holds a rose and a fan. Lamen (badge) can be either a spiral, a whorl, or a fylfot cross (the swastika—whirling creation of the universe).
ל lamed	feet	green	Poised. Graceful. Righteous. Humble. Intelligent. Well-proportioned. Winged. Crowned with a laurel wreath. Fair hair and eyes. Hands holding the scales and the sword of justice, the crook and scourge, or an ox-goad. Stands elevated above clouds. Lamen (badge) can be either the Feather of Maat (justice and truth), a Greek cross (equal-armed cross), or a cross crosslet (arms that end in crosses).

Figure 48: Literal Telesmatic Image of Shelachel.

There is a majority of feminine letters in the name, so the telesmatic image of Shelachel would portray her as female. She has a pale complexion and a graceful, gloried face framed by white wings that emerge from the sides of her head. She wears a strophion ornamented with the symbol of the pentagram. She is poised and well-proportioned. From her shoulders emerge large wings which partially cover the lower part of her body. She holds a scepter surmounted by a cube. Her lamen is the Feather of Maat. She wears a wide belt engraved with her name in Hebrew or Theban letters.[25] Her legs and feet are also winged and she stands elevated above the clouds. The scales and sword of justice are at her feet, and she wears a robe of pale yellow-green ornamented in pale red–violet.

Since you know that Shelachel is the intelligence of Luna, you could opt to add other symbols that would be appropriate for her. The crescent moon could be added to the top of her scepter, showing that the moon is over the cube of the earth. You could add blue tones (gimel), or silver—a traditional Luna color.

For another example, let's presume that you wanted to create a tarot talisman for protection, and your choice is the Seven of Wands. In this case you might want to work with Mahashiah, a decanate angel associated with this card. The name of Mahashiah is composed of the Hebrew letters mem, heh, shin, yod, and heh. If we place the letters in a vertical line, we can form the image of the angel:

Figure 49: Literal Telesmatic Image of Mahashiah.

Using our correspondences, the figure would look like a beautiful female warrior of slender build. Her face displays sensitivity, parental love, and wisdom. She has dark brown hair and eyes. Upon her brow she wears a strophion upon which is the symbol of the *tet* (the Knot of Isis) in blue. She is strong, fiery, and active. She wears red armor and chainmail. Upon her chest is a golden lamen of a pyramidal cross. In each hand she holds a red pyramid of flame. Her name in Hebrew is engraved upon a wide green belt. She has fiery red wings, and her wrists are also winged. She is seated upon a throne like a queen. A flaming glory is at her feet. The figure is surrounded by a red-violet light—the synthesis of all her colors combined.

It is also possible to create telesmatic images out of words which can be used to represent archetypal forces. For example, let's say that you had a strong affiliation with Egyptian magic and wanted to create a magical image out of the word *Egypt*. Such a figure might be considered an archangelic guardian of the Egyptian current of energy. The English letters of the word Egypt could be transliterated into the Hebrew letters aleph, gimel, yod, peh, and tau.

The telesmatic image of the name Egypt would appear male, since the majority of letters are male. The head of this angelic figure would be winged with fair hair and eyes. It would also wear the lunar horned headdress surrounding a disk containing the image of a spiral. The figure would have an attractive full body, and upon his chest is the lamen of the lunate

Figure 50: Literal Telesmatic Image of Egypt.

cross. In one hand he holds a lotus wand. The lower part of his body is strong and muscular, covered with a red linen kilt. The feet stand upon a vast field of stars. The entire figure is surrounded by a blue-violet aura, tinged yellow around the edges.

ELEMENTAL IMAGES

There are times when you may want to create an elemental form out of an angelic name. This elemental being would represent a synthesis of the elemental powers of the name corresponding to the world of Assiah. It would be a synthetic kerub or protective sphinx. The figure might well have the head of an animal. Its skin could be any color as indicated by its correspondences. For example, an elemental image created from the name of the great archangel Sandalphon has been described as consisting of:

ס samekh	blue	♐ Head fierce but rather beautiful
נ nun	blue-green	♏ Neck with eagle's wings from behind
ד daleth	green	♀ Shoulders feminine, rather beautiful
ל lamed	green	♎ Chest of a woman
פ peh	red	♂ Strong and shaggy hips and thighs
ו vav	red-orange	♉ Legs of a bull
נ nun	blue-green	♏ Feet of an eagle

This kerubic figure may be represented with its feet on the earth and its head in the clouds. The colors would synthesize a delicate and sparkling green.

> The uncovered parts of the body would be blue, the countenance belonging to Sagittarius would almost be that of a horse. The whole form would almost be that of a goddess between Athor and Neith holding a bow and arrows, that is if represented as an Egyptian symbol.[26]

In another example of a kerubic image, the elemental form of the name Mahashiah would look like this:

מ mem	blue	▽ Head of an eagle
ה heh	red	♈ Neck and shoulders shaggy
ש shin	red	△ Chest of a woman. Winged.
י yod	yellow-green	♍ Hips and legs are slender
ה heh	red	♈ Feet of a ram

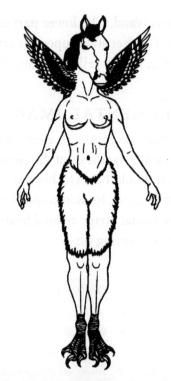

Figure 51: Elemental Image of Sandalphon.

Figure 52: Elemental Image of Mahashiah.

The result is a figure with the head of an eagle surrounded by a blue halo. The neck and shoulders are shaggy like that of a ram. There is a majority of feminine letters, so the figure will have the chest of a woman. Fiery red wings emerge from the shoulders and wrists. The legs are slender and athletic and the feet end in the hooves of a ram. The skin color is red. The figure is surrounded by a bright red-violet aura, a synthesis of all the colors.

Creating telesmatic images is an effective method for connecting with the godnames and angels of the tarot. But it is not the only method that may be used. You can also invoke these forces by drawing their sigils.

SIGILS

A sigil is a magical symbol that contains the essence of a godname, angel, or spirit. It is the magical signature, mark, or "calling card" of a spiritual entity. Hundreds of examples of sigils can be found in medieval magical texts known as grimoires. Drawing a sigil enables the magician to focus on a specific spiritual entity he or she wishes to invoke. A traditional sigil is made by determining the letters in a name and transliterating them into Hebrew. A sigil can also be created from the magician's own name or sacramental motto to represent his or her own magical "mark."

Magical Squares

The *qameoth*, or magical squares, are an important tool used to create sigils and talismans. These are a series of diagrams associated with the planets, consisting of grids filled with numbers or Hebrew letters[27] (see figure 53). If you wanted to draw a sigil for Anael, the archangel of Venus, you might want to use the sigil of this name created from the Venus square. If you wanted to invoke Iophiel, the intelligence of Jupiter, you could use the sigil of Iophiel created from the Jupiter square. Sigils of all the planetary angels and archangels can be drawn from their respective qamea.

The qameoth are assigned to the planets in accordance with their sephirotic numbers (Saturn = 3 Binah; Jupiter = 4 Chesed; Mars = 5 Geburah; Sol = 6 Tiphareth; Venus = 7 Netzach; Mercury = 8 Hod; and Luna = 9 Yesod).[28] The system is sephirotic as well as planetary, and therefore the godnames, angels, and archangels of the ten sephiroth could also be created from their respective magical square.

Two additional magical squares can be used as well. The first is the qamea of Malkuth and the elements, which can be used to create elemental sigils, such as the sigil of Chassan, the angel of air. The second is the qamea of haMazzaloth (associated with Chokmah) which can be used to create sigils for zodiacal angels—such as Zuriel and Chadaqiel, the archangel and angel of Libra[29] (see figure 54).

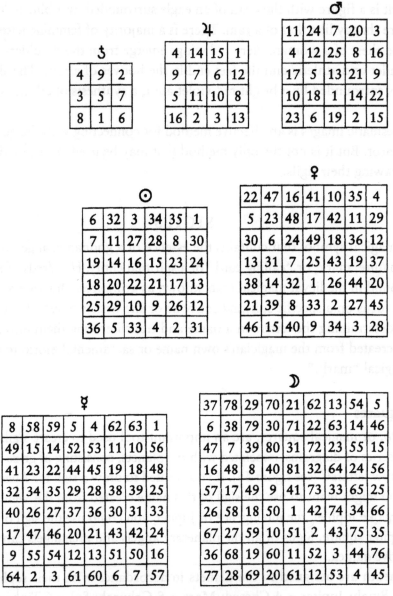

Figure 53: The Qameoth, or Magical Squares.

10	92	8	94	5	96	97	3	99	1
11	19	83	17	85	86	14	88	12	90
71	22	28	74	26	25	77	23	79	80
40	62	33	37	65	66	34	68	69	31
51	49	53	44	46	45	57	58	42	60
41	59	48	54	56	55	47	43	52	50
70	39	63	67	35	36	64	38	32	61
30	72	78	24	76	75	27	73	29	21
81	89	13	87	16	15	84	18	82	20
100	2	98	7	95	6	4	93	9	91

12	134	135	9	8	138	139	5	4	142	143	1
121	23	22	124	125	19	18	128	129	15	14	132
109	35	34	112	113	31	30	116	117	27	26	120
48	98	99	45	44	102	103	41	40	106	107	37
60	86	87	57	56	90	91	53	52	94	95	49
73	71	70	76	77	67	66	80	81	63	62	84
61	83	82	64	65	79	78	68	69	75	74	72
96	50	51	93	92	54	55	89	88	58	59	85
108	38	39	105	104	42	43	101	100	46	47	97
25	119	118	28	29	115	114	32	33	111	110	36
13	131	130	16	17	127	126	20	21	123	122	24
144	2	3	141	140	6	7	137	136	10	11	133

Figure 54: The Qamea of Malkuth and the Elements (top) and the Qamea of haMazzaloth (bottom).

300	30	3	200	20	2	100	10	1
ש	ל	ג	ר	כ	ב	ק	י	א
600	60	6	500	50	5	400	40	4
ם	ס	ו	ך	נ	ה	ת	מ	ד
900	90	9	800	80	8	700	70	7
ץ	צ	ט	ף	פ	ח	ן	ע	ז

Figure 55: Aiq Beker or the Qabalah of Nine Chambers.

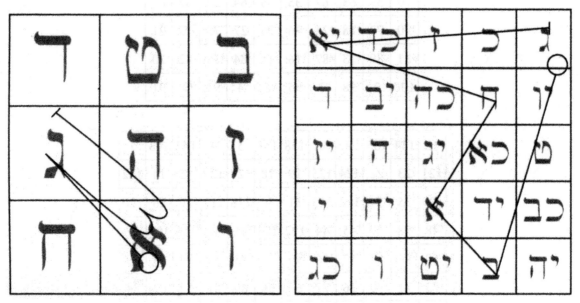

Figure 56: Sigil of Agiel on the Saturn Square (left); Sigil of Graphiel on the Mars Square (right).

In order to trace the sigil of an angel or spirit name on a qamea, it is important to first reduce the name to the lowest possible numerical value that will fit on a given qamea. This is done by referring to the *Aiq Beker* diagram, also called the Qabalah of Nine Chambers. This is a diagram that shows three rows and three columns (a total of nine chambers) of numbers that are grouped together according to their similarity (see figure 55). For example, in one chamber, gimel, lamed, and shin are placed together because of their numbers 3, 30, and 300. The numbers in this diagram, from 1 to 900, are read from right to left, in the same manner that Hebrew is read. The name Aiq Beker comes from reading the Hebrew letters in the first two chambers from 1 to 200: aleph, yod, qoph, and beth, kaph, resh.

If one wanted to trace the sigil of Agiel, the intelligence of Saturn, on the magical square of Saturn, the numerical value of each Hebrew letter of the name would have to be reduced to nine or less than nine (since nine is the highest number on the Saturn square). The letters in the name are aleph א = 1, gimel ג = 3, yod י = 10, aleph א = 1, and lamed ל = 30. The only letters that need to be reduced in this case are yod and lamed, which can be reduced to 1 and 3 respectively, using the Aiq Beker chart. The numbers obtained can be used to trace the sigil on the square—1, 3, 1, 1, 3. The Saturn square is one of the simplest of the useable qameoth, containing only nine cells. Other qameoth, such as the Mars square, are more complex, and some even contain cells of two-digit numbers such as aleph and yod (with a total numeric value of 11). Figure 56 shows sigils on two magical squares that have the Hebrew letter equivalents of the numbers.

Using the Aiq Beker diagram and the magical squares to create angelic sigils can be a complex method for some. A far simpler way to create sigils is to use the diagram of the Rose of Twenty-two Petals.

The Rose of Twenty-two Petals

The diagram of the Rose of Twenty-two Petals shows the twenty-two letters of the Hebrew alphabet arranged in the shape of a rose[30] (see figure 57). The three inner petals of the rose are assigned to the three mother letters: aleph, mem, and shin. The second ring of petals is composed of the seven double letters, assigned to the seven ancient planets. The third or outer ring of petals is composed of twelve petals that refer to the twelve simple letters and the twelve signs of the zodiac.

The Rose of Twenty-two Petals provides a simple yet ingenious system for creating sephirotic, planetary, and elemental sigils to be used in ceremonial workings. Sigils are created simply by tracing them on the Rose from letter to letter. Through this method an entirely new set of sigils can be drawn, vastly different from medieval sigils created from the traditional magical squares. Also, sigils created from the rose may be of more practical value than those made from

Figure 57: The Rose of Twenty-two Petals.

the qameoth, because there is no need to refer to a system of mathematical reduction such as Aiq Beker. Another advantage is that the Rose of Twenty-two Petals is a universal symbol—it is one diagram as opposed to the system of the qameoth, which depends upon several separate diagrams. You can also trace your own name or magical motto on the rose to create a personal sigil or symbol.

TRACING A SIGIL

When tracing a sigil on a either a qamea or the Rose of Twenty-two Petals, the first number or letter of the name is marked with a small circle. From there a line is drawn following the progression of the numbers or letters. When the final number or letter of the name is reached, a short line is drawn to indicate the completion of the sigil.

Variations in tracing sigils: If two letters of the same kind, such as two beths or two gimels are side by side within a name, this is represented in the sigil by a wave or crook in the line at that point. If there is a letter in the name that the line of the sigil passes straight through to meet another letter, a loop or noose is formed at that point to indicate that the letter is indeed a part of the name (figure 58 shows variations in sigils drawn on the qamea of the sun[31]).

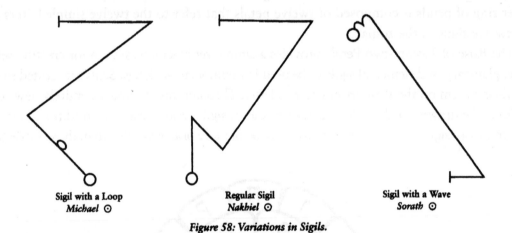

Sigil with a Loop
Michael ☉

Regular Sigil
Nakhiel ☉

Sigil with a Wave
Sorath ☉

Figure 58: Variations in Sigils.

Other Methods for Creating Sigils

Two other ways of creating sigils are explained by Agrippa in his monumental work *Three Books of Occult Philosophy*.[32] The first method relies upon the Aiq Beker diagram or the Qabalah of Nine Chambers seen in figure 55. The "nine chambers" of that diagram look much like the line divisions in a game of tic-tac-toe. The intersections of the four lines can be dissected into nine parts, resulting in the following nine figures that are used to symbolize the various Hebrew letters contained within the "chambers."

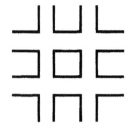

Figure 59: The Nine "Chambers" separated.

To indicate a particular Hebrew letter in the chamber, you would use a series of dots above the figure—one dot indicates the first letter of that chamber, two dots would denote the second letter, and three dots would indicate the third letter. Following this description, the name of the archangel Michael would yield the following five figures:

Figure 60: The "Chambers" of Michael.

These five figures are then combined down to three:

Figure 61: The "Chambers" of Michael combined.

The three final figures are then joined together and the dots are omitted, resulting in a single figure which can be placed within a circle and used as a sigil of Michael:

Figure 62: Final Sigil of Michael.

The other method mentioned by Agrippa for creating sigils is simply to combine the letters of a name into a single symbol. This can be done in any language you wish. The three sigils in figure 63 were all created from the name of Michael in Hebrew, Greek, and Latin, respectively.

Figure 63: Combined Letter Sigils of Michael.

VIBRATION

Visualized images and words of power are essential to the practice of ritual magic. "By names and images are all powers awakened and re-awakened."[33] The magician uses the *vibration* of sacred names that are connected to the divine forces they represent to empower both the word and the image. Talismans, telesmatic images, and sigils can all be charged or consecrated by means of vibration. Magicians have been using these divine names and linking their personal energy to them through centuries of living ritual work. We've already discussed how to create magical images of divine and angelic powers associated with the cards of the tarot. But it is also important to learn how to "vibrate" godnames and angelic names.

Divine names are not simply spoken in ritual. They are intoned or vibrated. Scientists have only recently become aware of what magicians have known for centuries —that all matter is vibratory energy. There is a physical phenomenon known as *harmonic resonance* which means that if one object starts to vibrate strongly enough, another object nearby will begin to resonate with the first, if both objects share the same natural vibratory rate.

The magician vibrates a godname in order to create a harmonic resonance between the deity *within* and the deity *without*—between the divine as it exists within him- or herself, and the divine as it exists out in the greater universe.

Words and names of power are also tools that the magician can use to focus the mind on the desired forces. Certain words or names of power, when properly vibrated or intoned, attract the energies that are associated with them. A technique known as the *vibratory formula* is a method by which divine names and words are spoken forcefully and with authority in a "vibration."

To vibrate a godname or angelic name takes practice. The basic method is this: intone the name slowly in a single note until you notice a strong vibration in the chest cavity, and even the entire body. Lower tones are generally better than higher ones. You may feel a tingling sensation in the face and afterward you may experience a slight sense of fatigue combined with exhilaration.

There are two more advanced methods of vibration known to adept magicians as the *Invoking Whirl* and the *Expanding Whirl*.[34] These should only be done when you have become fully skilled in the basic techniques of ritual magic.

The Invoking Whirl centers on the heart, which answers to the sephirah of Tiphareth. First, you should concentrate on the divine white brilliance of Kether above your head, all the while keeping your mind focused on the first sphere of highest aspiration. Next, imagine your consciousness in your heart center, bringing down the white brilliance from Kether to the sixth sephirah of Tiphareth. The letters of the divine or angelic name to be vibrated should then be imagined in white letters within your heart center. Pronounce the name slowly so that the sound vibrates throughout your entire body. One rule of thumb is to vibrate the name as many times as there are letters in it. If a name has seven letters, vibrate it seven times. You should imagine that the sound of your vibration reaches into every corner of the universe.

The Expanding Whirl of vibration is centered in the aura, rather than the heart. This method may be more useful for charging telesmatic images. To do this, visualize the brilliance of Kether, as before. Then imagine the image standing before you, or you may also have it drawn on a piece of paper. Next, visualize the Hebrew letters of the name in a brilliant cross of light in the air directly in front of you. Vibrate the letters of the name and imagine a brilliant flashing light around them. Visualize the telesmatic image of the form you have created absorbing the energy of the white brilliance. As you do this, vibrate the name of the figure. Vibrate it as many times as there are letters in the name. See the image growing larger until it fills the universe. Finally, draw the figure around you and absorb the white rays of the image, until you feel your aura radiating with its brilliance.

TESTING TOKENS

Any time you work with divine beings, there is a possibility that you may receive a spirit vision or angelic communication. There are certain symbols that you can use to help ensure the veracity of any visions you might receive during ritual work with angels. This is important, since you would not want your vision or angelic communication to be influenced by tricks of your own memory or imagination. The Hebrew letters of the seven planets can be used as important test symbols by tracing them in front of the angel as you vibrate the appropriate godname. Imagine these letters or planetary symbols in brilliant white light.

1. If you suspect that some image from your memory is influencing your vision, trace the symbol of Saturn or the letter tau ת. (Tau is the letter of Saturn, the planet that governs memory.)

2. If you think that you have constructed the scene in your imagination, rather than receiving a true astral image, trace the symbol of Jupiter or the letter kaph כ. (Kaph is the letter of Jupiter, the planet of construction.)

3. To vanquish feelings of revenge, anger, or hatred, use the symbol of Mars or peh פ, the letter of Mars.

4. To rid yourself of delusions of arrogance and inflated ego, use the symbol of Sol or resh ר, the letter of the sun.

5. If your vision lapses into a pleasure-seeking fantasy or intellectual vanity, use the Venus symbol or daleth ד, the letter of Venus.

6. If you suspect that what you are looking at is a deception or a falsehood, use the symbol of Mercury or beth ב, the letter of Mercury.

7. For wandering thoughts, use gimel ג, the letter of the moon.

If the angel disappears or your vision changes after tracing any of these symbols, banish with a pentagram or hexagram and start over with the vision to see if a different scene or being appears. Divine powers, archangels, and angels will not mind being tested.

---

1 Forrest, "This Holy Invisible Companionship," 188.

2 A term developed by William Stoltz. See *The Middle Pillar: The Balance Between Mind and Magic*, by Israel Regardie, edited by Chic Cicero and Sandra Tabatha Cicero (St. Paul, MN: Llewellyn Publications, 1998), 129–130.

3 Agrippa, *Three Books of Occult Philosophy*, 562. (Italics are the authors'.)

4 *The Book of Revelations*, 10:1.

5 Malcolm Godwin, *Angels, an Endangered Species*, 39.

6 The Book of Tobit 5:4–5, *The New American Bible*, St. Joseph Edition (New York: Catholic Book Publishing Co., 1970), 475.

7 The colors in this chart are often referred to as the colors of the *minutum mundum* or "small universe." This refers to the Golden Dawn's Tree of Life diagram (which most magicians use) wherein the ten sephiroth are in what is described as the "Queen Scale" of color and the twenty-two connecting paths symbolized by the Hebrew letters are in the "King Scale" of color.

8 Sometimes with a touch of gray.

9 The right-hand Pillar of Mercy with Chokmah (Yah) at its summit is masculine. The left-hand Pillar of Severity with Binah (YHVH Elohim) at its summit is feminine.

   Qabalists believe that even evil spirits cannot exist without divine permission from God. Therefore you will often find that evil spirits or qlippothic demons have the suffix "el" joined to their names. The suffix "yah" is only added to angelic names, never demonic ones. This is because the suffix "el" at the end of a name always represents severity and judgment, while "yah" always indicates mercy and generosity.

10 Five of the Hebrew letters have final forms which are used whenever the letter occurs at the end of a word or name. These also have additional numerical values. The final forms and their numerical values are: kaph ך 500, mem ם 600, nun ן 700, peh ף 800, and tzaddi ץ 900.

11 The qlippoth are unbalanced evil spirits belonging to the world of Assiah. We absolutely do not recommend making telesmatic images of any qlippothic name.

12 There is no "Tz" in Theban, so "T" and "S" are used in the transliteration.

13 From a paper entitled "Flying Roll No. XII: On Angelic Telesmatic Images & Vibratory Mode of Pronouncing Divine Names: The Particular Mode of Pronouncing the Divine Name Adonai ha-Aretz, the Particular Telesmatic Image allotted thereunto." Delivered by the Chief Adept G.H. D.D.C.F. to the College of Adepts in London. May 27, 1893. From the private archives of the H.O.G.D.

14 Hermaphroditic, tending toward male.

15 Hermaphroditic, tending toward female.

16 In Hebrew, vowels are indicated by marks or points called *dageshes*.

17 A vowel sound is created by the relatively *free passage* of breath through the larynx and oral cavity, usually forming the most primary sound of a syllable, while a consonant sound is produced by a partial or complete *obstruction* of the air stream by the constrictive action of the tongue, teeth, or throat.

18 Incidentally, in our amended list, the name of the great archangel Sandalphon has a predominance of feminine letters in her name.

19 The *djed* was a symbol of the backbone of Osiris.

20 The *nefer* symbolized a lute or some kind of stringed instrument. It was a symbol of good luck, joy, and strength.

21 The *menat* was heavy beaded necklace with a crescent-shaped front and a counter piece at the rear worn by deities and humans. It was a symbol of joy, life, potency, fertility, and birth.

22 The sistrum was a sacred percussion instrument consisting of a wooden or metal frame fitted with loose strips of metal and disks. The jingling sound it produced when shaken was thought to attract the attention of the gods.

23 The *sema* symbolized the trachea and lungs and was a symbol of unification.

24 Since this is an image of a divine Hebrew godname, we will use the letter shin to represent the element of spirit rather than fire.

25 The Theban alphabet can be found in the appendix.

26 Regardie, *The Golden Dawn*, 489.

27 The traditional magical squares have come down to us through the writings of magicians such as Trithemius and Agrippa, but they are derived from much earlier and unknown sources.

28 The qamea of Kether contains only one "cell" and number.

29 The qameoth of Malkuth and haMazzaloth were first published by Adam P. Forrest in "Mysteria Geomantica: Teachings on the Art of Geomancy," *The Golden Dawn Journal: Book I, Divination* (St. Paul, MN: Llewellyn Publications, 1994), 198.

30 The Rose of Twenty-two Petals is a diagram that was created by the Golden Dawn as an emblem of the Rosicrucian impulse behind the Order. This diagram was a portion of a larger symbol known as the rose cross lamen, which was used for various purposes, including the construction of sigils and talismans employed in practical magic.

31 Sorath is the spirit of the sun.

32 Agrippa, *Three Books of Occult Philosophy*, 561–562.

33 From the Neophyte Ceremony of the Golden Dawn. See Regardie, *The Golden Dawn*, 118.

34 The Golden Dawn recommends that the LBRP and the Rose Cross Ritual precede both methods of vibration.

7
TAROT TALISMAN RITUALS
AND MAGICAL IMAGES

At this point you have been given all the tools you need to understand how the various cards of the tarot can be used as tarot talismans. The next step is to make use of all the information supplied thus far—to choose your tarot talismans, set up ritual card spreads, invoke the divine and angelic powers of your selected cards, create magical images and sigils, and ritually charge your cards. Here we will provide numerous examples that you can draw upon to construct your own ritual spreads and consecration rites.

TO OBTAIN MORE TIME TO FINISH A PROJECT

The Golden Dawn Magical Tarot will be used to illustrate this spread. The tarot talisman card is planetary in nature and will therefore need to be invoked by a hexagram.

Card 1: For the significator, choose your own self-image card. Here we will choose the Magician card as an affirmation of the reader's confidence and skill in his own magical abilities.

Card 2: For the card of initial action, we choose the Two of Wands. This card is attributed to the decanate of Mars in Aries, associated with power, control, dominion, great energy, and rapid movement.

Card 3: For the card of progression, we will choose the Three of Pentacles. This card is attributed to the decanate of Mars in Capricorn, associated with hard work as well as taking pride in one's work. It is a card of industriousness and productivity.

Card 4: For the tarot talisman, we will choose the Universe, the last of the trump cards—attributed to Saturn, earth, time, and completion. This card denotes the objective of the ritual: to have more time allotted for the completion of a project.

The Ritual

Prepare your ritual space and include any items that might help you focus on your objective. Although the Universe card is attributed to both the planet Saturn and the element of earth, here we will concentrate on the correspondence of Saturn, since Saturn is the ruler of time. You might want to adorn your altar with supplemental items that will reflect this: for gemstones choose star sapphire, onyx, or pearl. For incense use civet, myrrh, or cinnamon. A blue-violet candle, symbolic of Saturn, can be added to your altar—you can carve the symbol of Saturn into the candle before dressing it with an appropriate essential oil. Include any items that will symbolize time such as a clock, a watch, a calendar, or an hourglass.

Prepare telesmatic images of the godname and angelic forces associated with the talisman card. These can be drawn or painted images, or merely written descriptions of the figures that you can visualize during the ceremony. Use an Atziluthic image for the godname of YHVH Elohim—a flaming cross of Hebrew letters of the type described in the previous chapter. Create Yetziratic or humanlike images of the archangel Kassiel and the intelligence Agiel. You may also wish to incorporate sigils in your magical images. For the purpose of this example, we will use a general telesmatic image of Kassiel and a literal telesmatic image of Agiel.

Begin with the opening ceremony.

Invoke the highest aspect of deity.

Lay out the cards in order and proceed with the work of visualization.

As the significator is placed on the altar, visualize yourself standing in your magical regalia, ready to bring all of your natural talents and magical abilities to bear in order to complete your project.

Lay down the initial action card of the Two of Wands. Visualize the hand in the card as your own hand—you grasp the two fire wands with authority and command. Imagine yourself taking firm, hands-on control of the project from this point forward. It is *your will* to have more time to complete your project.

Lay down the progression card of the Three of Pentacles. Visualize yourself using your new-found control as inspiration to get down to work. Picture yourself invigorated and enthusiastic about your project, scheduling your work time to get the job done efficiently. See yourself meeting with others who will help you and who are just as excited as you are to bring this project to fruition.

In the center of the spread, lay down the tarot talisman card—the Universe. Trace a circle clockwise over the talisman card.

Trace the Invoking Hexagram of Saturn over the card by starting at the point of Saturn on the upright triangle, going clockwise. Then start at the opposite point on the inverted triangle and trace clockwise (see figure 65).

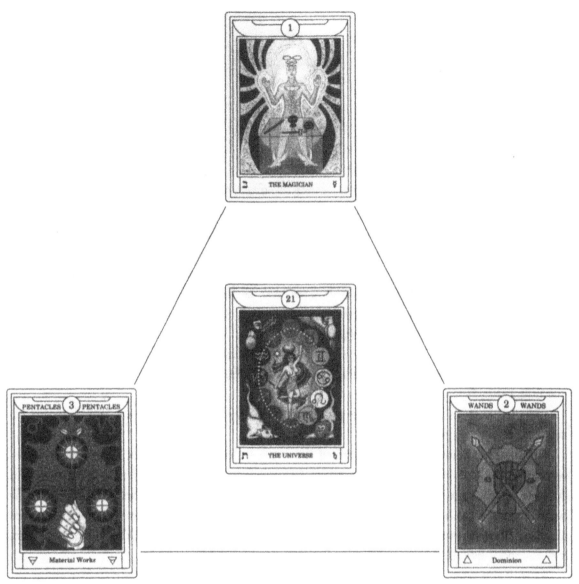

Figure 64: Sample Spread Invoking Time.

You have the option of tracing the hexagram in silence or you can vibrate traditional words of power associated with it. As you draw the two triangles that make up the hexagram, intone the name of unity **"Ararita"** (*ah-ra-ree-tah*). Next, intone the Hebrew godnames associated with the Saturn hexagram—**"YHVH Elohim"** (*yod heh vav heh el-oh-heem*) as you draw the symbol of Saturn in the center. Then say:

"I invoke the powers and forces governing the nature, place, and authority of the planet Saturn by the majesty of the divine name YHVH Elohim. I invoke the archangel of Saturn,

Figure 65: Invoking Hexagram of Saturn.

great Kassiel, who is called the 'speed of God!' Mighty Kassiel, who shows forth the unity of the eternal kingdom, I ask you to bless this sacred space with your presence."[1]

Visualize the general telesmatic form of Kassiel before you. The archangel appears as a mature man in a hooded robe of the deepest blue-violet trimmed with yellow-orange. On the front of his robe is the figure of a hexagram that contains the symbol of Saturn at its center. In his hand he holds an hourglass.

Vibrate the name of "Kassiel" a number of times (three times for Saturn or five times for the number of letters in the name). Pause for a few moments to visualize the archangel, using a testing token if need be, then say:

"Mighty Kassiel, send forth your great angel Agiel to aid me in this rite and bless this sacred space with his presence."

Visualize the literal telesmatic form of the angel Agiel. He appears as a fair-skinned adolescent male. On his head he wears a winged strophion with a small fylfot cross on the front. Around his neck he wears the symbol of the lunate cross on a silver chain. In one hand he holds a lotus wand and in the other, a lamp. He stands in the Sign of Isis Mourning. His hips and thighs are covered by a yellow-green kilt, ornamented with spirals. His feet are winged, and on either side of them lay the sword and scales of justice.

Vibrate the name of "Agiel" a number of times (three times for Saturn or five times for the number of letters in the name). Pause for a few moments to visualize the angel, using a testing token if need be.

At this point you should clearly state your purpose for consecrating the talisman and always be specific when vocalizing your stated goal. It could be something like the following:

"I, *(magical name)*, open this temple to perform a working in the magic of light. I seek an increase in the time I need to finish my project *(state the details)*. Look with favor upon this ceremony. Grant me what I seek, so that through this rite I may be enabled to successfully accomplish my endeavor with efficiency. Thus may I be enabled to make better use of time in all of my efforts, increase my esoteric knowledge, and thereby advance in the Great Work."

Personalized invocations may be added here. You may address an invocation to a deity associated with the Universe card and the planet Saturn listed in the chart on page 115. The following invocation includes some of them:

"I invoke all you powers and forces governing the nature, place, and authority of the planet Saturn by the majesty of the divine name YHVH Elohim! Hail Ptah, creator god of all eternity! Pre-existent father of time! Hail Anki, Chronos, and all you gods and goddesses who have the power to manipulate time! Mighty archangel Kassiel and great angel Agiel! Grant me what I seek! Charge and bless this talisman with your sacred force! May it bring me the power to increase the time allocated to my project. May it grant me control over the effective use of time in order to successfully complete my endeavor! With your divine aid it shall be done! So mote it be!"

Vibrate the name of "YHVH Elohim" three times for Saturn (or as many times as there are Hebrew letters in the name). Visualize the telesmatic images you have created. The aura surrounding these figure shines brilliantly upon the card of the Universe. Envision Kassiel as he makes a gesture of blessing over the card. Picture Agiel touching the card with his lotus wand.

Now concentrate on your stated goal as exemplified in the talisman card you have chosen. In your mind's eye, see yourself in the center of the Universe card, surrounded by the expanse of space and the belt of the zodiac. You are at the very center of the cosmos where time and space are completely fluid and non-linear. Around you are the stars of the constellations, shimmering like diamonds. You have the power to touch any one of them and set their energy in motion. You reach out with one hand to touch Gemini, drawing into yourself the speed and versatility of the Twins. With the other you touch Virgo, drawing into yourself the industrious nature of the sign of the Virgin. You have the ability to grasp the power of any constellation or planet that might help you increase your allotted time and use it wisely.

Next, visualize a calendar. See the month and date on the calendar when your project is due to be finished. Now look beyond that date and find the date by which you want to have your project finished. Envision a blue-violet circle around that date on your imaginal calendar. Visualize yourself moving forward in time to that date.

Then picture yourself having completed your project. See other people congratulating you on the efficiency with which you finished the task. Imagine the feeling of accomplishment you will experience when you are able to kick back and admire your own handiwork.

State the following affirmations, giving the Signs of the Four Magical Laws:

"I WILL that more time is granted to me to complete my project!

I CHOOSE to invoke those powers that conform to the planet Saturn!

I CREATE a facsimile in the astral light—an undeniable image of what will be!

I SEE myself as I WILL it to be! My allotted time has been extended and my project has been successfully completed."

Perform the closing ceremony.

TO INVOKE A GUARDIAN ANGEL

This ritual spread is designed to invoke a guardian angel for general protection and spiritual guidance. *The Universal Tarot* will be used to illustrate this spread. The tarot talisman card is zodiacal in nature and will therefore need to be invoked by pentagrams.

Card 1: For the significator, choose your own self-image card. For our example we will choose the Queen of Wands, which might represent the ritualist as a mature woman who is a fire sign.

Card 2: For the card of initial action, we will choose the Star. This card is attributed to Aquarius and is associated with hope, aspiration, and meditation.

Card 3: For the card of progression, we will choose the Ace of Cups. This card is associated with purity and divine aid.

Card 4: For the tarot talisman, we will choose Temperance to invoke a guardian angel.

The Ritual

Prepare your ritual space and include any items that might help you focus on your objective. The card of Temperance is attributed to the sign of Sagittarius. You might want to adorn your altar with supplemental items that will reflect this: for gemstones choose jacinth, for incense use lign-aloes, sage, cedar, or star anise. A blue candle, symbolic of Sagittarius, can be added to your altar—you can carve the symbol of the sign into the candle before dressing it with an appropriate essential oil. Include any items that will symbolize the divine, such as a chalice, a star, or a statue of an angel.

Prepare telesmatic images of the godname and angelic forces associated with the talisman card. These can be drawn or painted images, or merely written descriptions of the figures that you can visualize in detail. Use an Atziluthic image for the godname of Elohim—a flaming cross of Hebrew letters. Create Yetziratic or humanlike images of the archangel Adnakhiel and the angel Saritaiel. For the purpose of this example, we will use a general telesmatic image of Adnakhiel and a literal telesmatic image of Saritiael.

Begin with the opening ceremony.

Invoke the highest aspect of deity.

Lay out the cards in order and proceed with the work of visualization.

As the significator is placed on the altar, picture yourself dressed in your magical regalia with all of your natural talents and abilities.

Lay down the initial action card of the Star. Feel your capacity for imaginal thought and meditation expanding. Visualize a brilliant white light pouring down on you from a great star above your head, and see yourself opening up to this light, ready to receive it.

Figure 66: Sample Spread to Invoke a Guardian Angel.

Lay down the progression card, the Ace of Cups. Visualize the hand of the divine reaching down to you. The hand extends a sacred chalice filled with the waters of creation. Envision yourself accepting his holy gift and taking a drink of the pure water that the chalice contains.

In the center of the spread, lay down the tarot talisman card—Temperance. Trace a circle clockwise over the talisman card.

Trace the pentagrams associated with Sagittarius over the card. Practitioners of some magical traditions may choose to trace only the Invoking Fire Pentagram shown in figure 67.

start here

start here

Invoking Spirit Active   Invoking Fire (Sagittarius)

Figure 67: Pentagrams Invoking Sagittarius.

Ceremonial magicians may prefer to trace two pentagrams—the Invoking Pentagram of Spirit Active and Invoking Pentagram of Sagittarius. These are the same two pentagrams that you would normally trace when invoking the element of fire. The only difference is that you would trace the sigil of Sagittarius in the center of the Fire Pentagram, rather than the symbol of kerubic fire (Leo).

You have the option of tracing the pentagrams in silence or you can intone traditional words of power associated with them:

As you trace the Spirit Pentagram, intone the word **"Bitom"** (*bay-ee-toh-em*), a divine Enochian name associated with fire. Trace the spirit wheel in the center and intone the god-name of spirit active, **"Eheieh"** (*eh-hay-yay*).

As you trace the Fire Pentagram, vibrate the words **"Oip Teaa Pedoce"** (*oh-ee-pay tay-ah-ah pay-doh-kay*), three Holy Enochian names associated with Fire. Trace the symbol of Sagittarius in the center and intone the godname of Fire, **"Elohim"** (*el-oh-heem*). Then say:

"I invoke the powers and forces governing the nature, place, and authority of the sign Sagittarius by the majesty of the divine name Elohim. I invoke Adnakhiel, the great archangel of Sagittarius. Mighty Adnakhiel, I ask you to bless this sacred space with your presence."[2]

Visualize the general telesmatic form of Adnakhiel before you. The archangel appears as a red-haired man clothed in robes of blue trimmed and ornamented in orange. The figure of an upright fire triangle containing the symbol of Sagittarius is emblazoned on his chest. He carries a bow in one hand and an arrow in the other. His wings are covered with feathers of pastel blue and orange.

Vibrate the name of **"Adnakhiel"** seven times, once for each Hebrew letter in the name. Pause for a few moments to visualize the archangel, using a testing token if need be. Then say:

"Mighty Adnakhiel, send forth your great angel Saritiael to aid me in this rite and bless this sacred space with his presence."

Visualize the literal telesmatic form of the angel Saritiael. He appears as a slender young man with flowing red hair. On his head, which is surrounded by a flaming glory of light, he wears a strophion with a small Maltese cross on the front. He has a thoughtful, tranquil face which glows from within. His fair eyes are sharp and active. In one hand he holds a lotus wand and in the other he holds a lamp. Upon his chest is the symbol of the oroboros. His robe is yellow-green. His feet are winged, and on either side of them lay the sword and scales of justice. He stands upon flames.

Vibrate the name of "Saritiael" five times, once for each Hebrew letter in the name. Pause for a few moments to visualize the angel, using a testing token if need be.

At this point you should clearly state your purpose for consecrating the talisman, and be specific when vocalizing your stated goal. It could be similar to this:

"I, *(magical name)*, open this temple to perform a working in the magic of light. I seek to invoke a guardian angel. Look with favor upon this ceremony. Grant me what I seek so that through this rite I may acquire an angelic steward to provide me with aid, protection, and spiritual support. Thus may I advance in the Great Work."

Personalized invocations may be added here. You may address an invocation to a deity associated with the sign of Sagittarius listed in the chart on page 115. The following invocation includes a prayer to Neith:

"I invoke all you powers and forces governing the nature, place, and authority of the sign Sagittarius by the majesty of the divine name Elohim! Hail, great goddess Neith, the lady of the arrow and the bow! You who are both mother and daughter of the Sun! Holy huntress, goddess of wisdom and creator of light! You who are called the 'opener of the ways!' Great lady of the south, the one who is both father and mother, eternal and self-born! Self-sustaining and self-existent goddess! Be here now! Mighty archangel Adnakhiel and great angel Saritiael! All you powers and forces already named, grant me what I seek! Charge and bless this talisman with your sacred force! May it bring unto me a holy guardian angel. May this angel provide me divine guidance and protection. With your holy power it shall be done! So mote it be!"

Vibrate the name of "Elohim" five times for the number of Hebrew letters in the name. Visualize the telesmatic images you have created. The aura produced by these figures shines brilliantly upon the card of Temperance. Envision Adnakhiel as he makes a gesture of blessing over the card. Picture Saritiael touching the card with his lotus wand.

Now concentrate on your stated goal as exemplified by the tarot talisman you have chosen—Temperance. In your mind's eye, see the image of a mighty angel as portrayed on the card before you, with one foot in water and the other on dry land. Her face is beautiful and her expression is soft and compassionate. In each hand she holds a chalice of pure, sacred water. She pours water from one chalice to the other, and back again. Her wings stretch outward to fill the sky. Upon her brow she wears the symbol of the sun. Use testing tokens if need be.

Concentrate on the symbol of the sun on the angel's brow and sense a connection between this symbol and your own heart center. Feel the connection between the colossal angel and yourself grow stronger and stronger.

Envision the great angel holding out one of her chalices before you. You take the chalice and press it to your chest. The sacred cup is absorbed into your heart center. The angel then presses the other chalice to her own breast and it too is absorbed. You have created a link with a guardian angel.

Picture yourself receiving guidance from this angel. When problems arise, you are able to call upon the angel for assistance. When you need spiritual support, you are able to access her wisdom and grace. Imagine that the angel is always there for you whenever you need her.

State the following affirmations, giving the Signs of the Four Magical Laws:

"**I WILL** myself to invoke a holy guardian angel!

I CHOOSE to invoke those powers that conform to the sign Sagittarius!

I CREATE a facsimile in the astral light—an undeniable image of what will be!

I SEE myself as I **WILL** it to be! I have invoked and connected with my guardian angel."

Perform the closing ceremony.

FOR COURAGE IN A DIFFICULT SITUATION

The Babylonian Tarot will be used to illustrate this spread. The tarot talisman is a pip card and will therefore need to be invoked with a hexagram for the Qabalistic number of its sephirah, but since it is primarily zodiacal in nature it will then need to be invoked with pentagrams.

Card 1: For the significator, choose your own self-image card. Here we will choose Justice, which might indicate that the ritualist is a Libra and has a strong inclination for fairness and social justice.

Card 2: For the card of initial action, we will choose the High Priestess. This card is assigned to Luna and the divine feminine. In this deck it is attributed to Ishtar, the great goddess of magic.

Card 3: For the card of progression, we will choose the Nine of Wands, a card of "Power" and great strength.

Card 4: For the tarot talisman, we will choose the Seven of Wands, a card associated with "Courage" and heroism under fire.

The Ritual

Prepare your ritual space and include any items that might help you focus on your objective. The attributions of this pip card are fire (for the suit of Wands), Netzach (for the number seven) and Mars in Leo (the decanate).

For gemstones choose fire opal for the element of fire, emerald for the sphere of Netzach, and cat's eye for the sign of Leo. For incense use a mixture of rose and olibanum. Three can-

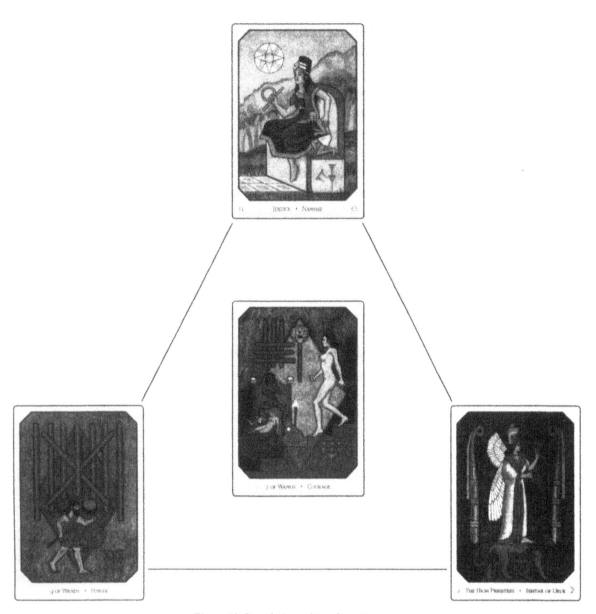

Figure 68: Sample Spread Invoking Courage.

dles may be added to the altar: a red candle for fire, a green candle for Netzach, and a yellow candle for Leo. If you desire, you can carve the following symbols into their respective candles: a fire triangle, the number seven, and the symbol of Leo.[3] The candles may then be dressed with an appropriate oil. Include any items that may symbolize courage for you, such as a statue of a lion.

Prepare telesmatic images of the godname and the angelic forces associated with the card. Use Atziluthic, flaming cross images for the godnames of YHVH Tzabaoth (Netzach) and Elohim (fire). Create Yetziratic, humanlike images of Verkhiel, the archangel of Leo, and the decanate angels Mahashiah and Lelahel. For the purpose of this example, we will use a general telesmatic image of Verkhiel and literal telesmatic images of Mahashiah and Lelahel.

Begin with the opening ceremony.

Invoke the highest aspect of deity.

Lay out the cards in order and proceed with the work of visualization.

As the significator is placed on the altar, visualize yourself dressed in your magical regalia, with all of your natural talents and abilities.

Lay down the initial action card of the High Priestess, who has all the powers of magic at her disposal. She is the guardian of the subconscious mind and she has the ability to extract courage that you did not know you possessed, from the depths of your own soul. Imagine yourself drawing upon her strength and finding your own courage within.

Lay down the progression card of the Nine of Wands. Imagine yourself as the figure shown in the card—a warrior who has fought battles and conquered enemies. Feel yourself growing larger as you are filled with tremendous strength. It gives you great self-confidence and assurance.

Finally, lay down the tarot talisman—the Seven of Wands, the card of "Courage." Trace a circle over it. Trace the Invoking Hexagram of Venus (attributed to Netzach) over the card by starting at the point of Venus on the upright triangle, going clockwise. Then start at the opposite point on the inverted triangle and trace clockwise (see figure 69).

You have the option of tracing the hexagram in silence or you can vibrate traditional words of power associated with it. As you draw the two triangles that make up the hexagram, intone the word of unity, **"Ararita"** (*ah-ra-ree-tah*). Next, intone the divine Hebrew name associated with the Venus Hexagram—**"YHVH Tzabaoth"** (*yod heh vav heh tzabah-oth*) while tracing the symbol of Venus in the center.

Our tarot talisman card of "Courage" is attributed to the third decanate of Leo (20°–30°), which is Mars in Leo. This is invoked by the figure of the pentagram. Over the talisman card, trace the pentagrams that are associated with Leo. Practitioners of some magical traditions may prefer to trace only the Invoking Fire Pentagram shown in figure 70.

Ceremonial magicians may opt to trace two pentagrams in this instance—the Invoking Pentagram of Spirit Active and the Invoking Pentagram of Leo.

You may trace the pentagrams in silence or you can intone traditional words of power associated with them:

As you trace the Spirit Pentagram, intone the word **"Bitom"** (*bay-ee-toh-em*). Trace the spirit wheel in the center and intone the divine name **"Eheieh"** (*eh-hay-yay*).

As you trace the Fire Pentagram, vibrate the words **"Oip Teaa Pedoce"** (*oh-ee-pay tay-ah-ah pay-doh-kay*). Trace the symbol of Leo in the center and intone the godname **"Elohim"** (*el-oh-heem*). Then say:

Figure 69: Invoking Hexagram of Venus and Netzach.

Invoking Spirit Active   Invoking Fire (Leo)

Figure 70: Invoking Pentagrams Associated with Leo.

"I invoke the powers and forces governing the nature, place, and authority of the sign Leo by the majesty of the divine name Elohim. I invoke Verkhiel, the great archangel of Leo. Mighty Verkhiel, I ask you to bless this sacred space with your presence."[4]

Visualize the general telesmatic form of Verkhiel in Figure 71. The archangel appears as a tall athletic man in robes of yellow trimmed with violet. His long golden hair frames his angular face like the mane of a lion. On the front of his robe is the figure of an upright fire triangle containing the symbol of Leo in violet. His right hand rests upon the head of the lion. His wings are covered with feathers of gold and pastel violet.

Vibrate the name of "Verkhiel" six times, once for each Hebrew letter in the name. Pause for a few moments to visualize the archangel, using a testing token if need be. Then say:

"Mighty Verkhiel, send forth your angels Mahashiah and Lelahel to bless this sacred space with their presence."

Visualize the literal telesmatic forms of the two decanate angels. The image of Mahashiah has already been described in the previous chapter. Give the following invocation to Mahashiah from the Book of Psalms:

"I sought Tetragrammaton and he answered me: and out of all my fears he delivered me. Seeking safety from trouble, I invoke Mahashiah who is called God the savior."

Vibrate the name of "Mahashiah" five times. Pause for a few moments to visualize the angel, using a testing token if need be.

Figure 71: General Telesmatic Image of Verkhiel.

Then invoke Lelahel with the following Psalm:

"Sing praises unto Tetragrammaton, who dwelleth in Zion; declare among the nations his deeds. I invoke Lelahel who is called praiseworthy."

The literal telesmatic image of Lelahel depicts the angel as an awesome valkyrie-like figure in green chain mail and buskins. Her head is crowned with a winged laurel wreath. Large pastel green wings spring from her shoulders. With one hand she grasps a red phoenix wand and in the other she holds a royal orb. Upon her chest is a lamen of a red pyramidal cross. Her hips and thighs are covered by a yellow kilt, ornamented with fylfot crosses. A golden belt surrounds her waist—on it are the letters of her name in violet. A sword hangs from her belt. Her feet are winged, and on either side of them lay the sword and scales of justice (see figure 72).

Vibrate the name of "Lelahel" five times. Pause for a few moments to visualize the angel, using a testing token if desired.

At this point you should clearly state your purpose for consecrating the talisman and be specific when vocalizing your stated goal. It could be similar to this:

"I, *(magical name)*, open this temple to perform a working in the Magic of Light. I seek to gain the courage I need to face a troubled situation. *(Be very specific.)* Look with favor upon this ceremony. Grant me what I seek, so that through this rite I may obtain the courage

Figure 72: Literal Telesmatic Image of Lelahel

and strength that I need to stand my ground and not give way in the face of great difficulty. Thus may I learn the virtue of valor and thereby advance in the Great Work."

Personal invocations or prayers might be added here. If desired, you may address an invocation to a deity from the pantheon of your choice. For this case in point, we will use an invocation to Ishtar, the Babylonian goddess who is featured in two cards of this ritual spread:

"Hail Ishtar, most awe-inspiring star goddess! Queen of heaven and earth. Bold mistress of love and war! Valiant lady who descended without fear into the dark abode of the underworld. I invoke thee! Grant me what I seek! Charge this talisman with your sacred power, your holy *me (pronounced 'may')*! O Ishtar, wise goddess of magic! Hear my prayer! May this talisman give me your bravery and daring! With your divine aid it shall be done! So mote it be!"

Vibrate the godname of "Elohim" five times. Visualize the telesmatic images you have created. The aura produced by these figures shines brilliantly upon the Seven of Wands. Envision Verkhiel as he makes a gesture of blessing over the card. Picture Mahashiah and Lelahel touching the card with their implements.

Now concentrate on your stated goal as exemplified in the talisman card you have chosen. In your mind's eye, see yourself confidently moving forward to meet the difficulty that you preciously feared, only now you have no trepidation about it whatsoever. Imagine that you have already confronted the trouble and all has been resolved to your liking. The adversity has passed. Conquering this problem has given you great satisfaction and self-assurance.

State the following affirmations, giving the Signs of the Four Magical Laws:

"I WILL myself to develop the courage I need to face a difficult challenge!

I CHOOSE to invoke those powers that conform to the third decanate of Leo!

I CREATE a facsimile in the astral light—an undeniable image of what will be!

I SEE myself as I WILL it to be! I have confronted the challenge and have prevailed!"

Perform the closing ceremony.

TO PROTECT AND FORTIFY A HOME

The Thoth Tarot Deck will be used to demonstrate this example. The tarot talisman is a pip card and will therefore need to be invoked with a hexagram for the Qabalistic number of its sephirah, but since it is primarily zodiacal in nature it will also need to be invoked with pentagrams.

Card 1: For the significator, choose your own self-image card. Here we will choose the Prince of Disks, which might indicate that the ritualist is a young man who is an earth sign, patient and pragmatic.

Card 2: For the card of initial action, we will choose the Ten of Cups. This card is attributed to "Satiety," wholeness, and happiness. It is also a card of home, family, and domestic harmony.

Card 3: For the card of progression, we will choose the Chariot, which corresponds to the sign of Cancer, the zodiacal sign of home and hearth.

Card 4: For the tarot talisman, we will choose the Four of Disks, a card associated with "Power" in the form of earthly security.

The Ritual

Prepare your ritual space and include any items that might help you focus on your objective. The attributions of this pip card are: earth (for the suit of disks), Chesed (for the number seven) and Sun in Capricorn (the decanate). For gemstones choose quartz for the element of earth, amethyst for the sphere of Netzach and onyx for the sign of Capricorn. For incense use a mixture of storax, cedar, and musk. Three candles may be added to the altar: a black (or green) candle for earth, a blue candle for Chesed, and a blue-violet candle for Capricorn. If you desire, you can carve the following symbols into their respective candles: an earth triangle, the number four, and the symbol of Capricorn.[5]

The candles may then be dressed with an appropriate oil. Include any items that may symbolize protection and security for you: a chain, a lock, or a statue of a guard dog.

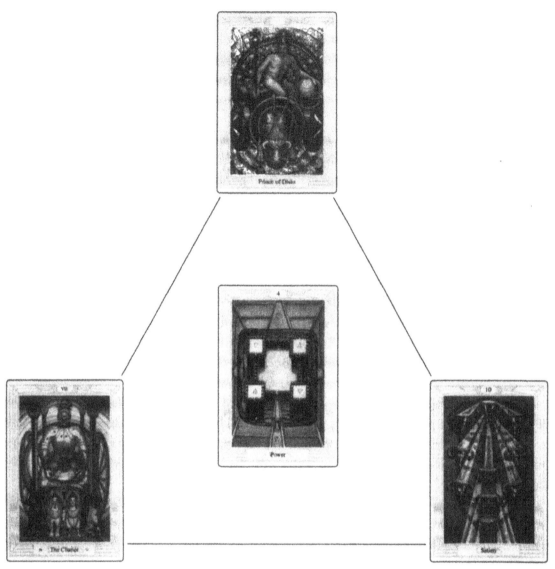

Figure 73: Sample Spread to Protect a Home.

Prepare telesmatic images of the godname and angelic forces associated with the card. Use Atziluthic, flaming cross images for the godnames of El (Chesed) and Adonai (Earth). Create Yetziratic, humanlike images of the archangel of Capricorn, Hanael, and the decanate angels Kuqiah and Menadel. For the purpose of this example, we will use a literal telesmatic image of Hanael and general telesmatic images of Kuqiah and Menadel.

Begin with the opening ceremony.

Invoke the highest aspect of deity.

Lay out the cards in order and proceed with the work of visualization.

As the significator is placed on the altar, visualize yourself dressed in your magical regalia, with all of your natural talents and abilities.

Lay down the initial action card of the Ten of Cups. See the light pouring into the ten cups that form the Tree of Life in the card. Now imagine yourself *as* the Tree of Life. The sacred light of the divine pours down on you from above, filling you with its essence. You are sated with its power and grace.

Lay down the progression card of the Chariot. Imagine yourself as the figure shown in the card—totally armored and protected against attack. You are in complete control of your chariot, which is a symbol of your home. Picture the four kerubic animals shown in the card as great sentinels posted at the four quarters of your home, keeping strict watch over the house.

Finally, lay down the tarot talisman—the Four of Disks, the card of "Power." Trace a circle over it. Trace the Invoking Hexagram of Jupiter (attributed to Chesed) over the card by starting at the point of Jupiter on the inverted triangle, going clockwise. Then start at the opposite point on the upright triangle and trace clockwise (see figure 74).

You have the option of tracing the hexagram in silence or you can vibrate traditional words of power associated with it. As you draw the two triangles that make up the hexagram, intone the word of unity, **"Ararita"** (*ah-ra-ree-tah*). Next, intone the divine Hebrew name associated with Chesed, **"El,"** as you trace the symbol of Jupiter in the center.[6]

Our tarot talisman card of "Power," is attributed to the third decanate of Capricorn (20°–30°), which is Sun in Capricorn. This is invoked by the figure of the pentagram. Over the talisman card, trace the pentagrams that are associated with Capricorn. Practitioners of some magical traditions may prefer to trace only the Invoking Earth Pentagram shown in figure 75.

Ceremonial magicians may opt to trace two pentagrams in this instance—the Invoking Pentagram of Spirit Passive and the Invoking Pentagram of Capricorn (the standard Pentagram for Invoking Earth, only with the symbol of Capricorn traced in the center, rather than the symbol of kerubic earth).

You may trace the pentagrams in silence or you can intone traditional words of power associated with them.

As you trace the Spirit Pentagram, intone the word **"Nanta"** (*en-ah-en-tah*). Trace the Spirit wheel in the center and intone the divine name **"Agla"** (*ah-gah-lah*).

As you trace the Earth Pentagram, vibrate the words **"Emor Dial Hectega"** (*ee-mor dee-al heck-tay-gah*). Trace the symbol of Capricorn in the center and intone the godname **"Adonai"** (*ah-doe-nye*).

"I invoke the powers and forces governing the nature, place, and authority of the sign Capricorn by the majesty of the divine name Adonai. I invoke Hanael, the great archangel of Capricorn. Mighty Hanael, I ask you to bless this sacred space with your presence."[7]

Figure 74: Invoking Hexagram of Jupiter and Chesed.

Invoking Spirit Passive   **Invoking Earth (Capricorn)**

Figure 75: Invoking Pentagrams Associated with Capricorn.

Visualize the literal telesmatic form of Hanael before you: The archangel appears as a graceful woman in robes of medium gray[8] trimmed with black. She has long red hair and red eyes. Around her brow she wears a strophion ornamented with a pyramid cross. She wears a necklace bearing the symbol of an ankh. In one hand she holds a flaming torch crowned with a laurel wreath. She wears a golden belt around her waist upon which are the letters of her name in violet. Her feet are winged, and on either side of them lay the sword and scales of justice.

Vibrate the name of **"Hanael"** five times, once for each Hebrew letter of the name. Pause for a few moments to visualize the archangel, using a testing token if need be. Then say:

"Mighty Hanael, send forth your angels Kuqiah and Menadel to bless this sacred space with their presence."

Visualize the general telesmatic forms of the two decanate angels. On the right-hand side, Kuqiah, the day angel and first angel of the decanate, appears as a fair-haired man wearing golden-yellow robes trimmed with violet. He has large wings with pastel yellow and violet feathers. Upon his chest is the symbol of the sun in violet.

On the left-hand side, the night angel Menadel appears as dark-haired woman in blue-violet robes with yellow-orange trim. She has large wings with pastel indigo and amber feathers. She bears the symbol of Capricorn on her breast. The two angels hold a large disk or pentacle between them.

Give the following invocation from the Book of Psalms:

"I rejoice in Tetragrammaton because he hath heard my voice and my supplications. I invoke Kuqiah who is called God who gives joy."

Vibrate the name of "Kuqiah" five times.

Then invoke Menadel with the following Psalm:

"O Tetragrammaton, I have loved the habitation of thy house, and the place where thine honor dwelleth. I invoke honorable Menadel who is called God adorable."

Vibrate the name of "Menadel" five times.

Envision the two decanate angels together with the great pentacle between them. Use a testing token if need be.

At this point, you should clearly state your purpose for consecrating the talisman and be specific when vocalizing your stated goal. It could be similar to this:

"I, *(magical name)*, open this temple to perform a working in the magic of light. I seek to shield and defend my home and family from all harm—from natural adversities and human malice alike. *(Be very specific.)* Look with favor upon this ceremony. Grant me what I seek, so that through this rite my household may be fortified and protected. Thus may I learn the virtue of strength and security and thereby advance in the Great Work."

Personal invocations or prayers might be added here. If desired you may address an invocation to a deity from the pantheon of your choice. For this example, we will use an invocation to Amon-Ra,[9] the Egyptian sun god:

"Hail Amon-Ra, most supreme king of the gods! Creator of the universe! O hidden god who is the giver of light to the world! O Amon, the concealed one, the opener of the day! I invoke thee! Grant me what I seek! Charge this talisman with your sacred power! O Amon-Ra, who abides in all things! Lord of Thebes, hear my prayer! May this talisman protect my home and family! With your divine aid it shall be done! So mote it be!"

Vibrate the godname of "Adonai" five times. Visualize the telesmatic images you have created. The aura produced by these figures shines brilliantly upon the Four of Disks. Envision Hanael as he makes a gesture of blessing over the card. Picture Kuqiah and Menadel touching the card with their hands.

Now concentrate on your stated goal as exemplified in the talisman card you have chosen. In your mind's eye, visualize your home and then picture it from above as if you were looking down upon your property from the clouds. Envision your home as the fortress portrayed in the talisman card. Your house has become a citadel—a stronghold maintained by the constant authority and vigilance of the divine forces. The walls have become impervious to the attacks of nature or the mischief of man.

State the following affirmations, giving the Signs of the Four Magical Laws:

"I WILL that my home and family be fortified and protected from all harm!

I CHOOSE to invoke those powers that conform to the third decanate of Leo!

I CREATE a facsimile in the astral light—an undeniable image of what will be!

I SEE my home as I WILL it to be! An impenetrable fortress! Safe from harm, a secure sanctuary."

Perform the closing ceremony.

TO LET GO OF PAST HURTS AND MOVE ON

This ritual spread is designed to give a passive person who has been emotionally injured the strength to put an end to the old wounds and move forward with life. *The Marseille Tarot Deck* will be used to demonstrate this example. The tarot talisman is a court card and will therefore need to be invoked with a hexagram for its sephirotic correspondence, but since it is primarily elemental in nature it will also need to be invoked with pentagrams.

Card 1: For the significator, choose your own self-image card. Here we will choose the Knave of Cups, which might indicate that the ritualist is a young woman who is a water sign: emotional, sensitive, and empathetic.

Card 2: For the card of initial action, we will choose Strength. It is a card of resilience, fortitude, control, and endurance. The strength it alludes to is an inner strength.

Card 3: For the card of progression, we will choose the Ace of Swords. This card depicts the exercise of willpower and conscious action to create change.

Card 4: For the tarot talisman, we will choose the Queen of Swords. She is a powerful, authoritative woman who is in control of her life. She is fearless and prepared to cut off whatever is old, outmoded, or unhealthy in favor of something better.

The Ritual

Prepare your ritual space and include any items that might help to focus on your objective. The attributions of this court card are Binah (for the Queen) and air (for the suit of swords). For gemstones choose star sapphire or pearl for the sphere of Binah and topaz or chalcedony for the element of air. For incense use a mixture of myrrh and galbanum. Two candles may be added to the altar: a black candle for Binah and a yellow candle for air. If you desire, you can carve the following symbols into their respective candles: the number three and an air triangle. The candles may then be dressed with an appropriate oil. Include any items that may symbolize moving forward into the future for you, such as fresh-cut flowers.

Prepare telesmatic images of the godname and angelic forces associated with the card. Use Atziluthic, flaming cross images for the godnames of YHVH Elohim (Binah) and YHVH (air). Create Yetziratic, humanlike images of Raphael,[10] the archangel of air, and Chassan, the angel of air. For the purpose of this example, we will use a general telesmatic image of Raphael and a literal telesmatic image of Chassan.

Begin with the opening ceremony.

Figure 76: Sample Spread to Put the Past Behind You.

Invoke the highest aspect of deity.

Lay out the cards in order and proceed with the work of visualization.

As the significator is placed on the altar, visualize yourself dressed in your magical regalia, with all of your natural talents and abilities.

Lay down the initial action card of Strength. Visualize yourself as the woman in the card. Feel yourself full of boundless strength. You have the inner fortitude needed to do whatever you wish. Draw upon this strength to overcome whatever is holding you back and

Figure 77: Invoking Hexagram of Saturn and Binah.

binding you to a hurtful situation—be it timidity, fear of change, or low self-esteem. The lion in this case represents the emotional pain that you wish to be rid of. Picture yourself grasping the lion's jaws and effortlessly pressing them shut. The pain cannot bite you again.

Lay down the progression card of the Ace of Swords. Now that you have found your inner strength, you must use willpower to keep from slipping backward into harmful old habits and routines that will only start the cycle of pain all over again. See yourself taking up the sword from the card as you claim your willpower and resolve to never go backward, only forward.

Finally, lay down the tarot talisman—the Queen of Swords. Trace a circle over it. Trace the Invoking Hexagram of Saturn (attributed to Binah) over the card by starting at the point of Saturn on the upright triangle, going clockwise. Then start at the opposite point on the inverted triangle and trace clockwise (see figure 77).

You have the option of tracing the hexagram in silence or you can vibrate traditional words of power associated with it. As you draw the two triangles that make up the hexagram, intone the word of unity, **"Ararita"** *(ah-ra-ree-tah)*. Next, intone the divine Hebrew name associated with Binah—**"YHVH Elohim"** *(yod heh vav heh el-oh-heem)* as you trace the symbol of Saturn in the center.

Over the tarot talisman card, trace the pentagrams that are associated with Air. Practitioners of some magical traditions may prefer to trace only the Invoking Air Pentagram shown in figure 78. Ceremonial magicians may choose to trace two pentagrams in this instance—the Invoking Pentagram of Spirit Active and the Invoking Pentagram of Air.

You may trace the pentagrams in silence or you can intone traditional words of power associated with them as follows:

As you trace the Spirit Pentagram, vibrate the word **"Exarp"** *(ex-ar-peh)*. Trace the Spirit wheel in the center and intone the divine name **"Eheieh"** *(eh-hay-yay)*.

As you trace the Air Pentagram, vibrate the words **"Oro Ibah Aozpi"** *(or-oh ee-bah-hay ah-oh-zoad-pee)*. Trace the kerubic symbol of air (Aquarius) in the center and intone the godname **"YHVH"** *(yod heh vav heh)*. Then say:

Invoking Spirit Active   Invoking Air

Figure 78: Invoking Pentagrams Associated with Air.

"I invoke the powers and forces governing the nature, place, and authority of the element of air by the majesty of the divine name YHVH. I invoke Raphael, the great archangel of air. Mighty Raphael, I ask you to bless this sacred space with your presence."[11]

Visualize the general telesmatic form of Raphael before you. The archangel appears as a tall, fair-haired man standing upon the clouds. He wears a strophion with the symbol of the air triangle upon his brow. He is dressed in yellow robes trimmed in violet with the symbol of the air triangle upon his chest. Huge wings of pastel yellow and violet feathers grace his shoulders. He bears in his right hand the caduceus staff of Hermes.

Vibrate the name of "Raphael" four times, once for each Hebrew letter of the name. Pause for a few moments to visualize the archangel, using a testing token if need be. Then say:

"Mighty Raphael, send forth your angel Chassan to bless this sacred space with his presence."

Visualize the literal telesmatic forms of the angel. Chassan appears as a bearded man with dark hair and eyes.[12] His head is crowned with a laurel wreath. He is dressed in a violet linen kilt[13] trimmed with yellow. Great wings of pastel violet and yellow letters adorn his shoulders. The lamen on the front of his chest is a yellow trefoil.[14] In one hand he holds an olive branch while in the other he grasps a palm frond. Around his waist he wears a blue-green belt engraved with the Hebrew letters of his name in red-orange.

Vibrate the name of "Chassan" three times. Pause for a few moments to visualize the angel, using a testing token if need be.

At this point you should clearly state your purpose for consecrating the talisman and be specific when vocalizing your stated goal. It could be similar to this:

"I, *(magical name)*, open this temple to perform a working in the Magic of Light. I seek to put a painful episode of my life behind me and move beyond it into a new phase of my life. *(Be very specific.)* Look with favor upon this ceremony. Grant me what I seek, so that through this rite I may put the pain of the past behind me and progress to a new, brighter future. Thus may I learn the virtue of personal growth and thereby advance in the Great Work."

Personal invocations or prayers might be added here. If desired you may address an invocation to a deity from the pantheon of your choice. For this example, we will use an invocation to the Babylonian air god Ellil:

"Hail Ellil, supreme king over all the lands! Lord wind! Master of fate! The god who bestows kingship and gives authority to mortals! I invoke thee! Grant me what I seek! Charge this talisman with your sacred power! O Ellil, whose word is wisdom that causes change! Lord of Eridu, hear my prayer! May this talisman give me the strength and willpower to end a sorrowful phase of my life and begin a new phase of joy and growth! With your divine aid it shall be done! So mote it be!"

Vibrate the godname of "YHVH" four times. Visualize the telesmatic images you have created. The aura produced by these figures shines brilliantly upon the Queen of Swords. Envision Raphael as he makes a gesture of blessing over the card. Picture Chassan touching the card with his olive branch.

Now concentrate on your stated goal as exemplified in the talisman card you have chosen. In your mind's eye, see yourself as the Queen of Swords. You now have her strength and power. You will no longer let your own happiness be put aside. You know that you must break the cycle of pain and move on. Visualize yourself having cut off a hurtful past once and for all. It is over and done. You are now in a positive place with a healthy frame of mind. Now you look forward to life. It is a new beginning for you.

State the following affirmations, giving the Signs of the Four Magical Laws:

"I WILL to cut the ties that bind me to a painful past! What is past is no more!
I CHOOSE to invoke those powers that conform to the element of air!
I CREATE a facsimile in the astral light—an undeniable image of what will be!
I SEE my future as I WILL it to be! I have moved forward into a brighter tomorrow."
Perform the closing ceremony.

---

1 When vibrating any of these Qabalistic names in this ritual, you may choose to trace their sigils over the talisman card. (Refer to the section on sigils in the previous chapter.)

2 See endnote 1.

3 Or the decanate symbols: Mars in Leo.

4 See endnote 1.

5 Or the decanate symbols: Sun in Capricorn.

6 See chapter 3, endnote 10.

7 See endnote 1.

8 The synthesis of all her colors.

9 Amon is a deity associated with Chesed-Jupiter. The sun god Ra (or Re) alludes to the decanate of this card, Sun in Capricorn. The compound deity Amon-Ra can be attributed to both Jupiter and Sol.

10 Raphael Ruachel or "Raphael of Air."

11 See endnote 1.

12 While most of the letters in this name are feminine, Chassan is traditionally a masculine name.

13 The synthesis of his colors.

14 From the spirit attribution of shin.

EPILOGUE

We hope that you come away from this book with a renewed appreciation for the many ways that tarot cards can be used as talismans. Please remember that the ritual spread method and amended telesmatic attributions that we have presented are certainly not the only ways to create such talismans. Much of what we have imparted here is traditional Golden Dawn information, and yet some of it isn't. Some of it is purely our own creation. No matter what the origin, none of this material is cast in stone. No one can show you "the one true way" of all magic, so don't bother chasing secret chiefs, or the guru of the month. What ultimately matters is what works for *you*, the reader: the spiritual seeker. Take what useful kernels you find here and there and create your own techniques.

Remember to always back up your magical work on the astral with physical work in the material plane—like the phrase says, "As above, so below." Another way of saying this might be "God helps those who help themselves." The gods won't reward spiritual slackers.

Perform ritual often. Do the work. And above all, inflame thyself with prayer. You may find that your journey with the magical tarot is just beginning.

APPENDIX

ADDITIONAL CORRESPONDENCES, FIGURES, AND SIGILS

The following chart gives additional gemstone and incense suggestions that can be used for optional ritual items in talisman consecration rites. Two color scales, the King Scale and the Queen Scale, are also given. The color attributions chart given on page 182 provides the most commonly used colors associated with the sephiroth and the Hebrew letters. These colors can be employed for any general magical purpose. However, there are other colors that can be used for more nuanced objectives if the reader desires to utilize them. The King Scale of color is considered masculine, positive, and projective, while the Queen Scale of color is regarded as feminine, negative, and receptive. Thus the colors of the King Scale can be used to create a talisman for another person—when you want to *project* the energy to someone else. The colors of the Queen Scale can be used to create a talisman for yourself—when you want to *receive* the force.

Attribution	Letter	Gemstone	Incense	King Scale	Queen Scale
Kether	—	diamond	ambergris	brilliance	white
Chokmah	—	star ruby, turquoise	musk	soft blue	gray
Binah	—	star sapphire, pearl	myrrh, civet	crimson (red-violet)	black
Chesed	—	amethyst, sapphire	cedar	deep violet	blue
Geburah	—	ruby	tobacco	orange	red
Tiphareth	—	topaz, yellow diamond	olibanum (frankincense)	rose pink	yellow
Netzach	—	emerald	benzoin, rose, red sandalwood	amber (yellow-orange)	green
Hod	—	opal, fire opal	storax	violet purple	orange
Yesod	—	quartz	jasmine	indigo	violet
Malkuth	—	rock crystal (colorless quartz), salt	dittany	yellow	citrine, olive, russet, black
△ Air	aleph א	topaz, chalcedony, opal	galbanum	yellow	sky blue
☿ Mercury	beth ב	opal, fire opal, agate, serpentine	mastic, storax, mace, white sandalwood	yellow	purple
☽ Luna	gimel ג	moonstone, pearl, quartz, fluorspar	camphor, aloe	blue	silver
♀ Venus	daleth ד	emerald, turquoise, amber, jade, malachite	sandalwood	green	sky blue
♈ Aries	heh ה	ruby, red jasper, diamond, garnet	dragon's blood	red	red
♉ Taurus	vav ו	topaz, emerald, red coral	storax	red-orange	deep indigo
♊ Gemini	zayin ז	alexandrite, tourmaline, agate	wormwood	orange	pale mauve
♋ Cancer	cheth ח	amber, pearl, moonstone	onycha	yellow-orange	maroon
♌ Leo	teth ט	cat's eye, ruby, sardonyx, chrysolite	olibanum (frankincense)	yellow	deep purple
♍ Virgo	yod י	peridot, sapphire	narcissus	yellow-green	slate gray
♃ Jupiter	kaph כ	amethyst, lapis lazuli, sapphire	saffron	violet	blue
♎ Libra	lamed ל	emerald, opal, malachite	galbanum	green	blue
▽ Water	mem מ	beryl, aquamarine, coral, moonstone	onycha, myrrh	blue	sea green
♏ Scorpio	nun נ	snakestone (fossil), topaz, blood-stone, obsidian	opoponax	blue-green	dull brown
♐ Sagittarius	samekh ס	jacinth (orange zircon), turquoise, blue zircon	lign-aloes	blue	yellow
♑ Capricorn	ayin ע	black diamond, jet, garnet, onyx	musk, civet	blue-violet	black
♂ Mars	peh פ	ruby, garnet, bloodstone	pepper, dragon's blood	red	red
♒ Aquarius	tzaddi צ	amethyst, aquamarine	galbanum	violet	sky blue
♓ Pisces	qoph ק	pearl, moonstone, bloodstone	ambergris	red-violet	buff-flecked silver-white
☉ Sol	resh ר	topaz, yellow diamond, chryoslite, heliodor, zircon, citrine	olibanum (frankincense), cinnamon	orange	golden yellow
△ Fire / ⊛ Spirit	shin ש	fire opal, ruby / diamond	olibanum	red / white	vermillion / deep purple
♄ Saturn / ▽ Earth	tau ת	onyx, jet, anthracite, obsidian / salt, moss agate, onyx	asafetida, sulfur scammony / storax	blue-violet / citrine, olive, russet, black	black / amber

PENTAGRAMS

Pentagrams are used to invoke and banish elemental and zodiacal energies. Used in conjunction with the pentagrams of spirit (active and passive), the standard pentagrams of the elements are traced with the kerubic (fixed) elemental symbols in the center. When invoking or banishing a zodiacal energy, use the pentagram(s) appropriate for the sign's element, but replace the kerubic symbol in the center with the symbol of the zodiacal sign with which you are working.

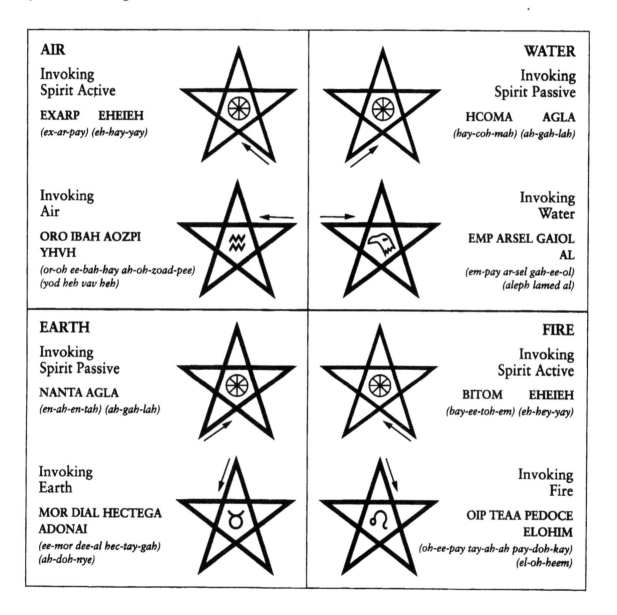

AIR

Invoking
Spirit Active

EXARP   EHEIEH
(ex-ar-pay) (eh-hay-yay)

Invoking
Air

**ORO IBAH AOZPI
YHVH**
(or-oh ee-bah-hay ah-oh-zoad-pee)
(yod heh vav heh)

WATER

Invoking
Spirit Passive

HCOMA   AGLA
(hay-coh-mah) (ah-gah-lah)

Invoking
Water

**EMP ARSEL GAIOL
AL**
(em-pay ar-sel gah-ee-ol)
(aleph lamed al)

EARTH

Invoking
Spirit Passive

NANTA AGLA
(en-ah-en-tah) (ah-gah-lah)

Invoking
Earth

**MOR DIAL HECTEGA
ADONAI**
(ee-mor dee-al hec-tay-gah)
(ah-doh-nye)

FIRE

Invoking
Spirit Active

BITOM   EHEIEH
(bay-ee-toh-em) (eh-hey-yay)

Invoking
Fire

**OIP TEAA PEDOCE
ELOHIM**
(oh-ee-pay tay-ah-ah pay-doh-kay)
(el-oh-heem)

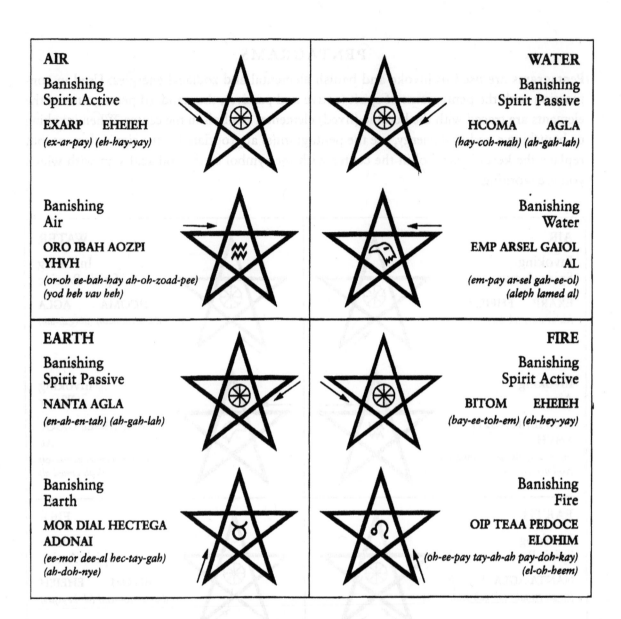

AIR

Banishing
Spirit Active

EXARP   EHEIEH
(ex-ar-pay) (eh-hay-yay)

Banishing
Air

ORO IBAH AOZPI
YHVH
(or-oh ee-bah-hay ah-oh-zoad-pee)
(yod heh vav heh)

WATER

Banishing
Spirit Passive

HCOMA   AGLA
(hay-coh-mah) (ah-gah-lah)

Banishing
Water

EMP ARSEL GAIOL
AL
(em-pay ar-sel gah-ee-ol)
(aleph lamed al)

EARTH

Banishing
Spirit Passive

NANTA AGLA
(en-ah-en-tah) (ah-gah-lah)

Banishing
Earth

MOR DIAL HECTEGA
ADONAI
(ee-mor dee-al hec-tay-gah)
(ah-doh-nye)

FIRE

Banishing
Spirit Active

BITOM   EHEIEH
(bay-ee-toh-em) (eh-hey-yay)

Banishing
Fire

OIP TEAA PEDOCE
ELOHIM
(oh-ee-pay tay-ah-ah pay-doh-kay)
(el-oh-heem)

HEXAGRAMS

Hexagrams are used to invoke and banish planetary and sephirotic energies. Starting from the appropriate planetary point, invoking hexagrams are traced in a clockwise direction, while banishing hexagrams are drawn anticlockwise. For Sol, which has no point but is attributed to the center of the hexagram, all seven hexagrams must be traced in their proper sephirotic order. The words of power are not vibrated and the sigil of the sun is not drawn until after the seventh hexagram is completed.

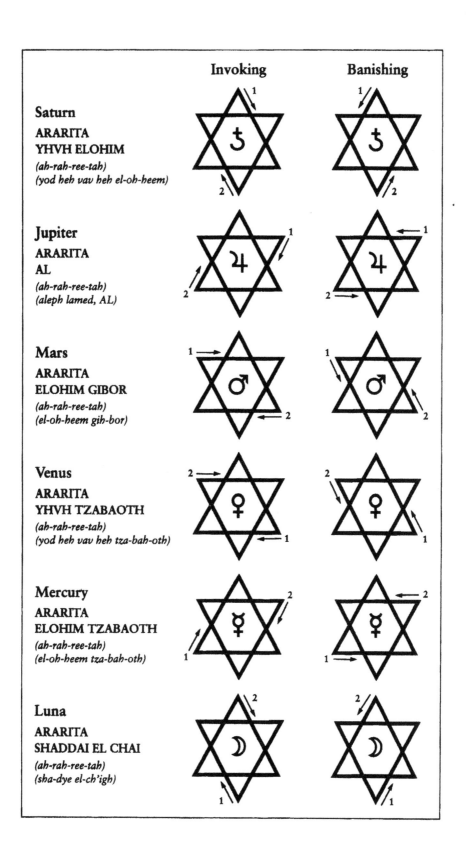

Invoking   Banishing

Saturn
ARARITA
YHVH ELOHIM
(ah-rah-ree-tah)
(yod heh vav heh el-oh-heem)

Jupiter
ARARITA
AL
(ah-rah-ree-tah)
(aleph lamed, AL)

Mars
ARARITA
ELOHIM GIBOR
(ah-rah-ree-tah)
(el-oh-heem gih-bor)

Venus
ARARITA
YHVH TZABAOTH
(ah-rah-ree-tah)
(yod heh vav heh tza-bah-oth)

Mercury
ARARITA
ELOHIM TZABAOTH
(ah-rah-ree-tah)
(el-oh-heem tza-bah-oth)

Luna
ARARITA
SHADDAI EL CHAI
(ah-rah-ree-tah)
(sha-dye el-ch'igh)

Sol

ARARITA
(ah-rah-ree-tah)

**YHVH ELOAH
VE-DAATH**
*(yod heh vav heh
el-oh-ah ve-da-ath)*

Invoking

Banishing

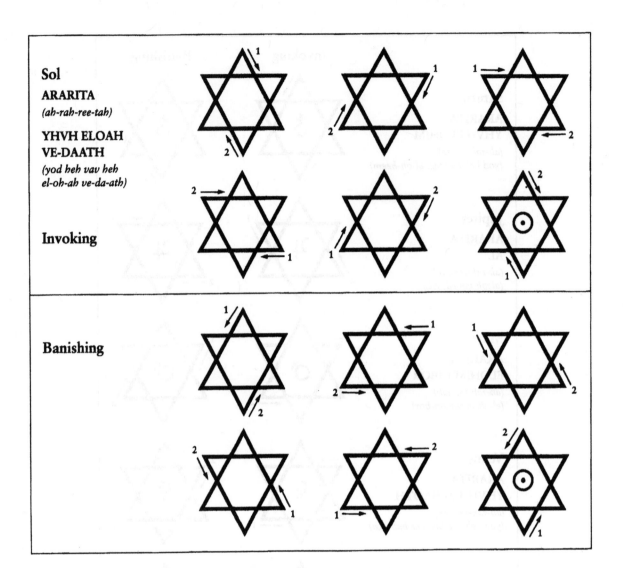

MAGICAL ALPHABETS

A variety of magical alphabets can be used in the making of sigils or as part of a telesmatic image. The following illustration from Francis Barrett's *The Magus* (1801) shows a number of magical alphabets including Theban, Celestial, Malachim, and Passing the River.

QAMEOTH, PLANETARY SEALS, AND SIGILS

The following pages show the seven traditional magical squares as well as the same squares translated into their Hebrew letter equivalents. The planetary seals are also given, along with the sigils of the planetary archangels, intelligences, and spirits, all of which are derived from their respective qamea.

SATURN

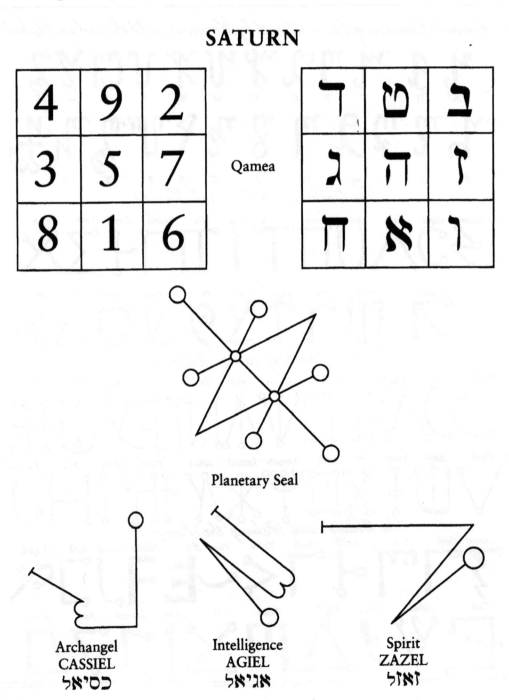

4	9	2
3	5	7
8	1	6

Qamea

Planetary Seal

Archangel
CASSIEL
כסיאל

Intelligence
AGIEL
אגיאל

Spirit
ZAZEL
זאזל

JUPITER

4	14	15	1
9	7	6	12
5	11	10	8
16	2	3	13

Qamea

ד	יד	טו	א
ט	ז	ו	יב
ה	יא	י	ח
יו	ב	ג	יג

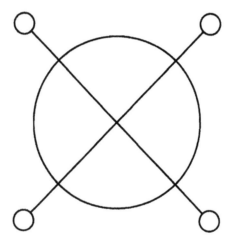

Planetary Seal

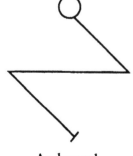

Archangel
SACHIEL
סחיאל

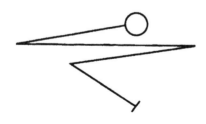

Intelligence
IOPHIEL
יהפיאל

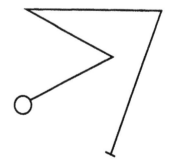

Spirit
HISMAEL
הסמאל

MARS

11	24	7	20	3
4	12	25	8	16
17	5	13	21	9
10	18	1	14	22
23	6	19	2	15

Qamea

יא	כד	ז	כ	ג
ד	יב	כה	ח	יו
יז	כא	יג	ה	ט
י	יח	א	יד	כב
יה	ו	יט	ב	כג

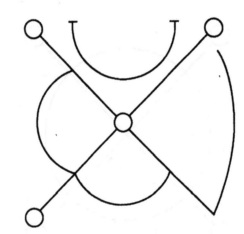

Planetary Seal

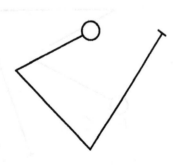

Archangel
ZAMAEL
זמאל

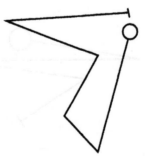

Intelligence
GRAPHIEL
גראפיאל

Spirit
BARTZABEL
ברצבאל

SOL

6	32	3	34	35	1
7	11	27	28	8	30
19	14	16	15	23	24
18	20	22	21	17	13
25	29	10	9	26	12
36	5	33	4	2	31

Qamea

ו	לב	ג	לד	לה	א
ז	יא	כז	כח	ח	ל
יט	יד	יו	יה	כג	כד
יח	כ	כב	כא	יז	יג
כה	כט	י	ט	כו	יב
לו	ה	לג	ד	ב	לא

Planetary Seal

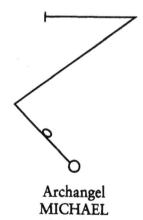

Archangel
MICHAEL
מיכאל

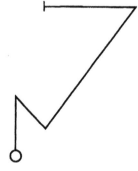

Intelligence
NAKHIEL
נכיאל

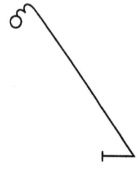

Spirit
SORATH
סורת

VENUS

22	47	16	41	10	35	4
5	23	48	17	42	11	29
30	6	24	49	18	36	12
13	31	7	25	43	19	37
38	14	32	1	26	44	20
21	39	8	33	2	27	45
46	15	40	9	34	3	28

Qamea

כב	מז	יו	מא	י	לה	ד
ה	כג	מח	יז	מב	מ	כט
ל	ו	כד	מט	יח	לו	יב
יג	לא	ז	כה	מג	יט	לז
לח	יד	לב	א	כו	מד	כ
כא	לט	ח	לג	ב	כז	מה
מו	יה	מ	ט	לד	ג	כח

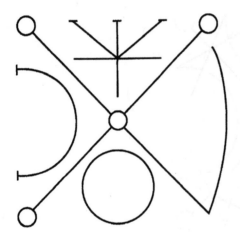

Planetary Seal

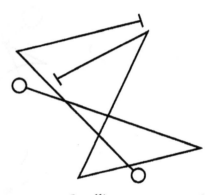

Intelligences
BENI SERAPHIM
בני שרפים

Archangel
ANAEL
אנאל

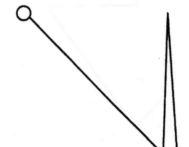

Intelligence
HAGIEL
הגיאל

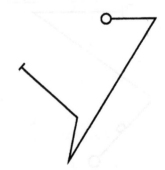

Spirit
QEDEMEL
קדמאל

MERCURY

8	58	59	5	4	62	63	1
49	15	14	52	53	11	10	56
41	23	22	44	45	19	18	48
32	34	35	29	28	38	39	25
40	26	27	37	36	30	31	33
17	47	46	20	21	43	42	24
9	55	54	12	13	51	50	16
64	2	3	61	60	6	7	57

Qamea

ח	נח	נט	ה	ד	סב	סג	א
נו	י	יא	נב	נג	יד	יה	מט
מח	יח	יט	מד	מה	כב	כג	מא
כה	לט	לח	כט	כח	לה	לד	לב
לג	לא	ל	לז	כז	כו	מ	
כד	מב	מג	כא	כ	מו	מז	יז
יו	נ	נא	יב	יג	נד	נה	ט
נז	ז	ו	ס	סא	ג	ב	סד

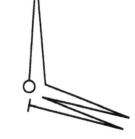

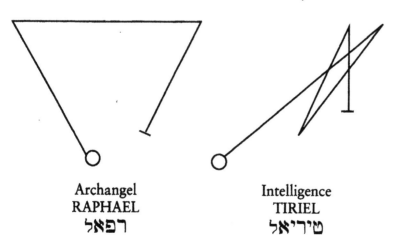

Planetary Seal

Archangel
RAPHAEL
רפאל

Intelligence
TIRIEL
טיריאל

Spirit
TAPHTHARTHARATH
תפתרתרת

LUNA

37	78	29	70	21	62	13	54	5
6	38	79	30	71	22	63	14	46
47	7	39	80	31	72	23	55	15
16	48	8	40	81	32	64	24	56
57	17	49	9	41	73	33	65	25
26	58	18	50	1	42	74	34	66
67	27	59	10	51	2	43	75	35
36	68	19	60	11	52	3	44	76
77	28	69	20	61	12	53	4	45

Qamea

לז	עה	כט	ע	כא	סב	יג	נד	ה
ו	לח	עט	ל	עא	כב	סג	יד	מו
מז	ז	לט	פ	לא	עב	כג	נה	יה
יז	מח	ח	מ	פא	לב	סד	כד	נו
נז	יז	מט	ט	מא	עג	לג	סה	כה
כו	נח	יח	נ	א	מב	עד	לד	סו
סז	כז	נט	י	נא	ב	מג	עה	לה
לו	סח	יט	ס	יא	נב	ג	מד	עו
עז	כח	סט	כ	סא	יב	נג	ד	מה

Archangel
GABRIEL
גבריאל

Spirit
CHASHMODAI
חשמודאי

Alternative Sigil
CHASHMODAI

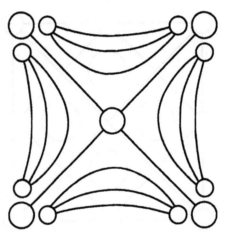

Planetary Seal

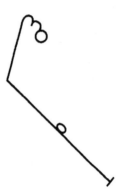

Intelligence
SHELACHEL
שלחאל

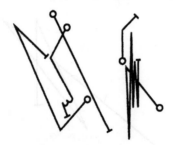

Intelligence of the Intelligences
MALKAH BE TARSHISM VE-AD
RUACHOTH SCHECHALIM

Golden Dawn Spelling	מלכא בתרשיסים ועד רוחות שחלים
Agrippa Spelling	מלכא בתרשיתים עד ברוח שחקים

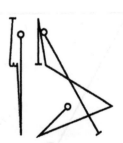

Spirit of the Spirits
SHAD BARSCHEMOTH
HA-SHARTATHAN

Golden Dawn Spelling	שד ברשמעת השרתתן
Agrippa Spelling	שד ברשהמעת שרתתן

264   *Appendix*

SIGILS OF THE DECANATE ANGELS

The decanate angels also have sigils associated with them, although these sigils have been somewhat controversial. They can be found in a Golden Dawn paper, "The Seals of the Schemhamphoresch,"[1] as well as in Robert Ambelain's *La Kabbale Pratique* (1951). By one account, the origin of these sigils was magician and cryptographer Blaise Vigenère.[2] Ambelain concluded that these sigils were not those of the decanate angels but of their unbalanced opposites. Sigils of this type appear to be derived from skryed or channeled sources and are difficult to verify. We include them here purely as a resource. We recommend that readers devise their own sigils for these angels, based on the diagram of the Rose of Twenty-two Petals.

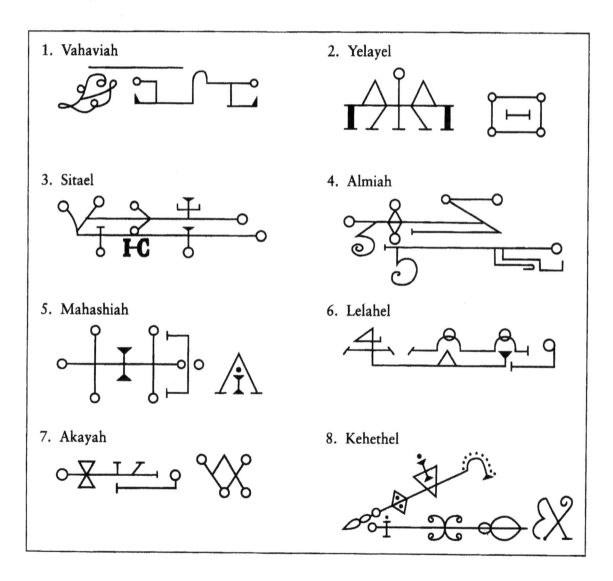

1. Vahaviah

2. Yelayel

3. Sitael

4. Almiah

5. Mahashiah

6. Lelahel

7. Akayah

8. Kehethel

9. Haziel

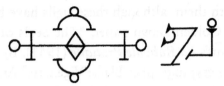

10. Eldayah

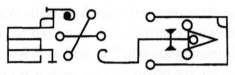

11. Laviah

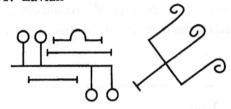

12. Hihaayah

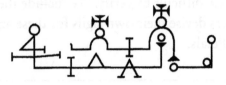

13. Yezalel

14. Mebahel

15. Hariel

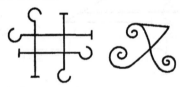

16. Haqamiah

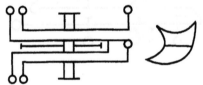

17. Levayah

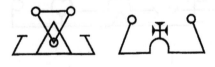

18. Keliel

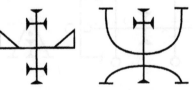

19. Luvayah

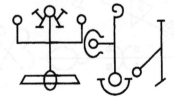

20. Phaheliah

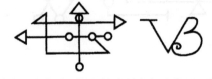

21. Nelakhel

22. Yeyayel

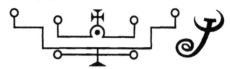

23. Melohel

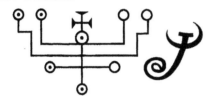

24. Chahaviah

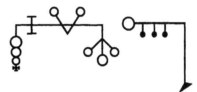

25. Nethahiah

26. Haayah

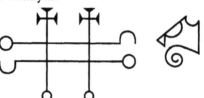

27. Yerathel

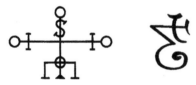

28. Saahiah

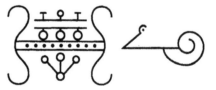

29. Reyayel

30. Umael

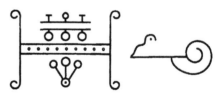

31. Lekhabel

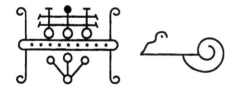

32. Veshiriah

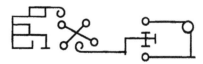

33. Yechaviah

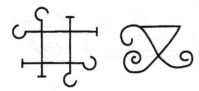

34. Lechachiah

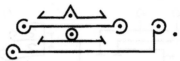

35. Kuqiah

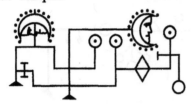

36. Menadel

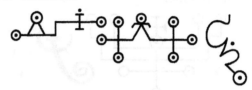

37. Eniel

38. Chaamiah

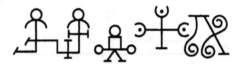

39. Rehael

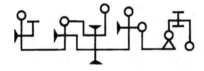

40. Yeyezel

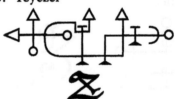

41. Hehakel

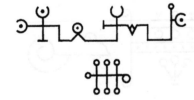

42. Mayakhel

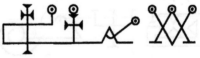

43. Vuliah

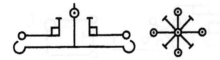

44. Yelahiah

45. Saaliah

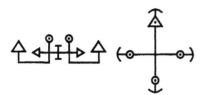

46. Eriel

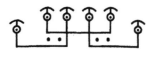

47. Esheliah

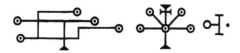

48. Mayahel

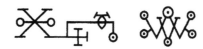

49. Vehuel

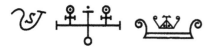

50. Deniel

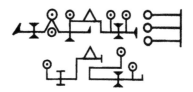

51. Hechashiah

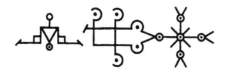

52. Amemiah

53. Nanael

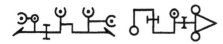

54. Nithael

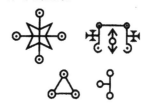

55. Mibahayah

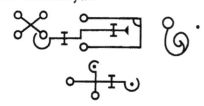

56. Puyael

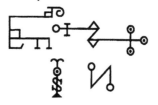

57. Nemamiah

58. Yeyelel

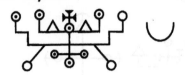

59. Herachel

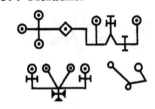

60. Mitzrael

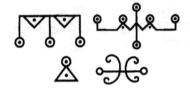

61. Vembael

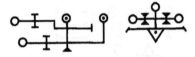

62. Yahohel

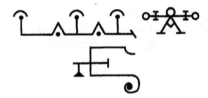

63. Anuel

64. Machiel

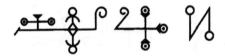

65. Dambayah

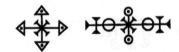

66. Meneqel

67. Ayael

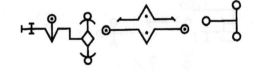

68. Chavuyah

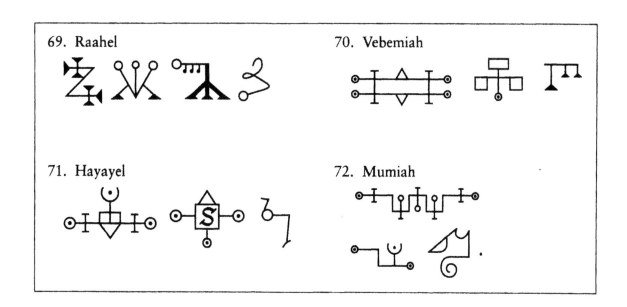

69. Raahel

70. Vebemiah

71. Hayayel

72. Mumiah

BREAKDOWN OF TELESMATIC IMAGE
TO THE NUMBER OF LETTERS IN A NAME

The following chart gives suggestions for how to build the telesmatic image depending on how many letters are in the name. Keep in mind that this is a guideline only.

1	crown	1	crown of head	1	crown, head, & face	1	crown, head, & face
2	head & face	2	face, neck, shoulders	2	neck & shoulders	2	neck, shoulders & chest
3	neck & shoulders	3	chest	3	chest, arms, & hands	3	arms, hands, & stomach
4	chest, arms, & hands	4	arms & hands	4	stomach	4	hips & legs
5	stomach & hips	5	stomach, hips & thighs	5	hips & legs	5	feet
6	thighs	6	legs	6	feet		
7	legs	7	feet				
8	feet						

1	crown	1	crown, head, face, & neck	1	crown, head, face, & shoulders
2	head & face	2	shoulders & chest	2	chest, arms, hands, stomach
3	neck & shoulders	3	arms, hands, & stomach	3	hips, legs & feet
4	chest	4	hips, legs & feet		
5	arms & hands				
6	stomach & hips				
7	thighs				
8	legs				
9	feet				

1 See Pat Zalewski's *Kabbalah of the Golden Dawn* (St. Paul, MN: Llewellyn Publications, 1993).

2 Blaise de Vigenére (1523–1596).

BIBLIOGRAPHY

Agrippa, Henry Cornelius. *Three Books of Occult Philosophy*. Edited by Donald Tyson. St. Paul, MN: Llewellyn Publications, 1993.

Ambelain, Robert. *La Kabbale Pratique* (1951). Partial translation of the French by Piers A. Vaughan.

Barrett, Francis. *The Magus: A Complete System of Occult Philosophy*. New York: Citadel Press, 1989.

Betz, Hans Dieter. *The Greek Magical Papyri in Translation: Including the Demotic Spells*. Chicago: The University of Chicago Press, 1992.

Black, Jeremy and Anthony Green. *Gods, Demons and Symbols of Ancient Mesopotamia: An Illustrated Dictionary*. Austin, TX: University of Texas Press, 1992.

Charles, R. H. *The Book of Enoch the Prophet*. York Beach, ME: Weiser Books, 2003.

Cicero, Chic and Sandra Tabatha Cicero. *The Essential Golden Dawn: An Introduction to High Magic*. St. Paul, MN: Llewellyn Publications, 2003.

———. *The Golden Dawn Magical Tarot* (kit). St. Paul, MN: Llewellyn Publications, 2000.

———. *The Magical Pantheons: The Golden Dawn Journal, Book IV*. St. Paul, MN: Llewellyn Publications, 1998.

———. *The New Golden Dawn Ritual Tarot*. St. Paul, MN: Llewellyn Publications, 1991.

———. *Secrets of a Golden Dawn Temple: Book 1: Creating Magical Tools*. Great Britain: Thoth Publications, 1991.

———. *Self-Initiation into the Golden Dawn Tradition*. St. Paul, MN: Llewellyn Publications, 1998.

Cirlot, J. E. *A Dictionary of Symbols*. 2nd ed. New York: Philosophical Library, 1983.

Coleman, Wade. *Sepher Sapphires: A Treatise on Gematria*. Austin, TX: Golden Dawn Trust, 2004.

Compton, Madonna. *Archetypes on the Tree of Life: The Tarot as Pathwork*. St. Paul, MN: Llewellyn Publications, 1991.

Crowley, Aleister. *777*. York Beach, ME: Samuel Weiser, Inc., 1982.

———. *The Book of Thoth*. New York: U. S. Games, Inc., 1982.

Cunningham, Scott. *The Complete Book of Incense, Oils & Brews*. St. Paul, MN: Llewellyn Publications, 1992.

———. *Cunningham's Encyclopedia of Crystal, Gem & Metal Magic*. St. Paul, MN: Llewellyn Publications, 1992.

Davidson, Gustav. *A Dictionary of Angels*. New York: The Free Press, A Division of Macmillan, Inc., 1992.

D'Olivet, Fabre. *The Hebraic Tongue Restored*. New York: Samuel Weiser, Inc., 1981.

Elworthy, Frederick Thomas. *The Evil Eye: An Account of This Ancient and Widespread Superstition*. New York: Bell Publishing Company, 1989.

Farrell, Nick. *Making Talismans: Living Entities of Power*. St. Paul, MN: Llewellyn Publications, 2001.

Forrest, Adam. "Mysteria Geomantica." *The Golden Dawn Journal, Book I: Divination*. Edited by Chic Cicero and Sandra Tabatha Cicero. St. Paul, MN: Llewellyn Publications, 1994.

———. "This Holy Invisible Companionship." *The Golden Dawn Journal, Book II: Qabalah: Theory and Magic*. Edited by Chic Cicero and Sandra Tabatha Cicero. St. Paul, MN: Llewellyn Publications, 1994.

———. *The Rhodostauroticon: The Angels & Spirits of the Hermetic Qabalah of the Golden Dawn*. Unpublished manuscript, 1997.

Fortune, Dion. *The Mystical Qabalah*. New York: Ibis Books, 1981.

Ginsburgh, Rabbi Yitzchak. *The Alef-Beit: Jewish Thought Revealed through the Hebrew Letters*. Northvale, NJ: Jason Aronson, Inc., 1991.

Gleadow, Rupert. *The Origins of the Zodiac*. New York: Castle Books, 1968.

Godwin, David. *Godwin's Cabalistic Encyclopedia*. 2nd ed. St. Paul, MN: Llewellyn Publications, 1989.

Godwin, Malcolm. *Angels, an Endangered Species*. New York: Simon and Schuster, 1990.

González-Wippler, Migene. *The Complete Book of Amulets & Talismans*. St. Paul, MN: Llewellyn Publications, 1991.

Greer, John Michael. *The New Encyclopedia of the Occult*. St. Paul, MN: Llewellyn Publications, 2003.

———. *Paths of Wisdom: Principles and Practice of the Magical Cabala in the Western Tradition*. St. Paul, MN: Llewellyn Publications, 1996.

Greer, Mary K. *Tarot for Your Self: A Workbook for Personal Transformation*. Franklin Lakes, NJ: New Page Books, 2002.

Jordan, Michael. *Encyclopedia of Gods*. New York: Facts On File, Inc., 1993.

Knight, Gareth. *A Practical Guide to Qabalistic Symbolism*. New York: Samuel Weiser, Inc., 1983.

Koch, Rudolf. *The Book of Signs*. New York: Dover Publications, Inc., 1955.

Kraig, Donald Michael. *Tarot & Magic*. St. Paul, MN: Llewellyn Publications, 2002.

Lang, Bernhard. "Why God Has So Many Names." *Bible Review*. August 2003.

Lehner, Ernst. *Symbols, Signs & Signets*. New York: Dover Publications, Inc., 1950.

Levi, Eliphas. *The Magical Ritual of the Sanctum Regnum*. Kila, MT: Kessinger Publishing Company, n.d. (originally 1896).

———. *Transcendental Magic*. York Beach, ME: Samuel Weiser, Inc., 1972.

Lewis, James R. *Astrology Encyclopedia*. Detroit, MI: Visible Ink Press, 1994.

MacMullen, Ramsay. *Christianity & Paganism in the Fourth to Eighth Centuries*. New Haven, CT: Yale University Press, 1997.

Mathers, S. Liddell MacGregor. *The Key of Solomon the King*. York Beach, ME: Samuel Weiser, Inc., 1974.

Meyer, Michael R. *A Handbook for the Humanistic Astrologer*. Garden City, NY: Anchor Books, 1974.

New American Bible, The. St. Joseph Ed. New York: Catholic Book Publishing Co., 1970.

Pollack, Rachel. *The Kabbalah Tree: A Journey of Balance & Growth*. St. Paul, MN: Llewellyn Publications, 2004.

———. *Seventy-Eight Degrees of Wisdom*. Great Britain: Thorsons, 1997.

Poncé, Charles. *Kabbalah: An Introduction and Illumination for the World Today*. Wheaton, IL: The Theosophical Publishing House, 1980.

Regardie, Israel. *The Art of True Healing*. San Rafael, CA: New World Library, 1991.

———. *The Complete Golden Dawn System of Magic*. Phoenix, AZ: Falcon Press, 1984.

———. *A Garden of Pomegranates: Skrying on the Tree of Life*. Edited and annotated by Chic Cicero and Sandra Tabatha Cicero. St. Paul, MN: Llewellyn Publications, 1999.

———. *The Golden Dawn*. 6th ed. St. Paul, MN: Llewellyn Publications, 1994.

———. *How to Make and Use Talismans*. London: The Aquarian Press, 1972.

Renée, Janina. *Tarot Spells*. St. Paul, MN: Llewellyn Publications, 2001.

Schaya, Leo. *The Universal Meaning of the Kabbalah*. Baltimore, MD: Penguin Books, Inc., 1973.

Sepharial. *The Book of Charms and Talismans*. Santa Fe, NM: Sun Publishing Company, 1992.

Shah, Sirdir Ikbal Ali. *Occultism: Its Theory and Practice*. New York: Dorset Press, 1993.

Thomas, William and Kate Pavitt. *The Book of Talismans, Amulets & Zodiacal Gems*. North Hollywood, CA: Wilshire Book Company, 1970.

Valiente, Doreen. *An ABC of Witchcraft Past & Present*. New York: St. Martin's Press, 1973.

Wang, Robert. *The Qabalistic Tarot: A Textbook of Mystical Philosophy*. York Beach, ME: Samuel Weiser, Inc., 1983.

Whitcomb, Bill. *The Magician's Companion: A Practical & Encyclopedic Guide to Magical & Religious Symbolism*. St. Paul, MN: Llewellyn Publications, 1993.

Williams, Brian. *A Renaissance Tarot: A Guide to the Renaissance Tarot*. Stamford, CT: U. S. Games, Inc., 1994.

Zalewski, Pat. *Kabbalah of the Golden Dawn*. St. Paul, MN: Llewellyn Publications, 1993.

Index

sistrum, 199, 221
Sitael, 149, 265
skhenet, 196
Smith, Pamela Coleman, 11
Sol, 32–33, 38, 46, 130–131, 178, 193, 201,
    211, 220, 247, 254, 256, 261
Stella Matutina, 188
strophion, 203, 207–208, 226, 230, 241, 246
Supernals, 86, 100, 110
swastika, 195

Taliahad, 127, 141, 191
talisman, 1–2, 1, 3–12, 15, 18–23, 25–71, 73–
    74, 78, 81–84, 86–87, 90–91, 93–94, 96–98,
    100–102, 106, 113, 121, 123, 126, 129, 131,
    135, 139, 180–181, 211, 218, 221, 224,
    226–229, 231, 234, 236–237, 240, 242,
    246–247, 249, 251
Tarot Consecration Ritual, 18, 20
Tau, 20, 30, 32, 134, 138, 181, 193–194, 196,
    202, 208, 219
Tau cross, 20, 202
Taurus, 36–37, 87, 110, 123–124, 169–171,
    196
telein, 4
telesmata, 181
telesmatic image, 180–181, 183–185, 187–191,
    194, 203–208, 211, 218–219, 221, 224,
    227–228, 231, 233–234, 236–237, 239,
    242–243, 247, 257, 271
telesmatic magic, 180, 188, 193
tet, 199, 208
tetelesmenon, 4
teth, 36, 191, 197, 203
Tetragrammaton, 23, 119, 136, 139–141, 143,
    146–173, 175, 193–194, 235–236, 242
Thelema, 11
Themis, 92, 94
Thirty-two Paths of Wisdom, 26, 71
Thoth, 11–12, 14, 23, 50–71, 82, 88–89, 103–
    105, 238
Three Books of Occult Philosophy, 118, 136–
    137, 175, 216, 220, 222
three magi, 80
three mother letters, 28, 30, 215
tilsam, 4
Tiphareth, 27, 46, 119–120, 130, 174, 193,
    211, 219

Tiriel, 82, 121, 263
Tree of Life, 8, 23, 25–27, 29, 42, 44, 46,
    48–49, 54, 62, 69, 116, 118, 133, 139, 141,
    174, 183–184, 191, 193, 220, 240
trefoil, 202, 204, 246
Triangle of Art Spread, 73–75, 79, 89
triangle of art, 74, 78
triangle of flame, 201
Triangle of manifestation, 202
trident, 201
trigram, 141, 146–173, 175
triple enclosure, 197
triple tau, 202
triquetra, 202
triskelion, 195
twelve simple letters, 28, 36, 192, 215
tzaddi, 36, 200, 220
Tzakmaqiel, 130

Uadj, 198
Uas, 196–197, 201
Udjat, 200
Umael, 152–153, 267
ur-uatchti, 201–202
uraeus, 197
Uriel, 20, 134–136, 141, 178
urs, 201
usr, 199, 201

Vahaviah, 148–149, 265
Vakhabiel, 130
vav, 23, 36, 97, 119, 137, 185, 191, 193, 196,
    203, 225, 234, 245, 253–256
ve-Geburah, 19
ve-Gedulah, 19
Vehuel, 146, 269
Vembael, 165, 270
Venus, 20, 32–35, 37, 39, 47, 84, 86, 100,
    122–123, 137, 147, 153, 157, 162, 172, 193,
    196, 211, 220, 234–235, 255, 262
Verkhiel, 125, 148–150, 233–237
Veshiriah, 167, 183–184, 267
vibratory formula, 218
Virgo, 36, 38–39, 79, 125, 171–173, 193, 198,
    227
Vuliah, 158, 268

Water Cup, 20
wheel cross, 202
Wiccan Rede, 10

Yah, 21, 100, 136, 146, 153, 160, 165, 167, 191, 220
Yahohel, 165, 270
Yebemiah, 154
Yechaviah, 168, 268
Yelahiah, 158, 268
Yelayel, 148–149, 265
Yerathel, 151–152, 267
Yesod, 27, 48, 121, 193, 211
Yetzirah, 71, 188–189, 204, 224, 228, 233, 239, 243
Yeyayel, 156–157, 267
Yeyelel, 170, 270
Yeyezel, 163–164, 268

Yezalel, 160, 266
YHVH, 19, 21, 82, 97, 119, 121–122, 124, 126, 130, 133–134, 136, 139, 141, 146, 150, 154, 157, 160–166, 168, 171, 175, 220, 224–225, 227, 233–234, 243, 245–247, 253–255
YHVH Eloah ve-Daath, 119, 130–131, 149, 156, 163, 170, 256
YHVH Tzabaoth, 122, 150, 157, 164, 171, 233–234, 255
yod, 23, 36, 97, 119, 132, 136, 141, 189–191, 193, 198, 204, 207–208, 214–215, 225, 234, 245, 253–256

Zamael, 129, 138, 181, 183, 260
zayin, 36, 197
Zuriel, 126, 160–161, 211

GET MORE AT LLEWELLYN.COM

Visit us online to browse hundreds of our books and decks, plus sign up to receive our e-newsletters and exclusive online offers.

- • **Free tarot readings** • **Spell-a-Day** • **Moon phases**
- • **Recipes, spells, and tips** • **Blogs** • **Encyclopedia**
- • **Author interviews, articles, and upcoming events**

GET SOCIAL WITH LLEWELLYN

Find us on Facebook

www.Facebook.com/LlewellynBooks

Follow us on twitter™

www.Twitter.com/Llewellynbooks

GET BOOKS AT LLEWELLYN

LLEWELLYN ORDERING INFORMATION

 Order online: Visit our website at www.llewellyn.com to select your books and place an order on our secure server.

 Order by phone:
- • Call toll free within the U.S. at 1-877-NEW-WRLD (1-877-639-9753)
- • Call toll free within Canada at 1-866-NEW-WRLD (1-866-639-9753)
- • We accept VISA, MasterCard, American Express and Discover

 Order by mail:
Send the full price of your order (MN residents add 6.875% sales tax) in U.S. funds, plus postage and handling to: Llewellyn Worldwide, 2143 Wooddale Drive Woodbury, MN 55125-2989

POSTAGE AND HANDLING

STANDARD (U.S. & Canada):
(Please allow 12 business days)
$30.00 and under, add $4.00.
$30.01 and over, FREE SHIPPING.

INTERNATIONAL ORDERS:
$16.00 for one book, plus $3.00 for each additional book.

Visit us online for more shipping options. Prices subject to change.

FREE CATALOG!

To order, call 1-877-NEW-WRLD ext. 8236 or visit our website

The Essential Golden Dawn
An Introduction to High Magic

CHIC CICERO AND
SANDRA TABATHA CICERO

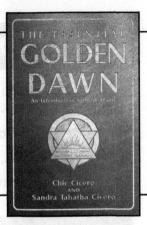

Is the Golden Dawn system for you? Today the Golden Dawn is one of the most sought-after and respected systems of magic in the world. Over a century old, it's considered the capstone of the Western Esoteric Tradition. Yet many of the available books on the subject are too complex or overwhelming for readers just beginning to explore alternative spiritual paths.

The Essential Golden Dawn is for those who simply want to find out what the Golden Dawn is and what it has to offer. It answers questions such as: What is Hermeticism? How does magic work? Who started the Golden Dawn? What are its philosophies and principles? It helps readers determine whether this system is for them, and then it guides them into further exploration as well as basic ritual work.

0-7387-0310-9
360 pp., 6 x 9 $19.99

Learning Lenormand
Traditional Fortune Telling for Modern Life

MARCUS KATZ
AND TALI GOODWIN

The Lenormand deck is a traditional French fortune-telling deck dating back to about 1850. It uses thirty-six cards, each with a symbolic image. This is the first comprehensive English workbook that explains its history, how to choose a deck, and how to use it for both fortune-telling and personal insight. It features the authors' signature methods of skill development and card-reading techniques to answer any question. This is the first well-researched book that fully explains and teaches the correct and unique methods of using the cards.

0-7387-3647-3
312 pp., 7½ x 9⅛ $16.99

365 Tarot Spreads
Revealing the Magic in Each Day

Sasha Graham

For many cartomancers, tarot is a hallowed daily practice. Now you can navigate important life choices every day, all year with *365 Tarot Spreads*. Featuring spreads for multi-cultural traditions, holidays, rituals, lore, and magic, this daily guide explores a tarot quest for every occasion and helps you discern answers to any question with interesting and magical results.

Use *365 Tarot Spreads* year after year with spreads falling on every possible calendar date. Each one is based on an important historical, magical, or fascinating occurrence on that particular date in history. This daily guide is concerned with the essential journey to find truth and answers, rooted in every spread with topics from love and money to career and life path. With an explanation of each spread and questions to focus on while reading, you'll achieve your quest for answers every day.

0-7387-4038-1
408 pp., 7½ x 9⅛ $22.99

Tarot Beyond the Basics
Gain a Deeper Understanding of the Meanings Behind the Cards

ANTHONY LOUIS

Take your tarot reading to a higher level. With an emphasis on tarot's astrological influences and a number of detailed sample readings, *Tarot Beyond the Basics* shows the way to becoming an advanced practitioner. Here, Anthony Louis shares how-to instructions for working with reversals, number symbolism, intuition, the four elements, and the philosophical roots of tarot.

Explaining astrology for tarot readers clearly and in a way that makes sense, Louis shows how to use the tarot to give powerful readings that change people's lives. The "real" tarot exists in the mind of each reader and is interlaced with his or her stories and experiences. The abundance of knowledge presented in *Tarot Beyond the Basics* is sure to make your readings come alive with meaning and significance.

0-7387-3944-8
408 pp., 7½ x 9⅛ $19.99

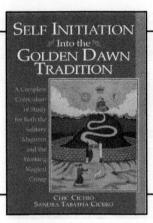

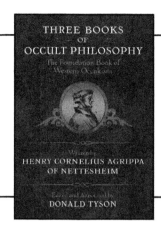

Three Books of Occult Philosophy
The Foundation Book of Western Occultism

HENRY CORNELIUS AGRIPPA,
EDITED AND ANNOTATED BY DONALD TYSON

Agrippa's *Three Books of Occult Philosophy* is the single most important text in the history of Western occultism. Occultists have drawn upon it for five centuries, although they rarely give it credit. First published in Latin in 1531 and translated into English in 1651, it has never been reprinted in its entirety since. Photocopies are hard to find and very expensive. Now, for the first time in 500 years, *Three Books of Occult Philosophy* will be presented as Agrippa intended. There were many errors in the original translation, but occult author Donald Tyson has made the corrections and has clarified the more obscure material with copious notes.

This is a necessary reference tool not only for all magicians, but also for scholars of the Renaissance, Neoplatonism, the Western Kabbalah, the history of ideas and sciences, and the occult tradition. It is as practical today as it was 500 years ago.

0-7387-5527-3
1,024 pp., 7 x 10 $65.00

To order, call 1-877-NEW-WRLD
Prices subject to change without notice
Order at Llewellyn.com 24 hours a day, 7 days a week!

Tarot & Magic

Donald Michael Kraig
Foreword by Mary K. Greer

Now you can take the information from a Tarot reading and modify your future—creating changes to, or enhancing, what the Tarot predicts. For readers of all spiritual paths, *Tarot & Magic* shows you how to use the Tarot to do magic on a practical level.

Create your own Tarot spells and discover a unique system for improving your life, simply by acting out the cards. Enter and work in the astral plane. Use the magical power of the cards as talismans. Learn three methodologies for working with the Tarot and sex magic, and much more.

0-7387-0185-8
192 pp., 6 x 9 $12.95

Tarot Spells

JANINA RENÉE

The Tarot has long been valued as a tool for meditation and divination, but its symbolism also performs perfectly as a focal point for working magic. *Tarot Spells* shows you how to deliberately arrange any deck of Tarot cards to state the goal that you want to achieve.

Want to lose weight? Looking for your dream lover? Want your boss to stop hounding you? With *Tarot Spells*, you'll be amazed at the phenomenal changes that can occur in your life. Begin doing spells as soon as you open the book. Each spell has a meditation/visualization that you do while you lay out the cards. To help you get results more quickly, some spells also suggest accessories (such as candles or crystals) or actions (writing or pouring water). Conclude with speaking the potent affirmation provided.

0-87542-670-0
336 pp., 7½ x 9⅛

$17.99

The Marseille Tarot Revealed
A Complete Guide to Symbolism, Meanings & Methods

YOAV BEN-DOV

Explore the deep symbolism of a frequently misunderstood deck and use the cards to answer the important questions of life. *The Marseille Tarot Revealed* explains everything you need to know to start or deepen your Marseille Tarot practice, including history, decks, readings, spreads, symbols, and much more. Yoav Ben-Dov shares the meaning of the Marseille art motifs and specific reading techniques that can be used with any tarot deck to help you tap in to your own intuition. With full-color illustrations and interpretations for each card, this book is a must-have for anyone who's interested in one of the world's most influential decks..

0-7387-5228-2
384 pp., 6 x 9

$22.99